Animals in the Fiction of
Cormac McCarthy

Animals in the Fiction of Cormac McCarthy

WALLIS R. SANBORN, III

McFarland & Company, Inc., Publishers
Jefferson, North Carolina, and London

Library of Congress Cataloguing-in-Publication Data

Sanborn, Wallis R., 1964–
    Animals in the fiction of Cormac McCarthy / Wallis R. Sanborn III.
      p.   cm.
    Includes bibliographical references and index.

    ISBN 0-7864-2380-3 (softcover : 50# alkaline paper)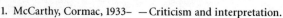

    1. McCarthy, Cormac, 1933– — Criticism and interpretation.
    2. Animals in literature.   I. Title.
    PS3563.C337Z895 2006
    813'.54 — dc22   2006003239

British Library cataloguing data are available

Cover photograph ©2006 PhotoSpin

Manufactured in the United States of America

McFarland & Company, Inc., Publishers
  Box 611, Jefferson, North Carolina 28640
  www.mcfarlandpub.com

To Craig and Victoria Young

Acknowledgments

I would like to express special thanks to Patrick W. Shaw of Texas Tech University, without whom this trek into Cormac McCarthy's fiction might never have begun, or ended. Dr. Shaw's critical commentary helped the document evolve, and his personal assistance helped me professionally and personally. Additionally, I would like to thank Wendell Aycock and B.J. Manríquez, who provided advice and support throughout the evolution of this project. I would also like to thank David Troyansky for his critical commentary regarding my early drafts of this project.

I am deeply indebted to Mary Valdez, Carolyn Cook, Daryl Lynn Davalos, and Juanita Ramirez; to Don Rude, Bruce Clarke, Michael Schoenecke, Bill Wenthe, Jill Patterson, Doug Crowell, Bryce Conrad, and Madonne Miner. You all have changed my life.

To the members of the Cormac McCarthy Society and *The Cormac McCarthy Journal* who assisted me with commentary or advice, thank you: Rick Wallach, Robert Jarrett, James Bell, John Wegner, and Nell Sullivan. I would also like to thank the various participants in the Cormac McCarthy Area at the 2002 and 2003 Southwest/Texas Meetings of the Popular Culture and American Culture Associations. The critical advice gleaned at these particular meetings proved to be quite valuable.

I would like to offer thanks to Thomas Sanborn and Mia Lane Burton-Sanborn, as well as to Amanda Burton and Laura Sanborn.

Oh, and thank you to Mister McCarthy.

Table of Contents

Introduction

The works of Cormac McCarthy have been critically studied as literature of the South and of the Border Southwest. While articles, anthologies and book-length studies have been devoted to McCarthy's body of work, little textual criticism exists regarding the omnipresence and presentation of non-human creatures in the McCarthy *oeuvre*. However, the abundance of zoology in the texts offers more than enough breadth and depth to make scholarly study worthwhile.

McCarthy's literature contains a panoptic of the beastly world, and as McCarthy's work deals with an ongoing, ceaseless battle for survival, non-human animals — wild, feral, stock, and domestic — exist in this battle for survival just as human characters do. The animals exist within McCarthy's fictional natural world, a world driven by biological determinism. Consequently, wild animals prey upon feral and domestic animals, horses exist as warriors, and the hunt is a ballet between man and hunting hound. Furthermore, hierarchies exist within genera so that proximity to and dependence upon man results in mistreatment and death, while distance from man results in survival and fitness; for instance, both felines and canines can be categorized hierarchically by the degree of their association with man and their domesticity. McCarthy also utilizes non-human animals within a text to serve as harbingers that preface specific types of events in the text. Repeatedly, the appearance in the text of a specific type of animal will signify a specific textual event to follow. Hogs, for example, are easily identifiable as harbingers of death, and specifically here, as harbingers of human death. Hogs appear in the text, and humans are killed by

1

malice or accident. Hogs and human death become so analogous that McCarthy's narrator and characters explicitly posit the theory that hogs are conjoined to the devil for a particular evil purpose.

Thematically, McCarthy uses human treatment of non-human animals to evince man's absolute desire to control the natural world and the beasts within it. In particular, McCarthy repeatedly offers scenes that argue man's obsession for dominion over flying animals, avians and bats in particular. Further, the many passages that lament and articulate the expulsion and extinction of the Mexican Gray Wolf from the Southwestern United States show man's innate ability to extinguish that which he cannot control and domesticate. If man cannot control an animal, man will attempt to kill that animal — individually, collectively or cumulatively. This desire by man to control or kill is also presented in lighter tones; bovines, stubborn and stupid, are often devices of levity, with which McCarthy contrasts scenes of gruesome seriousness. Universally, McCarthy's human characters possess a need to control the fauna — in the air, on land, or in the water — that exists in the natural world.

Clearly, McCarthy utilizes non-human animals within his texts for a variety of purposes. Specifically, felines, canines and horses are used as devices to present and argue biological determinism. Swine are harbingers of human death. Birds, bats, wolves, and bovines are receptors of man's obsession with control of the natural world, and, uniquely, hunting hounds are vehicles with which man controls the natural world. This study is an effort to apply the above animal based thesis to McCarthy's extant published body of work (excluding "Wake for Susan," "A Drowning Incident" and "The Wolf Trapper") on a text-by-text basis, in order to better understand the author's presentation of animals in the text; in each of the examples here, animals and death are conjoined in the texts, and the theme of death is the unifying theme in McCarthy's textual presentation of animals. The first analytical chapter examines animal presentation and death in *The Stonemason, The Gardener's Son,* and two rarely discussed 'short stories,' "Bounty" and "The Dark Waters." The next eight chapters focus on one text each, *The Orchard Keeper* to *Cities of the Plain,* one animal or type of animal —feline, swine, bovine, bird and bat, canine, equine, lupine, hound — and one sub-thesis which exists under the unifying theme of death. Each of these chapters also looks at the specific chapter-animal as it exists in other McCarthy texts and other works of literature. The final rhetorical chapter (before the conclusion) briefly examines the theme of animal death at the hand of man in *No Country for Old Men.*

Working Terms

As this study is literary and not scientific, an extended glossary is not necessary. However, a very limited number of working terms need to be explicated. "Biological determinism" refers to events that are causally determined by natural laws, which are, themselves, determined by a combination of environment and genetics; animals—genetic products—of all types, which endlessly struggle for survival, are victims of environmental forces beyond their control or understanding. "Domestic" refers to animals domesticated and trained through eons of breeding and training under man; for example, hunting hounds, house dogs, town dogs, and cats are domestic animals. "Feral" refers specifically to domestic cats and dogs that have gone wild, by choice or by force. "Stock" refers to animals that exist in a ranch or farm environment, as well as animals that pull carts, carriages or loads; cattle, swine, mules, oxen, and some unlucky horses are stock animals; additionally, horses that are ridden are stock animals. "Wild" refers to animals that are untamed by man, and usually untamable; as such, these animals are often hunted by man. Panthers, lynx, bobcats, birds and bats, wolves, and raccoons are examples of wild animals. The "natural world" refers to external nature; mountains, deserts, trees, rivers, oceans, flora, fauna comprise the natural world.

Chapter-by-Chapter Theses

Before entering the analysis of McCarthy's major texts, animal presentation and the theme of death in four other McCarthy texts must also be addressed. These four texts, the drama *The Stonemason*, the teleplay *The Gardener's Son* and two scenes from *The Orchard Keeper* published as titled short stories, "Bounty" and "The Dark Waters" all present animals and death prominently and are worthy of attention and analysis. *The Stonemason* is a bleak drama that calls attention to the end of the art of stonemasonry, while it also argues the theme of the unceasing mortality of all living things; everything and everyone dies, and the cycle of birth, life and death affects all. In the drama, members of the Telfair family die, and die, and die. The narrative protagonist, Ben Telfair, watches as his father, grandfather, nephew, and others die off; these deaths are analogous to the death of the trade and artistry of stonemasonry. As the practitioners of stonemasonry die, so does the promotion and practice of stonemasonry. Additionally, the Telfair family dog, Bossy, an animal featured prominently in the text, dies near the end of the drama. So in McCarthy's text, the relentless cycle of life includes beloved pets. In this text, the domestic canine is not maligned, but is nonetheless dead by the close of the action.

In his teleplay *The Gardener's Son*, McCarthy frames the opening and closing scenes of the text proper with passages in which mule teams are very prominently displayed. The teleplay, a revisionist account of a nineteenth-century murder and subsequent hanging, is akin to *Outer Dark* in that McCarthy uses a stock animal specifically as a harbinger of human death. In this case, though, the mule, in team on a wagon, is the signifier to death signified. So, where there are mule teams, there is human death, and the mule team as a framing device is analogous to James Gregg's and Robert McEvoy's deaths, as each team pulls and carries, literally and symbolically, the body of the dead.

In "Bounty," the first of two passages from *The Orchard Keeper* published as titled short stories prior to the publication of the novel, a boy finds a wounded sparrowhawk and takes the animal home; thus the boy takes control of the flying animal. After the animal dies, the boy takes the corpse to city hall for a one dollar—chickenhawk—bounty, with which the boy places down payment on a number of small animal traps. The boy is aware of the dead bird's value, as well as the value of other trapped animals. This bounty scene is the seminal scene of McCarthy's ongoing bounty theme; that is, a certain animal is worth more to man, dead than alive, and as such, man will take advantage of a found bounty animal, or man will seek to hunt, trap and kill a bounty animal.

"The Dark Waters" is the second passage from *The Orchard Keeper* published as a titled short story prior to the publication of the novel. This story is, in title, in theme, in action, a preface of McCarthy's ongoing textual battle between man and the natural world. In the short story, a boy is taken on a raccoon hunt by his mentor; what happens during the hunt initiates the boy into manhood. Of course this coming of age story is also a narrative of the hunt, the battle between man and hound, and wild animal, and as such, is the seminal scene of the ballet of the hunt. Both of the short stories above preface McCarthy's fascination with the animal world and man's ceaseless attempts to control the animals in the natural world. It is quite interesting that McCarthy chose to publish as short stories two passages with such prominent animal action and themes. Of course, as the stories were published in nineteen sixty-five, one must note that, thematically and textually, the early McCarthy reflects the later McCarthy, regardless of textual locale or era.

In *The Orchard Keeper*, Cormac McCarthy presents felines, domestic, feral, and wild, in an organized hierarchical structure. Each feline species exists in the hierarchy according to each species' proximity to and dependence upon man. In fact, McCarthy posits felines of all sorts in nearly all of his work. The Southern novels have domestic cats placed in the text periodically, and the novels of the Border Southwest include extended scenes with both domestic and wild felines, but only in *The Orchard Keeper* is feline hierarchy defined and presented in accordance with the manner in which man interacts with each feline species. For domestic felines, a litter of blind kittens, absolute dependence upon man has led to, symbolically at least, a plague of sightlessness and misery. These abject examples of the domestic cat exist at the bottom of the feline hierarchy. Neither fit nor survivors, the kittens' fate is to suffer and then die. Feral cats are those who have slipped the surly bonds of man, only to face a more surly natural world. In this case, one feral cat represents the paradox of freedom from man and dependence upon man. As a feral animal, the cat is burdened with thousands of years of environmental evolution, so survival away from man is a struggle. Yet the feral cat is gifted with the awareness of man's habits and behaviors, so scavenging smokehouses and sprung traps is a manner by which to survive. So it is that the feral cat survives, elevated above the lowly domestic cat. Next in the hierarchy are the wild felines, bobcats, lynx and panthers. Bobcats and lynx have value to man because of their bounty-value, a fact that is identified in a brief scene with John Wesley Rattner and his fellow bounty hunter, Warn Pulliam. The bobcats and lynx, though, avoid interaction with man, and are never present in the text, except in a trapping pamphlet shown to John Wesley by Warn. Of course, animals worth more to man dead than alive are wise to avoid man, and bobcats and lynx do so in the text. At the apex of the feline hierarchy, above even the former two wild felines, is the panther, a wild feline mythologized by John Wesley's "uncle," Artlur Ownby. The panther is a wild feline, whose fearsome reputation and legendary fantastic feats, such as invisibility and the ability to prowl without leaving paw prints, signify a forced respect on man's part. As well, the panther is the dominant predator in the southeast United States, and as such, the wild cat is the ringer in the genetic and environmental game of biological determinism. Feline hierarchy in *The Orchard Keeper* is but one of a number of different hierarchical systems that McCarthy uses in his texts; what each animal hierarchy has in common is the formula of proximity to and dependence upon man, and locus in the natural world. The feline's place in the hierarchy is inversely proportional to its proximity to man.

In *Outer Dark,* McCarthy uses stock swine as harbingers of death, in most cases, human death. Repeatedly, swine, or a swine, will be present in a scene, and almost immediately thereafter, death will show its presence in the narrative action. This technique of swine signifier to death signified, the sign of the swine or pig, so to speak, is one McCarthy uses in many of his other texts. In *The Orchard Keeper,* hogs starve to death and are purloined by panthers; *Child of God* contains a scene with a drowned sow, and very much death. *Suttree* contains a passage, both gruesome and hilarious, that has Gene Harrogate beating a juvenile pig to death. *Cities of the Plain* and *The Stonemason* also offer the sign of the pig. *Outer Dark,* however, is the text with the greatest use of swine as the harbinger, or signifier, of human death. Early in the text, in a brief, italicized passage, *"one screaming sow"* (35) announces the presence of death, in this case, the squire's death. Later, in another writing of the same scene, "a hog's squeal" (47) repeats the announcement of the squire's impending death. Finally, in two back-to-back passages, the squire is killed by The Three. McCarthy continues the sign of the swine when a boar in a slaughter lot, with death on *his* mind, chases the itinerant Culla Holme and immediately after, in an italicized passage, two wandering millhands are lynched. The sign of the swine occurs later in the text in a scene with a sow that has previously drowned her hoggets. In this scene, the sow is associated with Rinthy Holme, a young woman who has indirectly caused the eventual death of her own offspring. The lengthiest and most complex scene involving the sign of the swine is one near the close of the text, where a great drove of pigs scream and die, as does a pig drover named Vernon, who before his death expostulates on the evil of swine and their association with the devil. This example of the sign of the swine is unique in its length and direct argument of the swine as definably evil. In short, the image of swine as harbingers of death is one that McCarthy uses often in his texts, but only in *Outer Dark* are swine the signifiers of human death specifically.

In *Child of God*, McCarthy uses stock animals, primarily bovines—a couple of cows and an ox—to add levity to what may be conservatively labeled, a gruesome text. In addition, McCarthy includes a brief comic scene with a mule team before he closes the text on a horrifyingly descriptive note. In the former scenes, the scenes of bovine levity, McCarthy relies upon man's unquenchable desire to control the natural world. Man constantly seeks to control animal behavior and action, and McCarthy's characters are no different from any other men. As such, as usual, animals suffer at the hand of man; paradoxically, in this text, as the bovines suffer, the reader is amused. McCarthy's placement of bovines in the text is one he repeats in nearly all of his works; *The Orchard Keeper* has some slight mention of stock cattle, and *Blood Meridian* and the texts of the Border Trilogy, as novels of the Border Southwest, all have multiple scenes with bovines, primarily cattle. As well, *Cities of the Plain* has a scene in which cattle stampede and John Grady Cole actually makes a witticism to Billy Parham regarding a cattle stampede, geese and a flaming cat (124–7), but only the reader is in on the joke. So, McCarthy often uses cattle in his texts, and occasionally uses stock cattle specifically to add levity to his very serious works, but *Child of God* is the seminal text for the presence of extended passages that utilize bovines as devices of humor. Early in the text, seeking to control animal behavior and action, Lester Ballard shoots a cow that has muddied the river in which he had planned to shoot fish; the shooting is an act of impulse that results in death, as are so many of Lester's actions. Soon after, for example, in a shortsighted attempt to relocate the animal with a tractor and a rope, Lester partially decapitates a different cow. McCarthy uses bovine levity and man's attempt at control over a bovine a third time in a passage with a different human protagonist; this time, a young man named Trantham attempts to move a team of oxen by lighting a fire under the beasts; the results amuse, of course. McCarthy also utilizes a menagerie of other animals—cats, dogs, birds, mules—to add levity to the grotesque text. Paradoxically, *Child of God* is McCarthy's funniest and most gruesome novel.

In *Suttree,* McCarthy further expands his textual argument that man seeks to control the natural world, with emphasis on animals, specifically on flying animals. The character of Gene Harrogate, metaphorically an animal himself, the country mouse and the city rat, is McCarthy's vehicle to argue man's desire for control over avians and bats. Flying is an animal's ultimate act of freedom, and man's desire to control animals that fly is a desire that can be found in a number of other McCarthy texts. *The Orchard Keeper* contains a chapter where John Wesley Rattner captures a young wounded hawk, and thus takes control and possession over the dying animal. In *Child of God*, Lester Ballard catches and controls a robin; Ballard then gives the bird to an idiot boy, who subsequently bites off the bird's legs, gaining greater control over the doomed animal. Judge Holden, McCarthy's ultimate determinist, kills and dresses Mexican desert birds with a taxidermist's skill, and he also culls bat guano from the earth for gunpowder, thus capturing and controlling flying birds as well as flying mammals. The flawed protagonist of *The Crossing*, Billy Parham, dooms a hawk with the fly of an arrow. In *Suttree*, Harrogate, the master schemer, takes the lives of pigeons and bats in separate schemes, for separate reasons. Harrogate seeks pigeons for sustenance, and he seeks bats for bounty. In the first paragraph of the text, McCarthy introduces the bridge-pigeons that Harrogate is to kill; references to these pigeons are scattered through the text; Harrogate watches the pigeons, and watches them, and watches them. Eventually, he devises a plan to use grain and rat traps to catch and kill the birds. This plan evolves to one where Harrogate electrocutes the pigeons. Trapped or zapped, the pigeons are equally deceased, and as such, equally and completely controlled. Bats also fall prey to Harrogate's methodology of control. Told of a bat bounty (207), but ignorant of the fact that only rabid bats constitute bounty, Harrogate devises a manner to kill bats, en masse. After a failed attempt to kill the flying beasts with a slingshot, and a night of "heavy thinking" (212), Harrogate chooses poison as his method of execution, and puts his plan into action. Harrogate's plan results in the deaths of many, many bats. In *Suttree*, Harrogate's attempts at controlling birds and bats are but the two most evident examples of man's desire and ability to control flying animals through the killing of the wild, flying animals. Moreover, with a bit of ironic humor, McCarthy labels Harrogate the city rat; of course, in the lexicon, both bats and pigeons are popularly referred to as flying rats.

In McCarthy's first novel of the Border Southwest, the historiographic *Blood Meridian or the Evening Redness in the West*, the author again uses an animal hierarchy to posit species in a systematic order. In this text, canines are the focus of the animal hierarchy. Unlike the feline hierarchy in *The Orchard Keeper*, the canine hierarchy found in *Blood Meridian* can be entirely organized and structured around domestic canines. Additionally, this canine hierarchy is one structured on a canine and human analogy. Each canine is analogous to the human being who possesses that canine; for example, a warrior canine is possessed or owned by a warrior human. Canine presence in the text is not unusual in McCarthy's work, and canine hierarchy is not an uncommon McCarthy device. *The Orchard Keeper* is cataloged with scenes of canines and men, and the Border Trilogy offers many, many examples of canine hierarchy. Even *The Stonemason* and *The Gardener's Son* have canine scenes worth explicating and analyzing. What is unusual in *Blood Meridian*, though, is the analogous position in which the domestic canine is slotted in the animal hierarchy by its human keeper. For example, at the bottom of the hierarchy are town dogs, the least of which are the wretched specimens found in the primitive pueblos south of the Rio Bravo. The best, or least, example of this lowly canine's position in McCarthy's universe is a scene in which the judge purchases two puppies from a child "dogvendor" (192), and subsequently throws the short-lived animals into the river to drown; the little puppies are then shot by Bathcat. The hierarchic placement of the animals is not determined by the judge — he, of course, kills many things — but is determined by the child dogvendor. This ragged urchin is as doomed as the puppies he sells to the judge, for, as the reader is well aware, the judge is a child killer, and any type of child will do. So the town puppy, like the town child, is endangered and abject. Next in the hierarchy, are trained dogs that perform for man's amusement. This type of domestic canine is represented by a pair of Chihuahuas who travel in a caravan of *bufones*. The analogy here is clear; one is as one's master is. Third in the domestic canine hierarchy is Dr. Lincoln's "half-mastiff" (253). Prior to meeting Captain John Joel Glanton, Dr. Lincoln is top dog at the Yuma crossing on the Colorado River, and as such, his dog is afforded some honor and place. But at the top of the domestic canine hierarchy is Glanton's dog, described only as "large and vicious" (149). This unnamed dog incorporates into the gang of scalp-hunters and is the most prominently featured domestic canine in the text. And, as with the examples above, this beast lives a life analogous to his human master. Strong humans, who are consciously deterministic, dominate weak and apathetic humans, and domestic canines owned by strong humans fare better than weak and buffoonish canines; as well, the canines in *Blood Meridian* often live and die as their masters do, abjectly, clownishly or violently. This bloody canine/human analogy is how the domestic canine hierarchy in McCarthy's fifth novel is ordered.

In *All the Pretty Horses,* McCarthy argues the horse as a warrior. The horse is not merely a warrior animal but is at one with war and the existence of life as a warrior. As such, the horse is ideally suited for existence in a deterministic world. While horses or mules are present in all of McCarthy's works, warrior horses are few. The Southern novels offer the horse as a beast of burden, as in *Suttree,* or the horse as a panic-crazed dervish on a ferry, as in *Outer Dark*, or the mule as a plow animal, as in *Child of God.* In McCarthy's sixth text, the horse is a warrior, literally, as explained in the opening horse-ride of the text, where the ghosts of The People (the Comanche) and their equine warrior animals haunt the passage with their presence, for the Comanche existed as the greatest horsemen warriors of any era or locale, and their horses were bred, raised and tempered in war. Additionally, the warrior horse, like a captured ally, is worth rescuing, regardless of potential death to all involved. Men and horses both die in battle, as warriors should. And the horse is a warrior, metaphorically, as is presented via the sport of quarter-horse racing and the breeding value of winning quarter-horses. Subsequently, the sires of quarter-horses are shown to be the fittest of cattle handling equines. McCarthy's focus on the horse as a warrior animal is articulated through the character of Luís, a Mexican vaquero at La Purísima and a veteran of the Mexican Revolution. Luís argues the horse's common love for war and communal soul. Moreover, Luís argues that horses' souls mirror men's. Further, Alejandra Rocha, the scion of the ranch owner, rides an Arabian stallion, a warrior horse bred for war by a warrior people. Finally, John Grady Cole is forced, coerced and self-volunteered into a number of battle situations where horse and man must act as warriors under fire, and failure of the warrior horse will result in the man's demise. Also it bears mention that, but for a small number of domestic dogs and hounds, horses are the only named animals in the novels of the Border Southwest. Warrior horses are befitting of names, as are warrior hounds, and except for man and horse, the only other animal that coexists in honor with man is the hunting hound.

In *The Crossing,* though, the wolf is a warrior animal of honor that is McCarthy's metaphor for man's appetite for control over the natural world. Consequently, in the text, the absence of the wolf from New Mexico signals the presence of man. Man controls the animals he can, and he kills those animals he cannot. As well, the wolf, unlike the carrion scavenging coyote, is the bane of stock cattle, so the wolf must be annihilated. Man's desire to rid southern New Mexico of the wolf grants the wolf bounty-value, and as such, the wolf, previous to the chronology of the text, is exterminated from the southwestern United States. The absence of wolves in the area is why the presence of the she-wolf in Hidalgo county, in 1941 (J. Bell 40), is so exciting to Billy Parham. For in a scene of pre-chronology, a very young Billy watches the last of the New Mexico wolves run antelope in the winter moonlight; this type of hunt by these master predators is a scene Billy will never revisit, except in memory. Man seeks control of the natural world, and in the case of the wolf, man succeeds in his quest for control. But McCarthy promotes the wolf. In *Blood Meridian, All the Pretty Horses* and *Cities of the Plain,* the wolf is mythologized by articulate characters and brief but effective passages in the text. The wolf's past is explored in both *Blood Meridian* and *Cities of the Plain,* with Tobin and Mr. Johnson explicating the wolf's mythic, mystical and exalted place in the natural world. And Cole and Lacey Rawlins hear a wolf to "the southwest" (60), in Mexico, a sign that the two are entering the land of the wild, the land where not all is domesticated and civilized by man's hand and will. McCarthy honors and promotes the wolf in *The Crossing,* while concurrently arguing the unquenchable desire of man to control the natural world and the animals within it. For after the she-wolf is captured, a series of indignities occur to the beast. In addition to being captured by a child, the she-wolf, pregnant and forever separated from her life-mate, is dragged by Billy's horse, muzzled, attacked by ranch dogs, force-fed cold rabbit, nearly drowned while bound, stolen from Billy, poked and spit on by Mexican rabble, forced to fight for show until death, and finally, shot out of mercy. Of course, had Billy not initially caught and taken control over the wild animal, the wolf perhaps would have returned to the Animas Peaks and survived and birthed her litter, thus perpetuating her species. Man controls or kills that which exists freely in the natural world, and the absence of the wolf in the text and the southwestern United States is the direct result of the acts of man. In McCarthy's fiction, even honorable acts of control by man over beast have disastrous consequences.

In *Cities of the Plain,* McCarthy offers two very different hunting passages. Each passage contains a different bounty, theme and result, but, paradoxically, the very different passages argue the same thesis— the ballet of the hunt. For, other than the horse, the only animal that can coexist honorably with man is the domesticated, trained hunting hound. Domestic dogs exist in their own hierarchy, but hunting hounds exist isolated from the pueblo curs and beasts of *Blood Meridian, All the*

Pretty Horses and *The Crossing*. Hunting hounds, as well as various scenes of the hunt, can be found in the majority of McCarthy's texts. Beginning with a number of hunting scenes in *The Orchard Keeper,* McCarthy presents the argument that hunting wild and feral animals with trained hounds is a ballet between hound and man; the hound is immediately labeled an animal of honor, one that coexists in harmony with man. McCarthy furthers this argument through the Southern novels and the novels of the Border Southwest, up to the penultimate and ultimate hunting scenes in *Cities of the Plain*, rarely, if ever, presenting hunting hounds in a negative light. As the hunt is man's organized attempt at control of the natural world, in conjunction with trained hounds, which of course are specifically bred by man to hunt, the hunt evolves into a ballet between trained domestic animal and man. The goal of the hunt is to kill the hunted, and in this text, two hunts produce two results. The first hunt is one in which the prey is the wild feline, the mountain lion. Mountain lion is a provincial term synonymous with panther; the former is regional to the Border Southwest, and the latter is regional to the southeastern United States. McCarthy uses the dominant wild feline in the feline hierarchy to oppose the hunting hound; in doing so, McCarthy elevates the trained hound and transforms the master predator into a prey animal, thus man takes control over the natural. The second hunt in the text is one where the hounds hunt a pack of feral dogs. This hunt is quite different from the first in that this hunt also adds man and horse to the ballet of the hunt. The horse as warrior returns to war, this time conjoined and in harmony with man and hound. Again, though, as in the former hunt, man is seeking to control the natural world, for the feral dogs exist outside of man's control. Man is a creature easily captured in the text; man seeks control, and in *Cities of the Plain,* appears to achieve control.

In *No Country for Old Men*, McCarthy removes most of the animals from the text, but he nonetheless continues his theme of animal death at the hand of man. In the novel, characters discuss killing, kill or try to kill antelope, dogs, birds, and cattle, but very few animals of any kind are actually present in the text. By the year of the action, 1980, man has successfully killed off much of the fauna, especially the predatory fauna, of the Border Southwest. This being the case, the novel, unlike the previous eight, is nearly devoid of wild animal imagery. But as *No Country for Old Men* is a McCarthy novel, animals do die — just not as often as in previous works — and they do die at the hand of man.

The previous brief overview of the nonhuman animal scenes offers an idea of the breadth and depth of McCarthy's use of animals in his body of work. In the following chapters, I will further analyze and explicate these scenes in order to show that McCarthy's dominant theme of omnipresent death is one that can also be applied to the flora of the natural and man-influenced worlds. In McCarthy's universe, human characters die early and often in the texts, and the theme of death is pervasive; this theme of pervasive death can also be applied to the presentation of animals in McCarthy's *oeuvre*.

The literature of Cormac McCarthy contains a bounty of non-human animals and species-specific themes and arguments. Dominant among the themes are survival in a biologically deterministic world, animals as harbingers of human death and man's ceaseless desire and attempt to control the natural world. This study will analyze the animal themes and the use of animals in McCarthy's texts; the author's goal is to help fill the scholarly void that currently exists regarding this topic. Secondary sources will be limited to what currently exists regarding animals and literature, and the few discussions of McCarthy's use of animals. When appropriate, primary material will be cited for precedent value.

1

Animals and Death in
The Gardener's Son, The Stonemason,
"Bounty," *and* "The Dark Waters"

The dominant theme in McCarthy's major works, death, can also be found in the author's other texts. In keeping with the subject of animal presentation and death, four works other than the novels must be addressed. These four texts, the drama, *The Stonemason*, the teleplay, *The Gardener's Son,* and two scenes from *The Orchard Keeper* published as titled short stories, "Bounty" and "The Dark Waters," all present animals prominently and are worthy of individual attention and analysis. *The Stonemason* is a bleak drama, which calls attention to the end of the art of stonemasonry and argues the theme of the unceasing mortality of all living things; everyone and everything dies, and the cycle of birth, life and death affects all. The narrative protagonist, Ben Telfair, watches as his family is decimated by death and his father, grandfather, nephew, dog, and others, die off; these deaths are analogous to the death of the trade of stonemasonry; as the practitioners of stonemasonry die, so does the promotion, artistry and practice of stonemasonry. Additionally, the Telfair family dog, Bossy, dies near the end of the drama. In McCarthy's drama of family death, even the dog dies. Bossy dies, and so the canine's importance lies with its position as one of the dead family members. By killing off the dog, McCarthy is including the dog in the Telfair family.

In McCarthy's teleplay, *The Gardener's Son,* the author frames the opening and closing scenes of the text proper with passages in which mule teams are prominently displayed and play the role of harbinger to human death. In the teleplay, a revisionist account of a nineteenth century murder and subsequent execution, stock mules, teamed on wagons, signify human death. Where mule teams are present, pulling wagons, there is human death, and the mule team as a framing device is analogous to James Gregg's and Robert McEvoy's deaths, as a mule team pulls and carries, literally and symbolically, the body of the dead.

In "Bounty," the first of two passages from *The Orchard Keeper* to be published as a titled short story, a boy finds a wounded sparrowhawk and takes the animal home, thus he takes control of the avian predator and thus takes control of the natural world; after the bird dies, the boy redeems a one dollar chickenhawk bounty on the carcass. The boy uses the bounty as down payment on a set of traps to further his bounty-hunting career. This bounty scene is the seminal scene of a major McCarthy theme, the theme of the bounty-value of dead wild animals, and one of many in the body of work where a dead animal is worth more to man than a live animal. "The Dark Waters" is the second passage from *The Orchard Keeper* to be published as a titled short story. In title, in theme, in action, this short story is a preface of McCarthy's ongoing textual battle between man and the natural world in the constant struggle of biological determinism. In the short story, a boy is taken on a raccoon hunt by his mentor, and what happens during the hunt initiates the boy into manhood. Of course, this coming of age story is also a narrative of the hunt, the deterministic battle between man and coonhound, and wild animal, and as such, is the seminal scene of the ballet of the hunt. Both short stories foretell McCarthy's *oeuvre*-wide fascination with the animal world and man's ceaseless attempts to control the animals in the natural world, and as well, the drama and the teleplay slot well into the author's body of work, in that both texts deal primarily with the theme of death, human and animal.

The theme of death and animal presentation in *The Stonemason* is McCarthy's bleak argument regarding the unceasing mortality of all living things. The action chronicles the deaths that occur in the Telfair family, as a catalog of family members die or are alluded to as dead by the time the textual action is completed. Those chronicled as dead by the close of the text include Ben Telfair's paternal grandmother (6), paternal Uncle Selman (50–1), paternal great Uncle Charles (62), father Big Ben (102), nephew Soldier (120), beloved paternal grandfather Papaw (98–9), and all of Papaw's brothers, sisters and children (94). In fact, early in the text, Ben refers to all of the dead Telfair "ancestors black and white" (32). Additionally, as the drama is family-centric, a majority of the action occurs in the Telfair family kitchen. Those present in the Telfair kitchen or alluded to in the conversations within the Telfair kitchen are members of the Telfair family. This familial membership even includes the Telfair family dog, Bossy, who not coincidentally, is dead by the close of the text.

Early in the text, in fact in the very opening lines of the textual action, Act one, scene two, McCarthy posits Bossy in the Telfair family kitchen, thus McCarthy includes the dog in the Telfair family. McCarthy uses direction, not character attention and dialogue, in this introduction of Bossy [McCarthy's italics]: "*Early the following morning. The lights are on in the kitchen and outside it is just graying with daylight. Papaw is sitting in his chair by the stove as Ben enters ... Ben goes to the window and looks out at the yard. There is a small dog sleeping by the stove and it looks up*" (12). As the action of the drama opens, the two protagonists of the text, Ben Telfair and his paternal grandfather Papaw, are present in the family kitchen, the family meeting place. The importance of the two human characters is indicated by their introduction prior to the dialogue in the scene. Introduced immediately thereafter is the Telfair family dog. This immediate placement of the canine within the family, in the family kitchen, indicates that the dog is indeed a member of the Telfair family. Later in the same scene, as Ben and Papaw leave to work stone, the family dog is named, and the beast's advanced age is indicated:

> *Ben opens the door.*
> MAMA: And let Bossy out.
> BEN: (*To the dog*) Let's go.
> *The dog looks at him.*
> BEN: Let's go, I said.
> *The dog climbs slowly out of the box and goes to the door and looks out.*
> BEN: Hit it.
> *The dog goes out. Ben and Papaw turn up their collars and pull on their caps and let down the earflaps. Ben watches the dog out in the snow.*
>   BEN: Mama what are you going to do about this dog?
>   MAMA: Aint nothin wrong with that dog.
>   BEN: He raises his leg to take a pee and then falls over in it.
>   MAMA: You dont need to be worryin bout that dog. That dog's just fine [24–5].

In this comic passage, McCarthy names the dog, or more correctly, identifies the Telfair's name for the dog. And as only family have the right to give a name (*Outer Dark* 235–6), Bossy is identified as a Telfair family member — because he has been named by the Telfairs. Though circular in logic, this naming situation has precedent in *Outer Dark*, when the leader of The Three indicates to Culla that the tinker did not have the right to name the infant child, but Culla or Rinthy could have and should have named the doomed child — by right and by duty. Family members are to be named, and as the dog is a member of the Telfair family, the dog receives the inclusive gift of a name. Interesting also, is McCarthy's use of dialogue here. Ben says to the dog, let's go; in doing so, Ben is using a contraction with an inclusive pronoun — let us go. Using a pronoun such as us indicates that the dog is a part of the collective that encompasses the Telfair family. Again, McCarthy has clearly indicated that Bossy is a Telfair. Finally, the canine seems arthritic, or at the least elderly and unable to move about well, for he cannot balance long enough to void without falling into the waste. But Ben's mother indicates that the dog is acting as it should at that point in life, and as such, should be left alone to live comfortably. This acceptance of the creaky dog is the loving maternal acceptance of one who loves an elderly family member. Of course, as the text is McCarthy's, the dog is not going to be just fine, for death waits.

By Act five, scene one, Ben is the Telfair patriarch, for his father, Big Ben, has committed suicide and his beloved grandfather, Papaw, has died of old age. Literally and symbolically, the Telfair family has died, for the family no longer inhabits the same kitchen in the same home. From the stage-left podium, Ben articulates on family and death: "The big elm tree died. The old dog died. Things that you can touch go away forever. I don't know what that means. I don't know what it means that things exist and then exist no more. Trees. Dogs. People" (104). The familial structure of Ben's life has collapsed, and he searches in grief for a graspable, palpable meaning to the deaths that have occurred within his family, for the Telfair family, as a collective unit, is dead. McCarthy's direction indicates the family house is no longer lived in or even livable, while Ben's narrative lists a number of deaths unseen by the audience; the big elm in the front yard has died, as has the Telfair family tree. And as a dead tree must be cut down, the Telfair family has been cut down. The tree, now dead and in scraps or burned, is no longer touchable. The androcentric Telfair family tree has also fallen because the taproot, Papaw is dead, as is the trunk, Big Ben. Consequently, neither father figure is touchable, either. Also included in Ben's lament is Bossy, the now dead canine, for Bossy, as a beloved member of the Telfair family, is also mourned. Like the other dead, the Elm, Big Ben and Papaw, Bossy is now untouchable, and because of this untouchability, Ben mourns the loss of Bossy. Bossy's death is an inclusive act by the author, for the dog's death clarifies the canine's place within the Telfair family. Nowhere in McCarthy's *oeuvre* is a dead dog so lamented and so mourned as is Bossy in *The Stonemason*—a drama ultimately about the death of a family brought about through the deaths of the members of the family.

In McCarthy's teleplay, *The Gardener's Son*, animals and death again are conjoined, as mules are harbingers of human death. In *The Gardener's Son*, the author frames the opening and closing scenes of the text proper with passages in which stock mule teams play the role of harbinger to human death. As such, stock mules, teamed on wagons, signify human death. Consequently, where teams of stock mules are found in the text, human death is to follow. This theme is not unlike the stock animal as harbinger to human death theme found in *Outer Dark*, a text where the swine is the harbinger to human death. But *The Gardener's Son*, like *The Stonemason*, deals with human death and the destruction of the family, but unlike the drama, the teleplay incorporates violence and nineteenth century class schism into the nexus of familial destruction. In the teleplay, a catalog of family members from the wealthy Gregg family and the poverty struck McEvoy family die, but the focus of the action revolves around the murder of James Gregg, scion to mill owner William Gregg, by Robert McEvoy, scion to the mill's gardener, Patrick McEvoy, and Robert's subsequent execution by hanging. Prior to each man's death, mule teams are situated in either the text or the author's direction, signifying the death(s) to come.

In James Gregg's case, the first paragraphs of McCarthy's direction signify James as doomed (italics McCarthy's):

> *Series of old still shots of the town of Graniteville* [South Carolina] *and of the people.... They comprise an overture to the story to follow, being shots of the characters in the film in situations from the film itself, so that they sketch the story out in miniature to the last shot of an old wooden coffin being loaded into a mule-drawn wagon and a shot of the town.*
>
> *Freeze frame of the town, the rows of houses. Animate into action. A wagon comes up a street through the mud. Seated in three sets of spring seats are seven or eight stockholders of the Graniteville Company Mill and the son of the mill's founder who is named James Gregg.*
>
> *James Gregg is pointing out various features of the mill village* [5].

By presenting the photograph of the mule team, wagon and coffin as the final photograph of the montage, McCarthy immediately identifies the mule team with human death, and the position of the photograph can hardly be interpreted as an accident. Clearly, the author is developing a textual theme, for he posits the fated James Gregg in the paragraph that follows the opening montage. In this brief passage signifier and signified are quickly identified, and indeed James Gregg is later mortally wounded (56–7) by Robert McEvoy for crimes known and unknown to the reader. In this first example of mule as harbinger to human death, McCarthy introduces the theme of the mule team and human death, and then, the author presents, by name, the character whose death has been tolled.

Quickly caught, tried, found guilty, and condemned, Robert McEvoy is to die by hanging on 13 June 1876 (68–9). Regardless that the verdict comes before the mule, so to speak, McCarthy sees fit to continue to place the mule team in the text for the purpose of signifying human death, in this case, Robert McEvoy's death; again, the author uses direction to posit the mule team in the text:

> Exterior. Jail. Two men arrive on a wagon in front of the doors and one climbs down and taps at the door with the butt of his whip. The door opens and the jailer looks out. The teamster nods toward the wagon and they talk and the jailer nods and the teamster goes back to the wagon and the two teamsters slide a black wooden coffin off the tailboard and carry it in [83].

In this paragraph of direction, the mule team, identified by the fact that the drovers are teamsters, delivers the condemned man's coffin, McEvoy's black wooden box. In this example, as with the example with the mule team and James Gregg, the signifying mule team is easily identified with the signified. McEvoy is hanged at 1313 hours on Friday the 13th, June 1876 (84–5). To make the mule and human death conjugation even more explicit, McCarthy hauls McEvoy's coffined corpse off in a wagon pulled by a mule:

> Exterior. Long shot of jail and an empty wagon standing in the front with Patrick McEvoy waiting. The doors open and the men come out with the coffin and load it into the back of the wagon. The sheriff approaches McEvoy with a paper and gets him to sign it. The other men stand around somewhat uneasily. McEvoy looks at them and then turns and takes up the reins and chucks up the mule and they start off [86–7].

Here, no longer harbinger of Robert's death, the mule nonetheless signifies Robert's death. For the third time is this short text, McCarthy has conjoined the wagon-pulling mule with human death. The first time the theme is used, James Gregg is to be murdered; the second time the theme is used, Robert McEvoy is to be hanged; the third time the theme is used, McCarthy is presenting the death of the McEvoy family, as the only McEvoy son is now dead; there will be no more McEvoy scions. And the fourth and final time the theme of mule and human death is used in the text, McCarthy is presenting the death of the Gregg family, for James Gregg was the only remaining living Gregg son; there will be no more Gregg scions.

In the final directorial passage that contains the theme of the mule and human death, a team of mules removes the Gregg family plots and tomb-monument, prior to Mrs. Gregg's return to Charleston, her ancestral home:

> Exterior. Day. The Graniteville cemetery. A scaffolding of poles is erected over the monument of William Gregg and the monument is being hoisted with a block and tackle. A heavy freight wagon with an eight-mule team is waiting to be backed under and receive the monument. A crew of gravediggers wait on with shovels. Teamsters back the mules and the stone is lowered into the bed of the wagon and the diggers come forth with their picks and shovels and proceed to exhume the bodies of the Gregg family. Mrs. Gregg in her carriage waits on in the distance. It is a quiet and sunny scene [87].

In a lonely scene, not unlike the above scene with Mr. McEvoy, a lone remaining parent retrieves the dead for burial, or in this case, reburial. In each example, a mule team labors, carrying the weight of human death. Mrs. Gregg's material wealth means nothing, because her family has been destroyed, and she is without husband (18) and sons (15, 59), and she is as broken spiritually as is Mr. McEvoy, who has lost his son (85) and his wife (36). McCarthy's nexus to all of this human death is the mule team, for in *The Gardener's Son*, where mule teams are found pulling wagons, human death abounds, and the mule team as a framing device is specifically analogous to James Gregg's death and Robert McEvoy's death, as a mule team pulls and carries, literally and symbolically, the body of the dead.

In "Bounty," the first excerpt from *The Orchard Keeper* (77–85) published as a short story (*The Yale Review* 54.3), McCarthy offers the first scene that contains the theme of the bounty-value of dead wild animals. This bounty-value, of course, means that a dead wild animal is worth more to man than a live one. The bounty-value theme is a major theme in McCarthy's body of work, and is to be found, in some manner, in all nine of the novel length works of fiction. As man places bounty-value on specific animals, man kills said valued animals, and thus, controls the prey through killing. This act of controlling an animal through killing is one that man often repeats in McCarthy's fiction; using force, man controls the wild animals he can, and man kills the animals he cannot control. Either way, man seeks and gains control over the natural world. "Bounty" contains another important McCarthy theme as well, the theme of man's attempts to control flying animals. Flight symbolizes a freedom and a power that man does not possess. As such, man seeks to control avian freedom and power through controlling avians, often resorting to killing the flying animals, namely birds and the flying mammals, bats. All of McCarthy's novel length works except *Outer Dark* contain scenes of man explicitly attempting to control avians. Clearly, "Bounty" is an important work because the titled short story foreshadows the dominant, *oeuvre*-wide themes of bounty-value of a wild animal and control of the natural world — with attention here to a doomed sparrowhawk — through killing. And of course, bounty-value and control through killing are subthemes of McCarthy's omnipresent theme of death.

In "Bounty," an unnamed boy finds a wounded sparrowhawk, and he takes the little avian home. Thus the boy takes control of the natural world through control and capture, but the little bird dies in captivity:

> It was in August that he found the sparrowhawk on the mountain road, crouched in the dust with one small falcon wing fanned and limp, eyeing him without malice or fear — something hard there, implacable and unforgiving.... He carried it home and put it in a box in the loft and fed it meat and grasshoppers for three days and then it died [368].

This passage, excerpted from the first published paragraph of McCarthy's adult work, identifies McCarthy's naturalist bent, while additionally, the passage includes the theme of death and the theme of man controlling the natural world, specifically here, man controlling the flying wild animals of the natural world. The boy captures the wild bird, and he boxes the animal; the flying animal, no longer free, dies in captivity, for a broken wing is not necessarily a mortal wound, and a sparrowhawk, a master predator, is not meant to eat pieces of meat and insects from the hand of a boy. This idea that wild animals are not suited for captivity is also an important idea in McCarthy's later works, especially *The Crossing*. In McCarthy's body of work, wild animals do not do well in captivity. However, a dead wild animal still has value, bounty-value.

The boy still has use for the dead sparrowhawk, for there exists in the county, a chickenhawk bounty of one dollar, and the boy goes into town and to the courthouse to redeem his bounty:

There was a woman at a small desk just inside the door.... He stood for a few minutes looking around the hall and reading the signs over the doors and finally she asked him what it was he needed.
    He held the bag up. Hawk bounty, he said.
    Oh, she said. I think you go in yonder [369].

For the first time, the author presents the *oeuvre*-wide theme of the bounty-value of a wild animal; certain wild animals are worth more to man, dead than alive. The boy commences to the second clerk, and she asks if the dead bird is a chickenhawk. The boy replies in the affirmative and states that the dead bird is not yet full grown. The boy tells a lie, for the baby chickenhawk is actually a sparrowhawk, but the bounty is not for sparrowhawks; it is for chickenhawks. Chickenhawks prey upon chickens, and man invests time, money and energy raising chickens for eggs, meat, and feathers, and financial gain. As such, a wild animal that hurts man's profit must be controlled. One way to control the wild animals in the natural world is to kill the wild animals. One way to promote the killing of specific wild animals is to place a monetary bounty-value on the specific wild animal, in this case, the poultry ravaging chickenhawk. Subsequently, a wild animal's value to man increases after death, and so the boy lies about the type of hawk he possesses, for a dollar is a large sum to the boy, and the boy has a preplanned use for the bounty money.

After leaving the courthouse, the boy goes through town and arrives at a general store, where he gazes in the window and sees what he wants hanging from the wall. Concurrently, McCarthy continues his bounty motif. After entering the store, the boy is helped by an elderly gentleman:

Can I help ye, son? He said.
How much are they ... your traps there.
The man turned. Traps? Steel traps.
Yessir.
... what size?
Them. He pointed. Number ones [373].

The boy is going to invest in traps and enter the bounty-hunting business, for the boy understands bounty-value, in theory and in practice, and as such, believes that collecting bounty money is quite easy. The boy uses his bounty dollar to contract for twelve traps, four of which the boy receives at the time of the transaction. McCarthy dates the action, as well, as the traps are to be paid for in full by the first of January 1941 (374). As this scene is set in August, it becomes clear that the year of the scene is 1940. Returning to the traps and the themes of bounty-value and death in the text, typical of man in McCarthy's work, the boy seeks control of the natural world through the killing of wild animals; additionally, the boy understands the concept of bounty-value, and as such, seeks material gain through the trapping and killing of bounty-valued wild animals. Finally, the bounty-value concept is discovered when the boy captures and controls an avian, thus taking from the bird its freedom and its life. This seminal short story is an important work, regardless that it is an excerpt, because McCarthy's *oeuvre*-wide themes of death, control of the natural world, control through killing, and bounty-value are present from the first paragraph of the work. "The Dark Waters," also contains the dominant themes of the McCarthy body of work.

"The Dark Waters" is, in title, in theme, in action, a preface of McCarthy's ongoing textual conflict between man and coonhound, and wild animal, in a biologically deterministic world. In this titled short story (*The Sewanee Review* 73.2), also an excerpt from *The Orchard Keeper* (119–27), man, devolved to the point that he needs aid in hunting, uses coonhounds to hunt wild prey. As this titled short story is McCarthy's first published narrative of the hunt, it is also the seminal scene of the ballet of the hunt — man and coonhound hunting in an unseen balance, which is the product of more than five thousand years of canine domestication and training (see Chapter 9). This narrative of the ballet of the hunt is also a coming of age story, where a boy is taken on a raccoon hunt by his mentor, and the boy passes an initiation right into manhood. Of course, as this story focuses on the hunt, the theme of death is omnipresent through the narrative. So, as with "Bounty," "The Dark Waters" is a primer into the dominant themes in McCarthy's body of work.

The story opens with the ballet of the hunt as a man communicates with a coonhound, sight unseen, secondary to the pattern and direction of the canine's calls:

> Her first high yelp was thin and clear as the air itself, its tenuous and diminishing echoes sounding out the coves and hollows, trebling to a high ring like the last fading note of a chime glass....
> The strung-out ringing yelps came like riflefire. The boy was on his feet. Has she treed yet? he asked.
> No. She's jest hit now. Then he added: She's close though, hot [210].

In this scene, the coonhound and the man communicate; she bays, and he follows. As well, the man can ascertain how close she is to the wild

animal and whether or not the canine has treed the prey animal. This is
the balance between man and coonhound, each chasing the prey, but sep-
arately, not in geographic proximity. Easily understood by the reader is
the boy's secondary position in the hunt; the boy is obviously green,
and his questions and mannerisms indicate his freshness as a hunter.
The man is a willing mentor, and this relationship of paternal-
mentor/male student is one that McCarthy will use again and again in
the fiction.

As the action continues, the boy and the man race through the winter woods, above and parallel to a rushing, but freezing creek. The time
is winter, and the hunting pack and prey are ominously approaching the
water. Here, McCarthy is introducing a major motif, the drowning motif,
for many, if not all of the later texts contain scenes of animals drowning, and clearly the author understands the deadly power of water over
mammals human and nonhuman. Additionally, the winter setting
increases the deadly power of water, for hypothermia increases the risk
of drowning. The man and the boy continue their pursuit running
"down" (211) toward the creek as they can hear the "rush" (211) of the
freezing water of the creek, swollen from recent rain, which rumbles like
a "freight" (211) train passing in the distance. McCarthy increases the
danger of the water through the direction of the chase, downward, and
the fact that rain has recently fallen; the water in the creek is rushing,
not standing. Finally, McCarthy uses a simile of force and power and
mass and density, the freight train, to evoke the mighty power of the
water. The man, the boy, the coonhounds, and the prey animal must
converge at the creek:

> ... Lady's clear voice was joined by another, lower and less insistent....
> He could follow her progress.... Then she stopped.
> There was a moment of silence; then the other dog yapped once. Sounds
> of brush crashing. Two wild yelps just off to his right and then a concus-
> sion of water. A low voice at his side said: He's got her in the creek....
> [211].

The boy and the man race to the creek, and find the raccoon drowning
the lead coonhound: "The oval of the flashbeam ... came to rest on the
combatants clinching in the icy water.... They could see Lady's ear stick-
ing out from under the coon's front leg" (212–3). After the raccoon is
spooked off, Lady is swept down the creek and is again in great danger
of drowning. It is at this point that the boy risks his own life and leaps
into the frigid, rushing water and, and after some struggle, saves the

drowning coonhound (213–4). The boy proves himself adept at life and death, while he also impresses the seasoned hunters with his physical courage. This convergence at the creek, of hunter and hunted, wild and domestic, boy and man, is thematically indicative of the McCarthy body of work. The domestic canine attempts to hunt the wild raccoon in a deterministic battle, and in this case, the wild trumps the domestic, and but for the boy's actions, the domestic would have died through drowning. Concurrently, man attempts to control the natural world through killing, and the thematic and textual ballet of the hunt is born. Of course, the theme of death is the unifying force of the narrative, as it is in all of McCarthy's body of work.

McCarthy's lesser-studied works are important because these works contain the major themes, motifs and action that dominate McCarthy's major works. Both of the short stories, "Bounty" and The Dark Waters," foretell McCarthy's *oeuvre*-wide fascination with the animal world and man's ceaseless attempts to control the animals in the natural world — very often through the killing of the wild animals of the natural world for bounty-value. Additionally, "The Dark Waters" contains a deterministic battle for survival between Lady, the coonhound, and the male raccoon, and the theme of the ballet of the hunt, and "Bounty" is the seminal scene of McCarthy's bounty motif. As well, both *The Stonemason* and *The Gardener's Son* offer prominent thematic and textual displays of both human and animal death, with the former using the family dog in the cycle of life and inevitable death, and the latter using mules as harbingers of human death. In theme, text and action, all four of the lesser-known works bear the McCarthy imprimatur, and as such, fit quite well into the *oeuvre*.

Chapter 2 will be an analysis of the feline hierarchy present in *The Orchard Keeper*, Cormac McCarthy's first novel. In the text, a feline hierarchy exists, by which felines, domestic, feral, legendary, and wild, can be posited according to the animal's proximity to and dependence upon man. That is, the closer a feline is to man, the more dependent a feline is upon man, the lower the feline is on the feline hierarchy. A domestic kitten, utterly dependent upon man, exists at the abject position on the hierarchy, and a panther, a wild animal independent from man, exists at the apex of the hierarchy. In between the abject and the apex are felines in various states of existence.

2

Feline Hierarchy in
The Orchard Keeper

In *The Orchard Keeper,* Cormac McCarthy presents felines—domestic, feral and wild—in an organized hierarchical structure. Each feline species exists in the hierarchy according to each species' proximity to and dependence upon man. In fact, McCarthy posits felines—wild, feral and domestic—in all of his texts. The latter three novels of the South have cats placed periodically in the text, and the novels of the Border Southwest include extended scenes with both domestic and wild felines, but only in *The Orchard Keeper* is feline hierarchy so clearly defined and structured. What is more, the feline hierarchy in McCarthy's first text is presented in accordance with the manner in which each feline species interacts with man. Hierarchical placement is inversely proportional to each feline species' dependence on man, or lack of dependence upon man. So, domestic baby cats, completely dependent upon man, become blind, plagued, wailing kittens, born only to suffer and die in man's care. A feral cat, no longer purely domesticated, yet not wild in predatory activity and ability to survive, paradoxically becomes a prey animal, misplaced in the open and savage wild. Because of their social interaction with man, and their dependence upon man for their survival, domestic and feral felines exist at the bottom of the feline hierarchy, with the former in the abject position. Higher on the hierarchy are the wild felines, which exist in their own elevated hierarchy; bobcats, lynx, the supernatural wampus cat, and the panther, exist on the hierarchy in that order, with the panther holding the apex position. Because of their pelts, bobcats and lynx have bounty-value to man, and as such, are hunted for monetary purpose — as evidenced by the placement of a hunting pamphlet in the text and the recurring theme of animal bounty-value in this text specifically. In Anglo and Indian lore, the wampus cat, a legendary and supernatural feline, the product of feline and woman, must exist above the smaller wild cats on the feline hierarchy because of its cunning and savage exploits. The dominant predator in the feline hierarchy, and the dominant predator in the southeastern United States, and the only wild feline that strikes fear into man, is the panther, also known regionally as the puma, the mountain lion or the cougar. The panther exists literally, as do the lynx and the bobcat, and the panther exists in legend and in folklore, as does the wampus cat. As such, the panther is fact and fiction, hunter and haunter. In *The Orchard Keeper,* man promotes the panther through rumors and myths of its deeds and extraordinary predatory abilities, something man does not do with either the bobcat or lynx. This promotion of the panther signals a forced respect on man's part; man must respect the panther, and as such, man as myth-maker, mythologizes the feline at the highest position of the feline hierarchy.

Feline hierarchy in *The Orchard Keeper* is but one of a number of different animal hierarchies that McCarthy uses in his texts; what each McCarthy animal hierarchy has in common is the formula of proximity to and dependence upon man, in conjunction with locus in the natural world. With feline hierarchy, slotting in the hierarchy is inversely proportional to proximity to man. Man interrupts and affects biological determinism, as is evidenced by McCarthy's characterizations of the domestic and feral cats, and the manner in which each type of cat reacts to the struggle for survival. Man becomes an influencing environmental force upon biological determinism, though not necessarily one of the natural world, as evidenced by McCarthy's presentation of the wild cats— bobcat, lynx, wampus cat, and panther. In the text, only the panther seems suited and able to sway man's influence upon the outcome of biological determinism, and as a result, the panther seems to be the only feline suited to survive in a deterministic world where man is the most corrupting influence. For there can be no doubt, proximity to man adversely affects biological determinism. As panthers and other wild feline species exist in the natural world, entirely independent from man, these felines, at least the ones who are not hunted or trapped, propagate and survive. However, domestic and feral felines, close to and broken by man, may propagate, but these lowly and woefully mortal felines yield mortally wounded progeny. Biological determinism is exacted by a combination of environment and genetics, and in *The Orchard Keeper,* felines existing in an environment around man cease to exist, or fail to propagate effectively; consequently, the animals' familial lines cease. Conversely, the wild feline hierarchy, those species of felines existing independent of man, survive and fight and kill for the continuation of their familial lines. In *The Orchard Keeper,* through feline proximity to man, Cormac McCarthy succeeds in arguing a structured feline hierarchy, while also presenting the negative impact of man upon feline in a biologically deterministic natural world.

The use of felines in literature is not a new literary device, for cats of all sorts can be found in texts dating from 3000 b.c. to the present. In addition, the specific types of domestic and wild cats McCarthy uses in his feline hierarchy can be easily located in previously published Anglo and American literature. What is more, the felines in the precedent setting literature behave in similar manner as McCarthy's felines, and additionally, the topic fare in the previously published texts is analogous to the topic fare in McCarthy's text. For example, Beatrix Potter writes of a domestic kitten left in dire straits, "While Tom Kitten was left alone under the floor of the attic, he wriggled about and tried to mew for help. But his mouth was full of soot and cobwebs, and he was tied up in such very tight knots, he could not make anybody hear him" (60). This stranded domestic kitten is not unlike McCarthy's base domestic kittens, blinded and plagued, trapped and punished (180–2), and these examples of the scene or motif of the wretched, abused, ill kitten are but two examples of a common motif. In *The Orchard Keeper,* McCarthy uses this traditional device of the distressed domestic kitten to draw his scene of the domestic kittens. Gavin Maxwell, in *Ring of Bright Water,* also writes of "wounded and dying kitten[s]" (26); in this case, Maxwell refers to the doomed, domestic progeny of a semi-feral she-cat and a lynx. Of course, the domestic female cat with feral instincts is a very specific type of feline, a feline type McCarthy uses in *The Orchard Keeper,* and the lynx, a wild feline, is situated above the feral cat in McCarthy's feline hierarchy.

To locate precedent for Ather Ownby's wampus cat, one must look to regional American folklore, for the legend of the wampus cat is one that is time-honored in the southeastern United States, by both the Anglo and the American Indian cultures. While each version of the wampus cat legend is unique in its story up to the creation of the wampus cat, what is similar in either legend is the composition of the wampus cat; in each legend, the wampus cat is half-woman and half-cat. In the Anglo version, a witch transforms herself into a cat, but is caught in the act of retransformation; the result leaves her "half woman and half cat" (Legend 1). In the American Indian version, a woman commits a cultural taboo — watching the men's pre-hunting ritual — while wearing the skin of "a mountain cat" (Legend 2), and is subsequently "transformed into what is known as the Wampus Cat" (Legend 2). Additionally, what the two legends share, something present as well in the McCarthy text (59–60), is the emphasis on the non-natural scream of the wampus cat and the wampus cat's voyeuristic — rather than predatory — tendencies. All three versions of the wampus cat hint or argue the supernatural abilities of the wampus cat, an argument that leads to Ambrose Bierce's short story, "The Eyes of the Panther."

Bierce's short story is relevant to *The Orchard Keeper* for a number of reasons. First, the nineteenth century tale — like the oral legends of the wampus cat — precedes McCarthy's text and is a model from which McCarthy seems to draw; Bierce's tale (38–46) is an intergenerational story of a young married couple that live isolated in the southeastern United States and are visited upon by a nocturnal cat with "reddish-green" (41) glowing eyes. Three months after the nocturnal visit, a child is born, a girl with eyes of "feline beauty" (39), born perhaps of the coupling of the woman in the cabin and the cat, for the gestation period of a panther is three months. The baby girl grows into a woman with feline eyes and "lithe" (38) grace who is shot by her fiancé. The narrator tells though, that the man shot not a woman, but a nocturnal trespasser, a panther with "two gleaming ... shining eyes" (45). So, Bierce's panther seems to be what legend refers to as a wampus cat, a cat half-woman and half-panther, but Bierce is using the term panther to blur the line between the natural and the supernatural. McCarthy, however, seems to use the term panther for a natural, stealthy animal, while he uses the term wampus cat for a supernatural cat.

Besides the use of a young married couple isolated in the woods, Bierce uses a number of other motifs that McCarthy uses. Bierce's use of the eye motif to identify the supernatural cat as voyeuristic rather than predatory (42, 45), Bierce's use of a foreboding, prescient dream to announce the presence of the beast (40, 41), Bierce's appropriation of the wampus cat legend, and Bierce's use of the supernatural animal's "human [and] devilish" (46) scream all foreshadow McCarthy's tale of Ather Ownby and the wampus cat(s). Both authors draft the panther as a predator worth mythologizing, and the use of felines in literature is time-honored and tested. McCarthy furthers the use of this feline device. However, it is McCarthy who has created a structured feline hierarchy.

McCarthy's placement of felines within his texts is not, for McCarthy, unusual, for felines, domestic, feral and wild, can be found in all of the novel-length fiction that follow *The Orchard Keeper*. Very often in fact, the scenes in the latter texts contain domestic cats either dead, dying or being abused in some manner. In McCarthy's second published text, *Outer Dark*, domestic cats, and cats of any kind for that matter, are rarely located in the text, but one scene in a broken-down cabin illustrates the place of the domestic cat; seeking rest and shelter, Culla Holme enters a run-down cabin; on a dilapidated bed mattress, Holme spies "a dead cat leering with eyeless grimace, a caved and maggoty shape that gave off a faint dry putrescence above the reek of aged smoke" (196). Indeed this rotting, decaying beast is metonymously representative of the domestic cat, as presented in McCarthy's literature; the domestic feline is dead or dying at the hand of man. In *Blood Meridian,* McCarthy continues this domestic cat motif; while testing a Colt revolver for purchase, Captain John Joel Glanton uses a live target: "Glanton drew sight upon a cat that at that precise moment appeared upon the high wall from the other side ... Glanton leveled the huge pistol and thumbed back the hammer. The explosion ... was enormous. The cat simply disappeared. There was no blood or cry, it just vanished" (82). Here, McCarthy animates the cat via the animal's movement; he then sites the cat via Glanton; he then removes the cat, blood, guts and all, from the scene. Notice that McCarthy uses the term cat to refer to the living animal, and he uses the vague referent it to refer to the dead, disintegrated cat. The living domestic cat dissipates into a nonentity. In the third novel of the Border Trilogy, *Cities of the Plain,* McCarthy continues his abjection of the domestic cat. The voice of the ranching past, Mr. Johnson, is telling John Grady Cole about a long past trail ride; upon this ride, after some trouble, a rider from another outfit stampedes Johnson's herd by arson: "He come by in the night and set a cat on fire and throwed it into the herd. I mean slung it ... it looked like a comet goin out through there and just squallin" (125). Again, at the hand of man, a domestic cat is abjectified and abused until dead. McCarthy's presentation of the domestic feline is a rough one, on the cat, and he repeats the motif on a text-by-text basis. In regard to feral and wild felines in other texts, McCarthy is more kind to these cats than he is to the capitally punished domestic cat.

In *Suttree*, for example, McCarthy includes a number of scenes that contain feral cats, and analogous to the feral cat in *The Orchard Keeper*, the feral cats in *Suttree* are aware that sustenance can be gained around man. In one scene, a feral cat steals a cleaned fish from Cornelius Suttree's skiff; the feral beast is "a starved and snarling thing with the hackles reared along its razorous spine" (65). To retrieve his catch, Suttree pelts the feral cat with rocks, and the beast finally gives up the fish, but immediately after Suttree's departure, the wily feral cat returns to the skiff to sniff out a meal. With behavioral tendencies similar to the feral cat in *The Orchard Keeper*, feral cats in McCarthy's other literature have a parasitic, paradoxical relationship with man. However, in McCarthy's latter works, wild cats fare somewhat better than the feral or the domestic.

For example, in *Cities of the Plain*, McCarthy has a scene with two references to wild cats. The first is built into the scene; the scene is one of a hunt for a mountain lion; 'mountain lion' of course is a regional term synonymous with panther. In this brief scene (87–92), the hounds are unsuccessfully running a mountain lion, one that they have hunted before: "She aint goin tree, he [Travis] said ... How do you know it's the same lion? said JC. She's done us thisaway before, he said. She'll run plumb out of the country" (88). Here, the mountain lion is an animal of courage, cunning and endurance, running rather than getting caught, because to be caught is to be killed. The mountain lion will live to hunt and be hunted, unlike a hound mentioned in the same scene that was killed in Mexico by a jaguar. In both references to wild felines, McCarthy draws the animals as smart and predatory, determined to survive potentially lethal contact with man. In the former, the mountain lion chooses flight, and survives; in the latter, the jaguar chooses to fight, and survives. Each wild feline makes the correct choice under the circumstances. So, in the presentation of domestic, feral and wild felines, with regard to texts that follow *The Orchard Keeper*, McCarthy follows patterns of feline hierarchy originally established in the seminal text; domestic cats take the abject position; feral cats come next; then, lower wild felines follow; above them are wampus cats, and at the apex of the hierarchy, panthers are slotted.

Vereen M. Bell argues that *The Orchard Keeper* is "a meditation upon the irrelevance of the human in the impersonal scheme of things" (10). Bell's statement seems to argue that biological determinism in the natural world, Bell's "impersonal scheme of things," is unaffected by the intrusion of man. However, careful and in-depth analysis of the scenes that construct and define McCarthy's feline hierarchy shows that man indeed does have an effect upon "the impersonal scheme of things." As initial evidence, and abjectly speaking, the domestic kitten is where the feline hierarchy begins. The domestic cat *(felis catus)* has a long history of forced proximity to man. For at least 5,000 years, man has domesticated the feline (Cat Family). As such, for the domestic cat, proximity to man is the unchosen bane of its birth, and dependence upon man, while not always acknowledged by the cat, is as well an unchosen right of birth. In *The Orchard Keeper,* McCarthy realizes this fact, and as such, he places domestic cats, more specifically, domestic kittens, at the bottom of the feline hierarchy.

While domestic kittens only appear in one scene in *The Orchard Keeper,* their ignoble appearance in the scene easily places the domestic kitten at the base of the feline hierarchy. The scene takes place at Mr. Eller's general store, a locale of social, commercial and conversational intersection that McCarthy utilizes in a number of scenes. After filling his vehicle with gasoline, Marion Sylder converses and trades verbal jabs with Mr. Eller; the domestic kittens, accurately described by Vereen Bell as a "pathetic cat menagerie" (21), become the topic of the text and of the characters' conversation:

> A loosed box of kittens came tottering aimlessly over the floor, rocking on their stub legs and mewling. Their eyes were closed and festered with mucus as if they might have been struck simultaneously with some biblical blight.
> Them's the nastiest-lookin cats I ever did see, Sylder said.
> That's what Mrs Fenner said, droned the storekeeper. Young Pulliam told her she ought to see the ones back in the back propped up with sticks [180].

What is present in this scene is not one but two lots of domestic kittens. The first lot is the group of blind kittens in Eller's store, and the second lot is the group in the back of the store. The most abject of the abject — the kittens in the back of the store — are dead, and as such, the dead kittens are propped up on sticks for display, hence, Warn Pulliam's comment to Mrs. Fenner regarding the macabre presentation in the back area behind the store. Notice that the cats are not identified as bobcats

or lynx or panthers; the lack of specific wild feline signifier, in conjunction with the other plagued domestic kittens in the scene, leads one to
conclude that the dead felines on display are, indeed, dead domestic
felines, probably the siblings to the remaining kittens in the store. Thus,
the dead domestic kittens are not even present in the scene but are only
referred to as a matter of the characters' conversation. This absence of
the dead domestic kittens is somewhat humorous because the dead kittens remain unseen, while the living kittens cannot see.

The blind domestic kittens, those still living, are living to suffer.
The nasty-looking felines are aptly described as abject and very nearly
disgusting in appearance. The eyes of the beasts are actively festering and
producing what is likely to be some bacterial laden discharge. The disgusting creatures are runtish and squalling in physical and emotional
agony of biblical, Old Testament of course, proportions. The kittens are
fated to wander the floor of the store and would be better off dead,
propped up on sticks. Sylder even suggests that death would be better
for the kittens:

> A Cristian'd of drowned em.
> What's that? Mr Eller asked.
> Leaning over and grinning Sylder pointed at the kittens bobbing over
> the floor like brown lint.
> Mr Eller shooed his hand at him and he left [181].

What Sylder is stating is that the Christian thing to do with the little
wretches would be to put them out of their misery; and as the scene
occurs during a flood of biblical proportions, drowning would be a fit
way to stifle and help the little plagued beasts. Additionally, when Sylder
speaks to Eller, Eller seems to have forgotten that the kittens exist. The
kittens are out of sight and out of mind, so to speak. As such, literally
and symbolically, the domestic kitten is out of the scene when dead, and
out of Mr. Eller's mind while alive. It goes almost without stating that
if Eller had a loosed panther in his store, he would not forget the presence of the wild cat.

Lest the reader forget the presence of the pitiful creatures in Eller's
store, McCarthy conjoins the domestic beasts and the abject again before
closing the scene:

> One of the cats had wandered behind the meat block and ... it went
> by in a drunken reel, caromed off the meat case, continued. Lost, they
> [the kittens] wandered about the floor, passing and repassing each other,
> unseeing. One staggered past a coffeecan sat next to the stove, slipped, fell

in the puddle of tobacco spittle surrounding it. He struggled to his feet again, back and side brown-slimed and sticky, tottered across to the wall where he stood with blind and suppurant eyes and offered up to the world his thin wails [181–2].

The little beast rages and screams, thinly, and the reader empathizes with the humiliation of the suffering little feline. One notices, as well, that even at its most angry and expressive, the sickly kitten can only offer a thin wail, as if even the kitten's rage is abject. In this passage, as in the first cited passage, McCarthy refers to the little kitten's sightless, pus-producing eyes. It can be argued that in McCarthy's text, a feline's eyes are metonymic for the cat's place in the feline hierarchy; the blind and the unseen exist at the bottom of the feline hierarchy, while the sighted, especially those gifted with exceptional nocturnal sight, exist at the top of the hierarchy. Of course, the former are domestic and dependent upon man, and the latter are wild and independent from man.

As the domestic felines are entirely dependent upon man, it comes as no surprise that the doomed, sightless kittens are given some comfort and temporary reprieve by a young girl who enters the store and takes the sorry little beasts: "After a while a little girl in a thin and dirty dress came through the door behind the counter and gathered up all the kittens, now wailing louder and in broken chorus, carried them out again, talking to them in low remonstrances" (182). McCarthy's narrator notes the pitiful appearance of the little girl. This little urchin is in no position to offer any manner of veterinary help to the little kittens. It can be easily determined that the child can offer only emotional kindness to the little beasts; she cannot heal the festering sightless eyes of each kitten, and thus, the kittens remain doomed, even after rescue. The kittens exist in the scene but are removed from the store interior, thus the kittens become unseen, and symbolically speaking, dead. The unseen dead kittens and the suffering, wailing, short-lived blind kittens are merely a drawing of the entire life cycle of the domestic cat in *The Orchard Keeper*, with one exception, the feral cat. For except for the feral cat, one who has lived around and subsequently escaped man, the domestic cat is easily the most pitiful feline in McCarthy's feline hierarchy.

In *The Orchard Keeper*, the feral cat fares somewhat better that the domestic cat. For the curse of the feral cat is the paradox of domestication under man. The feral cat seeks an existence in the wild, but the feral feline cannot discount 5,000 years of domestication. As such, the feral cat seeks a life of biological determinism in the wild, but cannot quite sever its existence from the influence of and the dependence on man. The result is a cat that lives in the wild, yet returns to man in order to survive, a cat smart enough to leave man, yet too weak to survive without man. For the feral cat is aware that man is a predator, and, as such, man offers meat, sustenance, so the feral cat hunts in smokehouses and the like. As Ather states, in regard to cats, "Housecats is smart. Folks thinks they ain't on account of you cain't learn em nothing, but what it is is that they won't learn nothing. They too smart" (227). Feral cats are smart enough to escape man, but not smart enough to devolve from domestication. As such, the feral cat is a cat neither domestic, nor wild.

McCarthy intersperses *The Orchard Keeper* with scenes of an individual feral she-cat. In doing so, McCarthy elevates, by mere presence in the text at least, the feral feline above the domestic. However, when describing the feral she-cat, McCarthy hardly draws an attractive portrait of a master predator:

> The rain had plastered down her fur and she looked very thin and forlorn. She gathered burdock and the curling purple leaves of rabbit weed as she went; a dead stalk of blackberry briar clung to her hind leg. Just short of the road she stopped, shivered her loose skin, ears flat against her head. She squalled once, hugging the ground with her belly, eyes turned upward at the colorless sky, the endless pelting rain [176].

And another brief sketch of the feral feline is hardly flattering: "The cat trod the high crown of the road, bedraggled and diminutive" (174). Wet, cold, underweight, and battered by rain, McCarthy's feral cat is in poor circumstance and position, and this circumstance and position is the locus of the feral cat in the natural world, for the feral cat cannot exist and thrive in the natural world. As such, driven by misery, the feral cat returns to man.

Three times in *The Orchard Keeper*, McCarthy's feral she-cat looks to man for help. First, the feral cat seeks shelter from the rain in Ather Ownby's outhouse: "Rainwater seeped among the porous boards of the outhouse until the windrowed leaves in the cat's corner were black and lifeless and the cat left through the leaning door to seek new shelter" (172). The outhouse signifies the feral cat's proximity to man, but the outhouse offers little refuge from the incessant rain. After escaping the outhouse for a treebole and waiting for the duration of the day, the feral cat is forced to move again: "Hunger drove her out in the late afternoon, cautious, furtive, dusted with woodrot" (173). Here, McCarthy seems to imply that the feral cat is a hunter about to enter the hunt, but the inadequacy of the feral cat's hunting ability is quickly exposed, for McCarthy narrates that the feral feline moves about the wetted landscape with "a hunted look about her" (174). Hungry and hunted, the feral cat faces an uncertain future, but as indicated by her loose skin, sustenance is her most immediate need.

As she must feed to survive, she seeks out man, as is her habit. This time, the second instance in which the feral she-cat seeks comfort or food from man, the feral cat locates Mildred Rattner's smokehouse and subsequently feeds:

> A low sun fired the pine knots in the smokehouse wall till they glowed like rubies, veined and pupiled eyes, peering in at the gloom where the cat gnawed a dangling side of pork-ribs. The salt drew her mouth but she kept at it, pausing now and again to listen at the silence ... the cat heard nothing until the keys jangled just beyond the door and the lock rattled. She leapt to a high shelf, poised, sprang again, making for the air vent under the peaked roof. As the door let in she was hanging by one toenail from this opening, hindclaws flailing desperately for purchase, and then a sliver of the molded wood gave way and she lost her grip [174].

This paragraph opens with a serious tone as the feral cat attempts to survive through the theft of pork-ribs, but the scene quickly turns semi-comic as the hapless feline struggles to escape, but fails to and falls. McCarthy's next paragraph continues the cat's comic performance: "When Mildred Rattner swung open the door and stepped into the smokehouse she saw a cat drop with an anguished squall from somewhere overhead, land spraddle-legged facing her, and make a wild lunge at her, teeth gleaming in the dimness and eyes incandesced with madness" (174). The cat falls without grace and with great screeching fanfare; after falling, the feral cat, "with a long despairing wail flowed over her [Mildred] and was gone" (174). In both of the latter cited passages, McCarthy calls attention to the feral feline's scream, as he does again in the descriptive passage on page 176. McCarthy uses pejorative terminology, squall and wail, to describe the sorrowful creature's howl. The language, tone and comic action McCarthy uses in this scene are very different from the language, tone and violent action McCarthy uses in scenes with wild felines. The language here is condescending; the tone here is comic, and the action is farcical. McCarthy lends this feral she-cat no honor in her existence, and in doing so, he creates a pitiful wastrel of a beast, one who is little more than a scavenging mooch.

The graceless, undignified feral cat's third return to man involves John Wesley Rattner's trapped mink. Still hungry and after being chased from a field by a quartet of crows (a foreshadow of the feline's fate), the feral cat continues her ceaseless quest for sustenance at the hand of man and comes upon a deceased trapped mink. The she-cat's olfactory sense, a sign of the wild in the feline, alerts her to the carcass:

> She crept to it on cocked legs, leapt to a mud hummock and swatted it with a long reach downward ... it bobbed lifelessly ... and when she hooked her claws into the mink to pull it toward her it did not come. Finally she ventured one foot into the water and bit into the neck of the animal. The grit impregnated in its fur set her teeth on edge and she attacked it savagely, then stopped suddenly as if her attention had wandered or returned to something of importance which she has forgotten. She left the mink and set a course across the fields toward the pike road [175].

Why does she flee? The feral cat, hardly a predator, again seeks to feed off of man's labor, and it seems that she succeeds. The cat locates the mink carcass via her sense of smell, but the cat still has trouble tackling the dead mustela. However, once she gains footing, she attacks the mink, until she is interrupted, but what interrupts the feral feline's feeding? An owl on the hunt, for as Vereen Bell points out, the feral cat makes "her demented progress from one source of food to another, all the while being stalked herself by a great owl" (13). The scavenger becomes the prey, which comes as no surprise considering she cannot hunt, even to save her life, and she also has "a hunted look about her" (174).

McCarthy finally sees fit to remove the feral cat from the text, and coincidentally, the feral cat is carried away, just as the domestic kittens were carried away (182). But the feral cat is an owl's prey, while the kittens were a little girl's mission. Regardless, the feral cat is caught and soon to be dead and devoured, a fate befitting an herbivore not a carnivore:

> When she left the rocks, was clear of the overreaching branches of the tree, there grew about her a shadow in the darkness like pooled ink spreading, a soft-hissing feathered sound which ceased even as she half turned, saw unbelieving the immense span of wings cupped downward, turned again, already squalling when the owl struck her back like a falling rock [217].

In a hunger-driven search for food to scavenge, the feral cat exposes herself, unlike a wild cat would, and as such, the feral cat becomes a prey animal, not a predator, no longer a scavenger even. What is interesting here is that prior to the capture of the feral cat, McCarthy provides another opportunity to foreshadow the cat's fate, "A shadow passed soundlessly overhead, perhaps a flock of late-returning birds" (217). McCarthy juxtaposes the scavenging cat with the silent, stalking shadow. The pitiful, semi-helpless feral cat is deleted from the text in an overt act of biological determinism. McCarthy does not let the feral cat go quietly, however. As the cat is carried away, Mr. Eller, the harbinger of the dead or dying domestic and feral cat, is "arrested by the high thin wail of a cat coming apparently from straight overhead ... the squall sounded once more, this time more distant and to the ridge of pines behind the house" (217). Again, as with the doomed domestic kittens, McCarthy has used the term thin wail to describe the cry of the fated feline. And again, the feral feline squalls in misery. The feral cat attempts to survive, but cannot, because she relies upon man for assistance for her shelter and food. As well, in McCarthy's novel, the wild trumps the feral, and the wild lives to hunt again, while the feral is sacrificed to feed the natural world. Conversely, though, wild felines—bobcats, lynx, wampus cats, and panthers—endure to persevere and survive, and are unwilling to be prey, for man or beast.

Independent from man, bobcats, lynx, wampus cats, and panthers are more adept at survival than the domestic kitten or feral cat. The bobcat (*lynx rufus*) and lynx (*lynx canadensis*), in another scene of the seen and unseen feline, are present in *The Orchard Keeper* only in rumor and pamphlet. As such, the wild pair shows an amazing ability to elude both man, in the fictional text, and the omnipresent, omniscient narrator. For while the narrator describes floral and faunal minutia and cosmic level weather events, the narrator never shows the reader that bobcats and lynx exist on or around Red Mountain, Tennessee. But, rumors of the wild cats exist in the culture of the text. After Warn and John Wesley discover that John Wesley's trapped mink has been scavenged, by the feral she-cat no less, Warn immediately assumes that the carcass has been scavenged by a bobcat: "Sure raised hell with it, didn't he?" (206). In his misguided assumption, Warn has the incorrect animal and gender, but this can be forgiven, because Warn exists in an androcentric society, so he assumes the male gender as a matter of habit. In regard to the scavenging animal, Warn assumes that a bobcat has shredded the mink, and after returning to his house, Warn digs through the junk in his bedroom to locate something for John Wesley:

> Rifling through the mass he at length came up with a thin and dog-eared pamphlet, its cover decorated with an archaic and ill-proportioned

ink sketch of a trapped lynx. Across the top in black script was the title
TRAPPING THE FUR BEARERS OF NORTH AMERICA. Warn handled
the treasure reverently. I got this from Uncle Ather, he said. It'll have
something in it.

Under a section entitled *Lynx and Bobcat Sets* they found a plan of such
devious cunning as appealed to their minds [207–8].

Their plan is to trap the scavenger of the mink, but the two boys fail
to glean that the bobcat, their prey, is neither scavenger nor prey.
McCarthy's inclusion of the ancient pamphlet, with inaccurate draw-
ings of the wild cats, shows the historical place of the lynx and bobcat
as animals with bounty-value; the felines' pelts are worth money to
man. As such, the bobcat and the lynx have more value dead than
they do alive. Additionally, John Wesley wants equity for the devaluing
of his mink, and a mink is worth ten to twenty dollars, but only if
the pelt is not scavenged (206). This exchange is further confirmation
of the two boys' inaccurate assumption regarding the scavenger: "You
reckon it really was a bobcat? I dont know what-all else it could
have been, Warn said. Ain't nothin else around here got sharp claws
that I know of. I sure could of used the ten dollars, said the boy" (208).
What the boys fail to include in their assumption is that the bobcat
is a predator, which they should know, and as such, the bobcat
would not be scavenging trapped animals. Through this brief scene,
McCarthy notifies the reader that bobcats and lynx are a valued — by
man — part of the feline hierarchy, and by excluding the bobcat and lynx
from the text, except in rumor and pamphlet, McCarthy argues the
two wild felines' ability to elude man. And as wild felines with the
ability to elude man, the bobcat and the lynx are feline species that have
the opportunity to propagate their species, for a wild cat that is neither
seen, nor trapped and killed by man, is a wild cat that survives to propagate, thus furthering the species.

In *The Orchard Keeper,* McCarthy also includes supernatural wild
cats in his feline hierarchy. Wampus cats are legendary wild cats that are
bred of a cat or a panther and a woman. While the wampus cat in known
in both Anglo and American Indian folklore, the wampus cat in either
legend is always half-cat and half-woman. And, the cross-cultural promotion and generational retelling of this folk legend has been ongoing
in the southeastern United States since the middle to late nineteenth
century (Legend 1). Another common motif of the wampus cat story is
the supernatural feline's primal scream; the wampus cat does not wail

thinly, nor does the wampus cat squall in misery; the wampus cat howls like the savage beast that it is, for the wampus cat is a stalking predator that signals its proximity vocally. Further, the howl of the wampus cat is unlike the scream of the panther; the wampus cat's howl is unlike any in the natural world. In the text, Uncle Ather is well acquainted with the legend of the wampus cat; in fact, Ather dreams of the wampus cat:

> [Wampus] cats troubled the old man's dreams and he did not sleep well anymore. He feared their coming in the night to suck his meager breath. Once he woke and found one looking in the window at him, watching him as he slept ... but now he only lay there and listened for them. Very often they would not start until late and he would still be awake, his ears ringing slightly from having listened so long. Then would come a thin quavering yowl from some dark hollow on the mountain [59].

The wampus cat haunts Ather. Through the signifier of the cat's yowl, McCarthy allows that Ather's dreams are of a wampus cat. As well, in folk legend, the wampus cat watches humans, while the humans sleep. McCarthy includes this motif of voyeurism in the scene of Ather's dreams. Later in the scene, McCarthy identifies the wampus cat by name, while he also identifies the seminal source of Ather's fears and superstitions regarding the legendary wild feline:

> When he was a boy in Tuckaleechee there was a colored woman ... [who] told him that the night mountains were walked by wampus cats with great burning eyes and which left no track even in the snow, although you could hear them screaming plain enough of summer evenings.
> Ain't no sign with wampus cats, she told him [59–60].

In this passage, McCarthy confirms the folk position of the wild feline that haunts Ather's dreams. The legend of the wampus cat is cross-cultural and intergenerational, and the wampus cat is extant to Ather, as real as a bobcat, lynx or panther. Later in the scene, the narrator tells of a time when Ather thought, or dreamt, that the wampus cat was watching him from the cabin window, and he (Ather) subsequently shot out the window-frame with his shotgun; no evidence of the wampus cat's presence was to be found after the shooting, though, only splintered wood (60). Whether or not the wampus cat actually exists is not relevant, because Ather believes that the wild cat does indeed exist in the natural world. As such, the wampus cat exists in the feline hierarchy present in *The Orchard Keeper*, and because of the wampus cat's supernatural abilities, the wampus cat exists on a higher plane in the feline hierarchy than the bobcat or lynx. However, there is a wild cat whose existence cannot be disputed, the panther, which exists at the apex of McCarthy's feline hierarchy.

In *The Orchard Keeper,* it is the panther *(felis concolor)* that exists above all other wild, supernatural, domestic, and feral felines. The panther, or 'painter' as the feline is known locally, is the only non-legendary feline that strikes fear into men. This human fear factor is highlighted in the text a number of times. The first time McCarthy shows humans to be afraid of the panther is in Ather's retelling of a story of ten year's past; Ather, speaking to Warn Pulliam and John Wesley Rattner one evening, recalls to the boys a time when rumors of panthers were prominent among the men of Red Mountain. Warn asks, "What about painters ... was that a painter was hollerin around here one time?" (147). Ather answers, "Shore ... I heard it. Many's the time. Had folks stirred up and scared all of one summer. Yessir, stirred up a blue fog of speculatin" (147). Rumors of panthers, driven by fear of what is thought to be a panther's scream, stir up the local population. The problem is, as Ather notes to the boys, the sound rumored to be a panther's scream is only an owl's screech. One evening, Ather recalls, he went to Eller's store and while at the store, the screech-scream of the owl was heard; Ather tells Warn and John Wesley, "Boys, I mean it got quiet in that store to where you could hear the ants in the candy jar" (148). The men in the store, hearty souls all, are driven to absolute silence by the scream that they believe to be a panther's. When Ather, within the back-story, tells the men in the store that he has seen a panther, the men "all jumped up with something to ast then, how big it was and all" (149). What the men do not know is that Ather is funning them, and as such, only he knows that the scream the men fear is not a panther's and that his sighting of the wild feline is a bold-faced lie. Ather leaves the store, and the scared and impressed gentlemen in the store, after he tells the men that the panther he sighted was only a baby, but was nonetheless bigger than his hundred pound hound, Scout. Thus, the section ends. McCarthy places this back-story scene in the text in order to alert the reader to the mythic power of the panther; while the wampus cat, as dreamed by Ather, may be only a legend, the panther is a real wild feline. And interestingly, it only takes the misinterpretation of an owl's screech to begin the rumor mill of the panther's presence. While a panther is not present in this scene, the effect of the scene is successful; panthers, or rumors of panthers, strike real fear into man, and nowhere else in the text is man afraid of an animal. But here, in Ather's brief retelling of an event a decade past, man is shown to be afraid of the panther. Ather's second retelling of an event long past is one that clarifies the panther's status as the master predator, feline or otherwise, of late nineteenth century rural Tennessee. After drinking wine with the boys, Ather recalls a close encounter sixty years previous that he had with a she-panther and the panther's kit. It seems that one day, while blasting rock for the road crew, young Ather and another gentleman expose a den-hole with a collection of chewed bones and a litter of panther kits; all of the kits are dead except for one, which young Ather gathers up, only to be mauled: "Yessir ... he was a vicious critter. Must have weighed all of five pound ... Old Bill, he backed off some ... so I goes and grabs the little feller up by the scruff of the neck. That's when he hung his tushes in my thumb here" (151–2). This passage indicates a number of points about the panther and man's feelings in regard to the feline. Old Bill is afraid, not of the panther kitten of course, but he is afraid of the she-panther. For Old Bill is aware, correctly, that a she-panther will kill or die for her kits, and two unarmed men are no match for a frenzied postpartum she-panther. Regardless of this common knowledge concerning the panther, young Ather gathers the panther kit in his shirt and takes the animal home to his sod patch, hogs, and wife, Ellen. And thus, in a truly human act, young Ather and his wife attempt to domesticate the wild panther kit: "I brought him home and give him to Ellen. She took to it right off ... it got to where it'd folly her around the house like a everyday walkin-around cat" (152). But of course, the panther kit is not a domestic kitten, and the couple does not yet realize the folly of their attempt at domestication.

One evening, old Ather recalls, "I heard one of the hogs squeal. I got the lannern and went back out but I couldn't find nothin wrong and went on back in and never thought no more about it. Well, next morning they's a hog gone ... then two nights later anothern of em went ... the secont one never even squealt" (153). The hog thief is the she-panther, and she shows the ability to stalk and to evolve in her hunting methods. The first pig squeals, but the second pig does not. The night after the second theft, Ather watches all night for the thief, but she comes and goes, with another hog, without alerting Ather. Old Ather recalls to the boys, "I'd been mad afore but now I was scared" (153). Again, the motif of human fear appears in the text, fear driven and motivated by the panther and the panther's actions. So, three times in the text, the panther comes and goes without young Ather's notice. Smart, silent and stealthy, the panther preys upon Ather's stock, while Ather watches help-lessly. Old Ather continues, "Then one night Ellen went to the door to throw out a pan of water and I heard her holler. I run out and she grabbed on to me like she'd seen a hant or something, and I ast her what it was but she jest stood there and shook like she's freezin to death" (155). What Ellen has seen is the she-panther, and Ellen is understandably, physically terrified. At this point, old Ather stops the retelling of the long past story until he is prodded by Warn, "Did you ever find out what it was" (156). Of course the vague referent 'it' refers to what Ellen saw and what stealth-ily purloined the hogs: "Yessir, he [Ather] said. It was the old she-panther, come after the little one ... [I] never even seen her. I lost one more hog and then I give it up. I turnt the little one loose and that's the last I ever seen of it and the last hog I lost" (157). Again, the panther comes and goes without Ather's notice, this time, taking that which is hers, her kit. In this scene, McCarthy's panther shows herself to be a feline of extraordinary cunning and ability. Young Ather takes the kit, and the she-panther tracks, stalks and preys upon Ather's animals. The she-panther does not attack Ather or Ellen, but attacks the animals under their care; this act is analogous to what Ather does when he kills the she-panther's litter and takes the lone surviving kit. The panther gets close to man only to take her kit from man. This is one savvy panther, and through her actions and cunning and predatory ability, she proves that the panther is the wild feline at the apex of the entire McCarthy feline hierarchy.

In *The Orchard Keeper,* the feline hierarchy is one that is easily definable and clearly structured. The domestic cat, or woeful kitten, is in the base position of the hierarchy, doomed by proximity to and dependence upon man. The feral cat is posited on a plane slightly higher than the domestic cat, and although she tries, the feral she-cat cannot escape proximity to man. McCarthy transforms the feral cat into a prey animal, and she is ignobly deleted from the text and from eastern Ten-nessee. As naturally wild felines, bobcats and lynx are slotted higher in the feline hierarchy than are the domestic and feral felines. And while the two wild cats are not savage predators that strike fear into men, the bobcat and lynx are intelligent enough to avoid man, and thus survive. With its unnatural scream, the supernatural wampus cat strikes fear into men, or at least, the wampus cat strikes fear into Ather, and as such, haunts the old gentleman's dreams and dreamscape. The master pred-ator of the feline hierarchy, the panther, is the feline that exists at the apex of the feline hierarchy in *The Orchard Keeper*. For it is the panther that shows the desire and ability to survive, and the guile to outwit and terrify man to achieve its means.

In *Outer Dark*, swine do not inspire fear in man, nor do the beasts show too much guile, however, the porcine stock animals do act as harbingers of human death, for repeatedly in the text, swine are present in a scene, and almost immediately thereafter, a human character will be murdered or will die accidentally. This technique of swine as signifier of death is one McCarthy utilizes in many of his texts, but only in *Outer Dark* does the placement in the narrative text of a sow or a boar or a shoat indicate the imminent death of a human character. As such, throughout the text, McCarthy creates and builds the theme of swine as harbingers of human death; the author starts with loose associations of swine and human death, and eventually has a fated character articulating the evil of swine.

3

Swine as Harbingers of Human Death in *Outer Dark*

In *Outer Dark*, Cormac McCarthy uses stock swine as harbingers of human death. Repeatedly, swine are present in a scene, and almost immediately thereafter, a human character will be murdered or will die accidentally. This technique of swine as signifier to death signified, is one McCarthy utilizes in many of his texts, but only in *Outer Dark* does the placement in the narrative text of a sow or a boar or a shoat indicate the imminent death of a human character. As such, early in the text, a screaming sow announces the presence of the squire's death. Later, in the second writing of this scene, the hog's squeal repeats the announcement of the squire's impending death. Soon after, in two separate scenes of the same act, the squire is killed by The Three. For effect and attention, McCarthy writes and rewrites the brief passage of the screaming then squealing hog. In doing so, McCarthy emphasizes the theme of the swine as a harbinger of human death. McCarthy continues the sign of the swine when a boar in a stock-lot, with death on *his* mind, screams, and chases and slashes both the itinerant Culla Holme and an angry vigilante, who wants to lynch Culla for the death of the squire. Both Culla and the unnamed vigilante survive the boar's attack, but two wandering millhands are not so lucky and are wrongfully lynched immediately thereafter for the murder of the squire. McCarthy continues the use of the swine harbinger later in the text in a scene with a sow that has murdered all but one of her hoggets. In this passage, the sow is directly associated with Rinthy Holme, a young woman who has indirectly caused the death of her own offspring. The theme of swine as harbingers of human death is text-wide in *Outer Dark* and is culminated in a lengthy and complex scene near the close of the text, where a great drove of pigs stampedes and screams and dies, as does a pig drover named Vernon, who before his death, expostulates on the evil nature of swine and their associations with the devil. This example of the sign of the swine is unique in its length and direct argument of the swine as definably evil; rather than just placing the swine in the text prior to Vernon's death, McCarthy first has Vernon label swine as devilish. The swineherd appears, and he discusses the evils of swine with Culla, and the swine then stampede and carry him off a cliff and to his death.

Through the text of *Outer Dark*, McCarthy creates and builds the theme of swine as harbingers of human death; the author starts with loose associations of swine and human death, which are repeated for effect, as in the examples of the screaming sow and the squire's death. McCarthy then directly conjoins maternally driven infanticide to both swine and humans with the scene of Rinthy and the old woman and the murderous sow. Finally, McCarthy has a character who is fated to die at the hooves of swine expostulate on the evil and devilishness of the beasts. Ironically, the protector is killed by the animals he protects, and in this case, the swine are both harbingers and executors of the human death in discussion. So, it will be seen in detail that McCarthy creates the theme of swine harbinger to human death early in the text and expands upon the theme until the loose association of swine and human death become so tightly structured that swine are directly contributing to human death.

A pejorative view of the swine is not an idea unto McCarthy; for thousands of years, in both Talmudic and Biblical texts, swine have been cast as unclean and evil.

Commonly known, even among the secular of the early twenty-first century, is the idea of the swine as unclean. Precedent for the belief of the swine as an unclean animal can be traced to pre–Christian texts which direct both dietary law and the motivations behind such dietary edicts:

> The children of Israel were prohibited by God from eating pig (Lev. 11:7, Deut. 14:8). Some conjectured that this was for hygienic reasons. First, the pig as a frequent scavenger may pick up diseased material and either carry infection mechanically or itself become infected. Secondly, the pig is host of the tapeworm trichinosis; this passes into the muscles of a pig and can be transmitted only by being eaten. The tapeworm then invades various tissues in humans and can even cause death [Isaacs 17–8].

This passage identifies the prohibition and the precedent for abstaining from eating swine flesh, while the passage also identifies a number of reasons why swine should not be eaten. First, of course, is cleanliness. The swine is identified as a scavenging animal, one that eats what it finds. An accidental secondary effect of scavenging is the scavenging and consumption of diseased materials. As the swine scavenges, it consumes and comes in contact with rancid and rotting and diseased fleshes, and as such, the swine becomes a carrier, and not just a consumer, of disease. And of course, in pre-modern times, even minor illness would lead to human death. And while the ancients may not have known disease biology, even they would have made the direct association between eating diseased meat and disease transmission. In addition to scavenging and picking up disease, the swine is also a host to a potentially fatal — to humans — parasite, the trichinosis tapeworm. As Isaacs notes, the human who eats infected swine flesh, also ingests the tapeworm, and the ingestion of the worm can and does lead to human death. So here is an example, more than two thousand years old, of the swine as direct or indirect harbinger of human death. In Jewish thought and sacred tradition, the swine is both unhygienic and dangerously diseased, and external and internal contact with the animal can lead to human death. Further, Jewish proverbs and parables are rife with anti-swine rhetoric: "When [a man] drinks to excess, he becomes like a pig that wallows in mud (Tanchuma Noah 13:21 b) ... The pig sticks out its cloven hooves and says: 'See, I am clean' (Gen. Rabbah 75) ... Give a pig a soft branch to eat and he will still grub in the dirt (Talmud Berachot 43)" (Isaacs 122). Again, the negative connotations regarding the swine and humans' swine-like behavior are apparent. First, drunkenness, a negative human trait, is conjoined to wallowing in the mud; both are seen as dirty, slovenly behaviors. Next, the cloven hoof of the pig is alluded to; of course, in many descriptions of the devil, the devil's feet are cloven hooves, not anthropomorphic feet. The third observation refers to the piggish habits of the animal; a pig is a pig, and a pig will always act like a pig. So, in only a few lines of Jewish thought and observation, the pig is exposed as unclean — diseased externally and internally, dirty, devil-like, and piggish in behavior and habit. This pre–Christian doctrine sets the precedent for further anti-swine rhetoric and even links the swine with human death, and as Isaacs notes, "In Christian scriptures swine were connected with demons" (18).

The late Reverend J.G. Wood, author of the nineteenth century text, *Bible Animals: Being a Description of Every Living Creature Mentioned in the Scriptures from the Ape to the Coral,* states that under Mosaic law the pig is unfit for food because the pig is the only mammal that has a cloven hoof but does not chew its cud (292). As previously noted, the cloven hoof is but one of the pejorative associations between the pig and the devil, but most animals with cloven hooves are stock herbivores that exhibit fairly passive patterns of behavior. However, the swine exhibits devilish behavior in that the swine scavenges and wallows in the mire, while being quite intelligent and very destructive. On the swine's intelligence and benevolent behavior, Wood notes, "they play with the children, understand the language of their masters, and do not distain to play with the fowls, dogs, cats, asses, and horses, and are ... nimble" (299). Yet the swine is also an utterly destructive beast:

> If there should be any cultivated ground in the neighborhood, the boar is sure to sally out and do enormous damage to the crops. It is perhaps more dreaded in the vineyards than in any other ground, as it not only devours the grapes, but tears down and destroys the vines, trampling them under foot, and destroying a hundredfold as much as it eats ... breaking its way through the fences, rooting up the ground, tearing down the vines themselves, and treading them under its feet. A single party of these animals will sometimes destroy an entire vineyard in a single night [Wood 300–1].

In this passage, Wood describes the swine as overwhelmingly destructive. The beasts destroy that which man builds, indirectly injuring man and undermining his accomplishments. This description is conversely different from Wood's former passage. In the former passage, the swine are playful and intelligent, stock animals intelligent enough to socialize with children, but the swine of the latter passage is a very different beast, one that destroys not just what it eats, but destroys anything and everything in a given, man-made, area. The two very different descriptions of the same type of beast imply that the swine is a very complex animal, but complex in a negative way. The complexity of the swine confuses and perplexes the human, who, in turn, attempts to domesticate and control the animal but cannot. As such, in sacred text and parable, the human demonizes the swine and creates, justifiably or not, a pejorative portrait of the beast, which becomes time-honored and time-tested.

In the eighteenth-century text, *The History of the Robins,* author Sarah Trimmer deals with the paradox of the pig in a scene where a mother describes to her daughter the tricks that a learned pig can perform, and the motivations behind the performance. The mother states to the daughter, "'In respect to the learned pig, I have heard things which are quite astonishing in a species of animals generally regarded as very stupid'" (71). The pig, historically, is seen as stupid, but nonetheless, can be taught tricks by man. The mother continues by stating that the performing pig had "cunning eyes'" (72), which examined the audience and stage area "very attentively" (72), while the beast performed counting tricks and told time from a clock. The mother concludes by stating, "'I am fully persuaded that great cruelty must have been exercised in teaching him things so foreign to his nature ... and they [the pig trainers] exercise great barbarities upon them [the pigs]'" (72–3). This passage is interesting because it shows a compassionate mother, but nonetheless also shows man's ceaseless need to control the animals around him. The swine is both destructive and intelligent; as such, man attempts to use the animal's intelligence to control the animal's destructive tendencies. The result is another negative, if somewhat sympathetic, literary portrait of a swine. The precedent of the swine as a literary device of negativity and negative action can be found in sacred texts, oral tradition and literature. Cormac McCarthy furthers the use of this literary device of negativity, not only in *Outer Dark* but also in most of his texts— whether the work be novel, drama or short story, and in doing so, McCarthy follows precedent while setting precedent.

But why does McCarthy focus so heavily on the swine? While the theme of the swine as harbinger of death is present in many of the author's texts, and the theme of the swine as harbinger of human death is text-wide in *Outer Dark*, one must ask what motivates the author to include the animal in so many pivotal scenes, thus making the animal a literary device. First, as most of McCarthy's works are agrarian in locale and society, and set in times before the second half of the twentieth century, swine are available as both food source and commodity. In the texts, hogs can logically be found in slaughter-lots, small and large farms, and hovels, as well. Another reason McCarthy might use swine as literary devices, with negative connotations, is religion based. McCarthy's texts are filled with religious iconography, symbolism and characters. Churches, new, old, and ruined, litter the works, and preachers, priests, ex-priests, and the lay-religious are found in every text, while the presence of such characters gives birth to a litany of Christian religious philosophies. With this said, it is reasonable to assume that

McCarthy is well-read in both the new and the old testaments, and as such, is well aware of the dietary prohibitions and pejorative connotations associated with the swine. As such, the swine is a handy literary device, with which McCarthy can build a text-wide theme in *Outer Dark* and a recurring motif through many of his texts. Also helpful to the author is the almost immediate image of the swine as slop-eating, obese, and muck-covered. The swine is clearly a literary device of negative connotation, and is presented as such from McCarthy's first novel.

In McCarthy's first published novel, *The Orchard Keeper*, the author uses swine in two scenes of devastating loss in Ather Ownby's life. In the first example, a scene analyzed in Chapter 2, Ather, who is telling stories of yore to John Wesley Rattner and Warn Pulliam, tells of the she-panther that steals four of his hogs: "one evening I heard one of the hogs squeal ... next morning they's a hog gone" (153). Then the second, the third and the fourth hogs are purloined, and Ather's stock total of seven or eight hogs is depleted to a census of three or four. The stealing of the hogs is a negative textual action in that the stock is taken from Ather, and as such, the hogs are negated from Ather's tiny, but important, stock animal inventory. The loss of the hogs also represents a loss of money, for hogs are not free. As well, the loss of the hogs is the loss of a major food source; as Ather is not Jewish, it is doubtful that he has any qualms regarding the consumption of swine. In this scene, McCarthy uses the loss of the swine to call the reader's attention to Ather's multiple losses. In an italicized passage, which exists within the aforementioned scene, McCarthy also uses swine to symbolize another of Ather's losses; in this example, Ather's dying swine are analogous to the death of his marriage:

> [After his wife left], *he stayed for five more days, wandering about the house or sitting motionless, sleeping in chairs, eating whatever he happened to find until there wasn't any more and then not eating anything. While the chickens grew thin and the stock screamed for water, while the hogs perished to the last shoat. An outrageous stench settled over everything, a vile decay that hung in the air, filled the house* [155]

Here, as in the first scene, the hogs are harbingers of loss and death. In the former scene, the deaths are the hogs' themselves, and in the latter scene, the hogs, cattle and horse-stock, and fowl, all perish. In both of these scenes from *The Orchard Keeper*, the presence of hogs in the text is a harbinger for death, the deaths of the hogs, the deaths of the stock and fowl, and the death of Ather's brief marriage. This interassociation of swine and death is one McCarthy repeats in all of his fiction of the South, including of course, *Child of God* and *Suttree*, the author's third and fourth published novels.

In *Child of God*, McCarthy uses a scene of a flood of biblical proportions to again conjoin swine and death. McCarthy's murderous, necrophilic protagonist, Lester Ballard, walks along a swollen creek, watching the refuse of the flood pass by: "Ballard studied the water and moved downstream. After a while he was back. The creek was totally opaque, a thick and brickcolored medium that hissed in the reeds. As he watched a drowned sow shot into the ford and spun slowly with pink and bloated dugs and went on" (155). This scene, again a scene of swine death, is one of what can be seen and what cannot be seen. The river is opaque due to the sweeping downstream of loose clay and sediment, secondary to the rain and flood, so Lester cannot see what is in the river. However, the pink sow is contrasted by color against the river. This color contrast for effect alerts the reader to the theme of swine and death. What bears attention though, is the phrase, bloated dugs. Dugs of course are teats, which become swollen with pregnancy, and because McCarthy does not write by accident, it can be concluded from McCarthy's very specific text that the sow is pregnant or has recently given birth; swollen teats equate to mammalian pregnancy. It can also be concluded that the sow's hoggets are dead, for the offspring could not survive the flood that killed the sow. In addition, the hoggets would need the lactated milk for sustenance, and would, therefore, not be able to survive the sow's absence, even without the forced separation brought about by the rain and flood. If the sow is pregnant and yet to give birth, the pre-born hoggets have died with the pregnant swine. In any situation, the sow and her progeny are dead, and again, McCarthy has utilized a swine as a harbinger of death.

In *Suttree*, McCarthy uses a loose covey of red shoats and ideastricken buffoon Gene Harrogate to create a scene of death both disturbing and hilarious. Again, pigs serve as harbingers of swine death, but only one young pig is butchered in this instance. As the scene opens, Harrogate spies a loose covey [McCarthy's word] of red shoats—young pigs under a year in age. Being an opportunist, Harrogate immediately seeks out a shoat for capture and slaughter: "Coming past a collection of old waterheaters he started them and they flushed into the wall of ivy with high raspy snorts. He picked one out and dove after it. It ... disappeared with an agonizing squall" (138). Notice McCarthy's language and word choice. Harrogate dove after the pig, but Harrogate is no Dove of Peace; he seeks to commit bloody violence. As well, the shoats are red (137), the color of blood. These swine reek of death; it is McCarthy's way. Harrogate repeatedly fails at attempts at stealthy stalking of the swine, but finally resolves "upon a rush, the pigs being too wary for stealth" (138); as seen in precedent, pigs— regardless of being stock animals— are not stupid, and the animals seem to possess a strong sense of survival, even though many die at McCarthy's hand. Of course, Harrogate's rush fails, as his choice is "the fleetest of the pack" (139), but as luck would have it, "he came upon a pig with its head in a bucket. As he approached it went running. It crashed into a tree and fell back and lay there squealing" (139). The pig is blindfolded, like a condemned prisoner. The shoat is doomed, but McCarthy's executioner is skill-less:

> Harrogate launched out birdlike and fell upon the shoat with an enormous splash ... [he] selected a stick and laid the pig down, pinning the rear feet ... He began to beat the back of the pig's head ... denting in the bucket, raising bloody weals along the pig's neck ... until the stick broke ... He came up with the pig ... the bucket against the side of his face and blood running all down ... hugging it while it kicked and shat ... He picked it [a piece of pipe] up and hefted it ... He laid the pig down ... and then he raised the pipe and swung with all his strength. Blood spewed from under the edge of the bucket ... Harrogate swung again ... A whitish matter was seeping from its head and one ear hung down half off ... He bashed it again, spattering brains over the ground. It stretched out, trembled and quit [139–40].

The rightful owner of the pig, Rufus Wiley, comes upon the scene of Harrogate, the blood and brains, and the dead shoat, and he enquires as to who is going to pay the ten dollar value of the dead swine. Harrogate, of course, must go to work at fifty cents an hour to pay off the price of the dead animal, or face legal retribution. This scene again supports the theory that swine are harbingers of death, even swine death, even when the executioner is a hapless buffoon.

Cities of the Plain, McCarthy's third novel of the Border Trilogy, conjoins swine and death, but in a more subtle way than the Harrogate scene. The scene involves a brutal dog hunt, the second of two in the text, where hunting-hounds, horse and men, hunt a pack of marauding feral dogs on a vast floodplain. McCarthy's fated American cowboy, John Grady Cole, lassoes and strangles a dog also being chased by another rider, Joaquín [no last name]. After the first cast of dogs is killed, the riders take a break from the work, "He [Cole] came back trailing the empty rope, paying it up and recoiling it as he rode. Travis and Joaquín and Billy were sitting the horses and taking a blow ... Joaquín was grinning. I hogged your all's dog, I reckon, John Grady said" (163). On this day, the men's work is the killing — slaughtering — of the feral dogs, and killing on horseback is hard work. When the men meet for a break, Cole, in apology, uses the verb, hog, to mean *to take and to kill*, with emphasis on kill. Traditionally, to hog something is to take it, but McCarthy evolves the denotation and connotation of the word to the point where the word means and implies, to take and to kill, as in, Cole took and killed Joaquín's dog. Additionally, Cole is a doomed character, fated to die by text's end, and it is Cole who uses the bastardized form of the verb. So here McCarthy conjoins swine and death, the feral dog's death. As well, he also uses swine as a harbinger of human death, Cole's death. McCarthy's patterns of animal association are repetitive; in his drama, *The Stonemason*, the author again conjoins swine and death, and swine and human death.

In Act II, scene 3, of the drama, set in the Telfair kitchen on a Sunday after church, family patriarch Papaw Telfair and his grandson, Ben Telfair, the last of the family stonemasons, discuss work, racism, death, and the murder of Papaw's beloved Uncle Selman, a master stonemason. Papaw states that skill at work goes beyond race and racism, and that those who kill because of racial hatred are fools— people who cannot see that skill transcends race. And, indeed, Papaw's Uncle Selman was murdered by such a fool, a man who was not a mason of course, over a water bucket:

> PAPAW: ...that white man was all lie. And he killed him. He killed Uncle Selman with a timber maul, hit him blind side with it and laid him out graveyard dead. They come and got me. Oh I was a heartbroke boy. A heartbroke boy. We picked him up out of the dirt and carried him out under a shadetree and he was bloody as a hog [51].

Here is an example of an unjust killing of an honorable man by a dishonorable man. Note the simile McCarthy uses to describe the murdered man; the deceased was bloody as a hog. Those who have witnessed the butchering of a hog will affirm that the bleeding of the carcass is a very bloody mess. When Papaw states that his dead uncle was bloody as a hog, the mind's eye conjures up a scene of gruesome redness, for his uncle's head was laid open with a timber maul, a wooden sledge hammer used for driving wooden wedges into dense, heavy wood. As well, McCarthy's use of the hog simile calls to mind the idea of a slaughter;

Papaw's uncle, Uncle Selman, was slaughtered, without chance for survival, by a murderer who saw him as nothing more than an animal. Once again, in the text, McCarthy has bonded the swine and death. In this example, McCarthy uses simile to conjoin swine and death, more specifically, McCarthy adheres the swine to human death, something that he repeatedly does in *Outer Dark*.

In *Outer Dark*, the McCarthy text with the most extensive use of the swine, McCarthy uses the swine as a harbinger of human death, as well as an equalizer of human death. Robert Jarrett argues that *Outer Dark* is a study where those of the propertied class are killed by those of lower class and caste, in a sort of class reciprocation, where the "murders often function as a type of revenge against the ideology of the propertied classes, who associate wealth with morality and ignore their own exploitation of the lower classes" (28). But it will be seen that those who are killed and die in the text are of all three presented classes, landed, working and poverty-stricken, and those humans who die are identified by the swine harbinger, not class separation and reciprocal angst. Consequently, swine are the signifiers of human death in *Outer Dark:*

> *They entered the lot at a slow jog, the peaceful and ruminative stock coming erect, watchful, shifting with eyes sidled as they passed, the three of them paying no heed, seeming blind with purpose, passing through an ether of smartweed and stale ammonia steaming from the sunbleared chickenrun and on through the open doors of the barn and almost instantly out the other side marvelously armed with crude agrarian weapons, spade and brush-hook, emerging in an explosion of guinea fowl and one screaming sow, unaltered in gait demeanor or speed, parodic figures transposed live and intact and violent out of a proletarian mural and set mobile upon the empty fields, advancing against the twilight, the droning bees and windtilted clover* [35].

This punctuated sentence seems to support Jarrett's assertion that murder in *Outer Dark* is an act of proletariat revenge, which in the text is often meted out by The Three, an unholy trinity of essentially efficient killers. In fact, this scene does preclude the death of the character nicknamed the squire, a semi-wealthy gentleman who gives Culla Holme a job. However, attention must be given the stock and fowl alluded to in this italicized passage, for human death occurs often in the text, and The Three are not the lone mechanics of human death. Above, present of course is a pig, in this case, a sow — an adult female swine. This swine screams as The Three burst forth from the barn. In doing so, the sow is foreshadowing the human death and deaths to come, the first of which is the squire's. McCarthy even uses a very aggressive verb, screams, to call attention to the swine's call; ironically, people scream when they die, but in this text, human beings die silently, without call. McCarthy even sees fit to repeat this passage, from a different point of focalization.

The second passage, which is synchronous chronologically to the first cited passage, is one where Culla and the squire discuss the day's wages for Culla's labor; in this brief paragraph, McCarthy rewrites the former scene, and in doing so, identifies the location of the former scene: "Holme was looking down, one hand crossed over the back of the other the way men stand in church. There was a commotion of hens from beyond the barn, a hog's squeal, ceasing again into the tranquility of birdcalls and cicadas" (47). Three associations between the two passages can immediately be made. One, the presence of the hog and the outcry of the animal are synonymous in act, if not in verb; in either case, a disturbance rouses the single swine, which calls forth. Two, the presence of a plural number of barnyard fowl, hens and guinea fowl not ducks or geese, in both scenes is more than associative; the number and the type of bird are too similar to be ignored. Three, each scene closes peacefully, the former to the drone of bees, and the latter to the harmonies of birds and cicadas. The two scenes are one scene, and only the sow and the fowl are in each scene. And, both scenes are prequels to the death of the man whose swine called out the warning, the squire.

Later, in a rush to catch Culla, who has stolen his boots, the squire takes wagon and horse to a "log road" (50, 51). However, the squire is caught and killed by The Three:

> They were coming along the road. One of them said something and then one of them said Harmon and then one of them was alongside seizing the horse's reins. The squire... . [50] ... *rising in remonstration from the wagon box so that when the next one came up behind him sideways in a sort of dance and swung the brush-hook it missed his neck and took him in the small of the back severing his spine and when he fell he fell unhinged sideways and without a cry* [51].

It bears noting that McCarthy separates the scene of the squire's death into two different sections of the text, which occur on separate but continuous pages; the first scene is part of a longer chapter and not in italics, and the second scene is a free-standing section and is written in italics. And even though McCarthy sees fit to end the former death scene at the moment the squire rises, what follows in the latter scene is his falling down to death. The harbinger sow, who warned of impending human death, does so two times; as well, the squire's death scene, written in two passages, occurs two times. Consequently, the sow's two screams were the harbingers of two textual human deaths. McCarthy repeats this single swine dual human death motif later in the text.

The second instance of a single swine's scream as signifier to dual human death occurs when Culla is being chased by a lynch mob — a mob that collectively seeks retribution for the death of the squire. In this example, Culla again is situated near a stock-lot, specifically, "a hoglot" (93); as a fleeing Culla runs through the lot, an angry swine appears: "a boar came up out of a wallow with a scream and charged him and across the far fence and into the upper pasture" (93). Again, McCarthy uses a swine that screams. An uncastrated male, the boar pursues Culla until one of the vigilantes follows Culla into the hoglot: "He could hear the man behind him saying Goddamn, Goddamn, leaping and stepping as the boar came at him ... the boar screaming and cutting at him [the vigilante] and him sliding and dancing in the mud" (93). This boar is absolutely aggressive and actively attempting to injure the vigilante through tusk slashing. McCarthy writes that the swine cuts with its tusks while it screams and chases. McCarthy's use of verbs of panic and destruction when describing the actions of the boar is a recognizable trait. Additionally, McCarthy is using verbs usually applied to human beings, who cut with bladed implements and scream when dying. Even though both Culla and the vigilante survive the boar, human death has been signified and is only a page-turn away, again in an italicized scene of dual human death.

In this scene of human death to boar signifier, the italicized free-standing passage is bifurcated into two paragraphs. In the first paragraph, which occurs on the night of the squire's death, a crowd gathers around a wagon which contains a dead man in the bed; the decedent is the squire, whose name is finally revealed to be Salter. An announcement of vigilante intent is made, and the second paragraph, which occurs at dawn the next morning, illustrates the result of this example of vigilante action. The second paragraph is the scene of dual human death: "*In the cool and smoking dawn there hung from a blackhaw tree in a field on the edge of the village the bodies of two itinerant millhands. They spun slowly in turn from left to right and back again. As if charged with some watch. That and the slight flutter of their hair in the morning wind was all the movement there was about them*" (95). Previously, the boar screamed at and chased and attempted to kill both Culla and his pursuer, but both men escaped, scraped and cut, but alive; the scene of signification was very busy with physical pursuit and harried movement. However, this scene of human deaths signified by the boar's presence in the text is a serene, peaceful scene. These humans are quietly dead, just as Salter is quietly dead in the preceding paragraph. The swine scream, and the humans are silent in death. This example of human death, it should be noted, refutes Jarrett's argument that *Outer Dark* is a text of proletariat recompense, for the murdered millhands here are as poor and as lost and as misery-struck as are Culla Holme, and his estranged sister, Rinthy — the agonist of the text, and a character directly interassociated with swine and human death.

Rinthy Holme is a tragic character, adrift in a world of pathos. Her nameless infant child is the product of an incestuous conception; her miscreant brother has abandoned the hours old infant in the woods; her post-partum life is one of ceaseless lactation and endless wandering, endured while she searches for her unnamed "chap" (113); her suffering is manifest, and she is honorable and noble in her actions.

Regardless of honorable intent and noble actions, Rinthy, directly through incest, or indirectly through inaction, is responsible for the unnamed child's eventual gruesome but soundless death (236). Culla's actions notwithstanding, Rinthy has failed as a mother in the duty to protect her child, and as such, the child dies, and what is more, Rinthy wears the authentic aura of guilt. During an extended scene (108–16) in which a wandering Rinthy seeks comfort and aid and food from an old woman in the woods—a tried and true literary device — the old hermit can read that Rinthy is postpartum, and more importantly, the old woman can read the guilt of Rinthy's maternal neglect and the eventual outcome of the maternal neglect; the old hermit asks of Rinthy's destination, and Rinthy replies that she has no destination, but a mission, "... no special places. I'm a-huntin somebody" (111), and then "The old woman's eyes went to her belly and back again" (111), and she invites Rinthy into her shack. In the old "anthropoid's" (108) home is a sleeping sow — another failed mother, another who kills her children, another swine harbinger of human death.

Upon entering the shack, Rinthy and the old woman engage in a question and answer dialogue, which is driven by the old woman's accusatory questions:

> Get ye a chair, the woman said.
> Thank ye.

She was at the stove, turning the fire up out of the dead gray ashes. Are ye not married? She said.

No mam.

She added wood ... Her voice was hollow and chambered: Where's your youngern.

What?

I said where's your youngern.

I've got nary.

The babe, the babe, the old woman crooned.

They ain't nary'n.

Hah, said the old woman. Bagged for the river trade I'd judge. Yon sow there might make ye a travelin mate that's downed her hoggets save one.

... Cradled among stovewood against the wall was a sleeping hog... [112].

The old "androgyne" (112) directly accuses Rinthy of filialicide. Additionally, the sow seems to be aware of Rinthy's situation and of their [the sow's and Rinthy's] interassociation: "The sow reared half up and regarded them with narrow pink eyes and a look of hostile cunning" (114). By conjoining Rinthy's act with the murderous acts of the sow — also a mother who killed her young — and the common knowledge of all involved, McCarthy, via the old woman, explicates Rinthy's guilt in the eventual death of her infant son, for even if the child is not yet dead, only the unaware reader would ever expect the child to survive. As such, the sow, a murderous mother, is the harbinger of the infant chap's death, and a gruesome death it is, not unlike the slaughter of a hog.

The child's death — signified by the scene that includes and conjoins Rinthy and the murderous sow — is a throat-slitting death like one would see at a homestead butchering of a hog: "Holme saw the blade wink in the light like a long cat's eye slant and malevolent and a dark smile erupted on the child's throat and went all broken down the front of it. The child made no sound" (236). The child, tortured from birth to this moment, has his throat slit and dies without a cry or a scream. Rinthy contributed to the child's death; Culla witnessed it; The Three committed the act; and the offspring-murdering sow was the harbinger that announced the inevitability of the child's demise, for the sow is a disastrous mother, as is Rinthy, and the sow's actions led to the hoggets' deaths, as Rinthy's actions lead to her child's death. While the scene of the child's death does not directly follow the signifying scene with the swine, as the previous scenes of human death have, the interassociation between Rinthy and the sow conjugates this specific scene and swine to the scene of the child's murder, and while Rinthy does not wield the knife, she nonetheless contributes to the death of her progeny, just as the harbinger sow did. Additionally, at the close of the scene, the old woman and Rinthy discuss the two hanged millhands; Rinthy mentions, "This morning. I seen two fellers hung in a tree" (116). The old hermit woman replies, "They was supposed to of killed old man Salter over there" (116). In this text, tragically, comically and gruesomely, the swine signifies human death — landed rich or itinerant poor, full grown adult or toddling child. Finally, and logically, the presence of many swine in a scene will announce the death of a working class hog drover, for the occupation of swine-herd and the death of such a professionally occupied character is the apex of the theme of the swine as signifier of human death.

In a culminating scene late in the text, which McCarthy uses as a summary conclusion of the swine as harbinger of human death theme, the author includes the appearance of an enormous herd of swine followed by the death of a single human character, a philosophical, biblically literate pig drover named Vernon. The scene is important for a number of reasons. First, the scene is the longest scene (213–27) involving the motif of swine and human death. Interestingly, the scene is an inverse of earlier scenes where a single swine is a harbinger for multiple human deaths. In this scene, only the drover/philosopher Vernon dies. This scene is also important because this is the only scene where the swine directly contribute to the death of the human being. In this example, the herd of swine washes a helpless Vernon over a cliff and to his death. Culla's presence bears attention, too, because he is always very close to death, but he somehow lives on and on, while many others die. Absolutely important in this scene is biblical allusion and the philosophy of hogs, topics discussed by Vernon and Culla prior to Vernon's demise. Noticeably absent from this scene are The Three, the lynch mob, the squire, and Rinthy.

The scene opens "ON A GOOD [McCarthy's caps] spring day" (213), which would seem to indicate that one year has passed since the opening of the text. Culla is resting by the side of the road when below him come the herd of swine:

> ... suddenly the entire valley was filled with hogs, a weltering sea of them that came smoking over the dusty plain and flowed undiminished into the narrows of the cut, fanning on the slopes in ragged shoals like the harried outer guard of schooled fish and here and there upright and cursing among them and laboring with poles the drovers, gaunt and fever-eyed with incredible rag costumes and wild hair [213].

Notice the language McCarthy uses in describing the herd; the herd is a great sea of swine, a liquid mass; Vernon will die in the water, after being pushed off of a cliff by a great wave of stampeding swine. As well, drowning is a common manner of meeting death in McCarthy's *oeuvre*. The valley is filled with hogs, as if the valley is flooded with the hogs. Additionally, the edges of the herd are like the fringe of a school of fish. All of this language of liquid and the sea is not accidental. As Wood notes, in Matthew VIII, 28–34, a swine herd is drowned in the sea by God for the sins of their owners (297). Here, the swine-herd is downed and drowned by the swine, so the swine-herd dies, while the swine survive. Furthermore, in Jewish tradition, there was no occupation "so degrading" (Wood 294) as swine-herd, so the precedent dictates that at least one swine-herd must die, and one does. McCarthy labels the drovers, upright and gaunt and fever-eyed — bipedal, underfed and fatigued. This description hints of the drovers' exhaustion and potential inability to control the herd. That they are underfed alludes to the fact that the drovers do not own the stock; as such, the drovers cannot slaughter hogs for sustenance. Clearly, these unkempt drovers are of the poor but employed class, a socioeconomic class above Rinthy and Culla and the itinerant millhands, but of a lower socioeconomic class than the squire. So, the swine harbinger is not socioeconomically choosey.

Culla seeks shelter from the herd up a "rocky slope" (213) as the "first of the drovers was beating his way obliquely across the herd ... the hogs flaring and squealing and closing behind him again like syrup. When he gained the open ground he came along easily, smiling up to where Holme sat on a rock" (213). McCarthy allows this drover, Vernon, some intellect and dignity, "Howdy neighbor, called out the drover. Sweet day, ain't she?" (214). Unlike the majority of the characters in the text, this drover seems likable and genuinely friendly. When Culla asks how many swine are in the herd, "God hisself don't know, he [the drover] said solemnly" (214). This solemn reply notifies the reader that the drover is a religious man, one who does not speak disrespectfully of his God. Additionally, by the drover's answer, there seems to be an infinite number of hogs; ironically, the drover's life is very finite, and he has only moments to live. The topic of conversation — swine —continues, with Vernon explicating on "the mulefoot" (214) hog, a mountain hog with the hoof of a mule, not a cloven hoof. As previously stated, swine, with cloven hoof and sans cud, were thought by the Israelites to be both diseased and dirty. As well, the devil also was thought to be cloven hoofed, like the swine. As such, the swine was associated with the devil, a point that Vernon makes to Culla: "I heard it preached in a sermon one time. Feller knowed right smart about the subject. Said the devil had a foot like a hog's. He laid claim it was in the bible so I reckon it's so" (215). Here the junction is clear; the hog is a devilish and devil-like animal. The conversation continues and both men agree, a hog is a hog is a hog, with or without feet, cloven or not. The point is, hogs behave like hogs, and if swine are devilish, they will behave in a devilish manner. After this agreement, Vernon philosophically states, "Yessir. Makes ye wonder some about the bible and about hogs too, don't it?" (215). As the conversation evolves, Vernon muses some more on the nature of hogs:

> Hogs is a mystery by theyselves, he said. What can a feller know about one? Not a whole lot. I've run with hogs since I was just a shirttail and I ain't never come to no real understandin of em. And I don't doubt but what other folks has had the same experience. A hog is a hog. Pure and simple. And that's all ye can say about him. And smart, don't think they ain't. Smart as the devil. And don't be fooled by one's that ain't got nary clove foot cause he's devilish too [216].

This paragraph sums up the place of hogs in the text, as well as in the scene. Hogs—from the pre-twelfth century Old English *hogg*—are devilish and smart, regardless of their hoof shape, and as such, hogs cannot be trusted. Vernon, a swine-herd since childhood is on his final drive, yet he does not know this, but he knows hogs are hogs, and he will die with this knowledge, though little good the knowledge does him. After this monologue, McCarthy narrates, "They [the drovers] seemed together with the hogs to be in flight from some act of God, fire or flood, schisms in the earth's crust" (216). Remember in Matthew, God drowns the herd of swine; here, the swine will drown Vernon, in a river situated in a valley, a schism in the earth's crust. McCarthy through biblical allusion, precedent and swine, has doomed a drover, and he shall be Vernon.

Vernon leaves Culla and returns to the herd, which collectively panics while going through a narrow gap and stampedes upon exit of the flume:

> Hogs were pouring through the gap and building against the ones in the meadow until these began to buckle at the edges [of the cliff]. Holme saw two of them pitch screaming in stifflegged pirouettes a hundred feet into the river ... the entire herd had begun to wheel wider and faster along the bluff and the outermost ranks swung centrifugally over the escarpment... [217].

The hogs pour through the gap, like water. The herd surges and panics, out of the control of the drovers. Two swine scream, two harbingers of one human death, Vernon's. For Vernon is caught in the swell of swine, and he cannot save himself; Culla, the survivor, goes to higher ground, while the harbinger hogs that have fallen do not necessarily die: "Hogs were beginning to wash up on the rock, their hoofs clicking and rasping and with harsh snorts" (218), but Vernon does:

> The drover who had spoken him swept past with bowed back and hands aloft, a limp and ragged scarecrow flailing briefly in that rabid frieze so that Holme saw tilted upon him for just a moment out of the dust and pandemonium two walled eyes beyond hope and a dead mouth beyond prayer, borne on like some old gospel recreant seized sevenfold in the flood of his own nether invocations ... until he passed over the rim of the bluff and dropped in his great retinue of hogs from sight [218].

This death is another example of a silent human death, signified to the screams of swine. Vernon is *swept* past Culla and *washed* (italics mine) over the cliff by the stampeding wave of hogs. McCarthy narrates, "Holme blinked and shook his head. The hogs boiled past squealing" (218), while the remaining drovers watched "as if there were some old injustice being righted in this spectacle of headlong bedlam" (219). Of course, the injustice being righted is the Biblical slaughter of the swine by God, an act perpetuated by the misdeeds of the owners of the swine. Jarrett was correct about the theme of revenge in *Outer Dark*, but it is the revenge of the swine on the drovers, not of the lower socioeconomic classes on the landed class. Later in the scene, a wandering parson happens upon the post-stampede situation; the drovers seem to believe that Culla stampeded the hogs and caused Vernon's death. This of course is not true; the hogs panicked and stampeded, but the parson asks the drovers, "What possessed them hogs anyways?" (221). With this question, through the use of the verb, possessed, McCarthy reminds the reader of the devilish nature of swine, a topic Vernon postulated upon just before his death; swine are devilish in nature, intent and act. The scene closes with Culla leaping from the same cliffs that Vernon washed over, while he (Culla) is being pursued, again, by a lynch mob with vigilante vengeance as its goal (226–7).

In this final scene of swine harbinger to human death, McCarthy's character expresses the evils of the swine, which explains the motivation behind the theme of swine as harbinger of human death. It is arguable that the swine are righting an ancient wrong, at least in the case of Vernon's death. What is clear, however, is that in *Outer Dark*, swine appear in the text in a nexus with human death, and that the appearance of a swine or swine will lead to the death of at least one human character. Also, ironically, swine — as harbingers— scream in notification, while humans die silently, again and again. Additionally, swine signify human death of humans who exist in all three primary socioeconomic classes represented, the landed, the working poor and the poverty-stricken. And too, the age of the human fated to die is irrelevant, and the very young, the adult and the mature die secondary to the scream(s) of swine. In *Outer Dark,* swine are the great equalizers of age, class and caste, and once the swine is presented in the text, the human will die.

Cormac McCarthy's third published novel, *Child of God,* also has a harbinger of death, Lester Ballard. But the text additionally has, amidst the gruesomeness of Ballard's actions, a great deal of humor and levity. Chapter 4 will examine that levity in the context of man's ceaseless desire to control the natural world, and it will be seen that man can control some stock animals, while others he cannot, and that Lester Ballard is as ill-adept with bovines as he is with living people.

4

Bovines and Levity in
Child of God

In Cormac McCarthy's third published novel, *Child of God,* a work grotesque and gothic, the author includes levity with the horror of protagonist Lester Ballard's murder and necrophilia. McCarthy uses agrarian stock animals, primarily bovines—two cows and an ox—to add levity to what may be conservatively labeled, a gruesome text. Additionally, McCarthy includes a brief comic scene with a disappearing mule team before he closes the text on a horrifyingly descriptive note. In the three individual scenes of bovine levity, the author relies upon man's unquenchable desire to control the natural world, with special desire to control the fauna of the natural world. Man constantly seeks to control animal behavior and action, and McCarthy's characters are no different than any other men. As such, as usual, animals suffer at the hand of man, but paradoxically, in *Child of God,* as the stock bovines suffer, the reader is amused. Moreover, McCarthy includes other scenes of levity and humor in the text. A cat's judgment of Lester Ballard is an inside joke between the narrator and the reader; and Lester is later abandoned by a dog who chooses to face survival alone rather than with Lester. Even the animals are aware that Lester is not right. McCarthy also allows Lester three moments of physical happiness, as defined through Lester laughing or grinning.

Lester is given brief moments of levity in an otherwise bleak, bleak existence, and both Lester's in-text levity and the interpolated first-person narrated stories of levity are important breaks from Lester's endless existence of violence, an existence Lester has lived since childhood, for Lester's father hanged himself — Lester discovered the body — when Lester was nine or ten years old, and suicide is the ultimate act of self-violence. As such, John Lang argues, Lester has been a victim of violence since childhood (90–1). And in the text, in addition to at least seven human murders, Lester kills spiders, frogs, fish, rats, assorted birds, and at least one dog. Lester is an individual who uses violence as a problem solving methodology. Consequently, Lester kills through the text, often with his "totemic rifle" (Ciuba 77), as in one of the two examples of the cows he kills. As such, McCarthy's use of bovines, and other animals, to produce humor succeeds because the levity creates a nice respite to the ghastliness.

Writing of agrarian life in rural Tennessee and the cowboy life in the Border Southwest, McCarthy uses stock animals in all of his texts; and as well, he includes scenes of human and stock animal levity in at least two other texts, *Suttree* and *Cities of the Plain*. *Child of God*, however, is the seminal McCarthy text for the presence of extended passages that utilize bovines as devices of humor. Early in the text, seeking to control animal behavior and action, Lester shoots a cow that has muddied the river in which he had planned to shoot fish; the cow is not his, and the shooting is an act of impulse that results in death, as are so many of Lester's actions. Further, later in the text, Lester nearly decapitates a cow in a shortsighted attempt to relocate the animal with a tractor and a rope. A third bovine passage is a retelling of an oxen incident, this time with a different human antagonist seeking control over the animals. McCarthy also includes in the text, a menagerie of other animals—cats, dogs, birds, fish, rats, mules— to add levity to the grotesque text by playing Lester's comic foils. So, *Child of God* is quite funny and quite gruesome.

McCarthy's use of stock animals as literary devices in the text is not a new idea; much historical precedent can be found of stock, here specifically oxen, cattle and mules, through the course of literarily recorded knowledge. In his *Natural History*, Pliny the Elder (AD 23–79) writes of oxen and of the Egyptian deification of the ox. Pliny was a Roman Fleet Admiral, who traveled the Roman ruled Mediterranean world and chronicled that which he saw. Pliny's study covers agriculture, astronomy, botany, cosmology, foreign culture, custom and theology, geography, medicine, zoology, et cetera, and he was one of the first authors whose work contains a secondary source bibliography (Biographies 1). Pliny has this to say about Egyptian custom, theology and ritual bovine sacrifice:

> In Egypt an ox is even worshipped as a deity; they call it Apis. It is distinguished by a conspicuous white spot on the right side, in the form of a crescent. There is a knot under the tongue, which is called 'cantharus' [beetle]. This ox is not allowed to live beyond a certain number of years; it is then destroyed by being drowned in the fountain of the priests. They then go, amid general mourning, and seek another ox to replace it; and the mourning is continued, with their heads shaved, until such time as they have found one [Book 8. Chapter 71].

Intended or not, Pliny's shift from deification of the exalted beast to sloppy sacrifice by drowning of the beast is somewhat stunning, and when the passage is reread, and Pliny's tone understood, the reader can see that Pliny seems somewhat amused by the fact that the ox must be hailed as a god, then killed, and then, the priests must mourn, secondary to the killing of the ox, until a new ox-god can be found; the redundancy of the process seems to be that which amuses the author. This passage has a bit more levity, for the deified ox insults the potential emperor: "It gives answers to individuals, by taking food from the hand of those who consult it. It turned away from the hand of Germanicus Caesar, and not long after he died" (8.71). The author, from a different class and caste strata, does not seem too bothered by the death of the young, royal general. Pliny closes the passage on the ox deity, "when it comes forth in public, the multitudes make way for it, and it is attended by a crowd of boys, singing hymns in honour of it; it appears to be sensible of the adoration thus paid to it" (8.71). The caveat of the passage is in the final sentence, after the semi-colon, the ox seems to understand. The understatement and irony here, intended or not, is quite funny, for the reader is aware that the ox is to be horribly killed, but the ox, a deity, while seeming to understand the song, does not foresee its own brutal death. Read differently, but still humorously, by the last sentence cited, Pliny seems to believe that the ox does understand the song. This two thousand year old passage includes a textual trinity that can be found in much of McCarthy's work, with emphasis on *Child of God*, the bovine, the bovine death, and levity. And in addition to the precedent of the ox in ancient recorded literature, cattle have long been suitable fodder for authors.

Authors unknown and renowned have written about cattle, and what seems to be a common motif or topic in much of the literature is the fact that cattle wander on their own and must be actively driven to where the humans need the beasts to be. As such, in literature, scenes of humans attempting to control the animals can be easily cited; Thomas Hardy narrates an 1891 search for wandering cattle:

> On the gray moisture of the grass were marks where the cows had lain through the night — dark-green islands of dry herbage the size of their car-casses, in the general sea of dew. From each island proceeded a serpentine trail, by which they found her ... then they drove the animals back to the barton, or sat down to milk them on the spot, as the case might require [103].

The animals sluggishly wander after waking, and the human controllers of the stock beasts force the animals to do what the humans desire of them. The cattle, as stock animals, are under the control of man, so their wandering does no good. Man always finds the bovine, and then he puts the animal to work. The topic of cattle being driven, that is being forced by men to go where man wants, is common fodder in literature of the first half of the twentieth century, "There were railings along the road leading to [Silver Street] bridge ... and often people were glad to dodge behind them to escape from the terrified and terrifying herds of cattle, which were driven with bangs and shouts, through the streets to the Monday cattle-market" (Raverat 44). In this example, the author includes a number of common cattle literary motifs. Of course, the men who drive the cattle are an example of man controlling the animals around him; the herd of cattle is obviously under man's control. As well, the animals are terrified; man controls through fear, and as such, those under man's control live in fear. The animals are going to market, and then to slaughter, so, again, the idea of bovine death is alluded to. Iron-ically, the cattle are terrified, but the beasts are not yet aware of their fate, and will probably remain ignorant up until the moment of death. As animals that must be driven and controlled, but yet can be easily led to slaughter, cattle are not too intelligent, even for stock ani-mals, and this bovine lack of intelligence can be found in poetry as well as in prose.

When Lester kills the first cow, the animal has wandered into a river, and the characteristic of wandering river bound bovines is specifically discussed by Sylvia Townsend Warner:

> I think you should know about our remarkable cow.
> She is a black & white Holstein, one of the herd that grazes in the oppo-site field. During the drought, when there was nothing to graze on, she

took to wading in what was left of the river, & grazing on brooklime; and developed this into long solitary walks up the river [291].

This pragmatic cow takes to the river for sustenance during a time of drought, and the animal consumes the green growth on the rocks of the drying river. And then the bovine extends her wanderings as she sees fit, up the river. This passage of a wandering, water-seeking bovine is similar to one from *Child of God*, a scene in which Lester is less impressed than Mrs. Townsend Warner. So, it can be seen that cattle and cows are situated in nineteenth and twentieth century literature, and that in the literature, the stock bovines possess a specific number of characteristics, wanderlust, stupidity, a herd mentality which assists man in driving the beasts, and an affinity to water during times of drought. McCarthy utilizes all of these literary cattle characteristics in his fiction, and additionally, adds levity to the cattle based scenes. McCarthy also utilizes a team of mules in his writing, as does Charles Darwin.

In *Voyage of the Beagle*, Charles Darwin alludes to the mannerisms of mules and to the mules' inherent ability to exist in a team — socially and in an environment of labor:

> The madrina (or godmother) is the most important personage. She is an old steady mare, with a little bell around her neck; and wheresoever she goes, the mules, like good children, follow her.... It is nearly impossible to lose an old mule; for if detained for several hours by force, she will, by the power of smell, like a dog, track out her companions.... The mule always appears to me a most surprising animal. That a hybrid should possess more reason, memory, obstinacy, social affection, and powers of muscular endurance, than either of its parents, seems to indicate that art has here outsmarted nature [333–4].

The mule, a hybrid cross between a mare and a male donkey, has an inbred sense of social order and belonging, and as such, is impossible to lose. The mule knows, through smell apparently, where to go when mislocated. And, consequently, the muleteer never has to worry about losing his loose mules. Darwin seems puzzled that a human-created hybrid, the mule, can be a better beast of burden and social being than the two animals from which it was created, and he seems to see the mule as a feat above evolutionary biological determinism; man has interrupted evolution, and the result is an animal better than those that have biologically evolved. What is more, the creation of the mule is another attempt by man to control the natural world, a successful attempt, for, according to Darwin, the mule is an intelligent and tireless work animal, one that will always follow the lead-mule, and even a missing mule cannot be forever lost. But of course, McCarthy will show the reader that the mule can indeed be lost, or killed, or starved, sometimes humorously. First, however, we must address the topic of bovines and bovine death in McCarthy's work.

McCarthy places bovines of some sort in nearly all of his works, and both primary locales of action, agrarian Tennessee and the Border Southwest of the United States and Mexico, offer ample opportunity for the author to include stock bovines in the fictive action. In the first locale, the agrarian South, stock bovines appear in the texts sporadically, but in crucial scenes. In *The Orchard Keeper*, a young Ather Ownby, recently bachelored, exists in depression, "*While the chickens grew thin, while the stock screamed for water*" (155). In this example, the stock referred to is bovine and equine (and porcine), for Ownby mentions that at the time he had "a cow and a wore-out mule" (152). This example of the presence of stock animals in the text, and of the stock dying, is McCarthy's first in-text killing of a bovine and a mule, and it will be seen that in other texts, the killing of stock animals is a motif McCarthy repeats for effect. Additionally, and not surprisingly, the author continues to kill off stock animals in *Blood Meridian* and the novels of the Border Trilogy.

For example, in *Blood Meridian*, McCarthy includes brief scenes of mules that die, and interestingly, the mules die from falling, not unlike the mules in *Child of God*. In the first scene of a mule dying, Glanton's scalphunters are riding in the mountains of Mexico, between slaughters:

> The following evening as they rode up onto the western rim they lost one of the mules. It went skittering off down the canyon wall with the contents of the panniers exploding soundlessly in the hot dry air and it fell through sunlight and through shade, turning in that lonely void until it fell from sight into a sink of cold blue space that absolved it forever of memory in the mind of any living thing that was [147].

This scene of mule death deletes the animal from thought and existence, as if the mule never was. The beast slips away, gravity bound, and disappears. McCarthy's precedent for falling and disappearing mules is *Child of God*, and in that text, the disappearing mule(s) scene is not one of narrative philosophy, but is one of levity. The second mule falling scene in *Blood Meridian* is a scene of human controlled multiple mule deaths. Glanton's gang, again in the mountains, comes across a "conducta of one hundred and twenty-two mules bearing flasks of quicksilver for the mines" (194). The conducta is "twenty-six days from the sea [the Pacific Ocean] and less than two hours out from the mines" (194), but the conducta will not arrive to complete its mission, because the scalphunters shoot the drovers and ride the mules off of the ledge: "The riders pushed between them and the rock and methodically rode them from the escarpment, the animals dropping silently as martyrs, turning sedately in the empty air and exploding on the rocks below in startling bursts of blood and silver" (195). In this longer scene of mule carnage and slaughter, McCarthy repeats the manner of mule death, but on a grander scale, sans philosophic rhetoric; he writes that the scalphunters push the mules off the cliff, and the beasts explode on impact. In the former scene, neither the reader nor the scalphunters see the mule die, but here, the mules die in impressive explosions. The former scene, where the mules disappear, is more akin to *Child of God*, but the manner of mule death in all three examples is the same, falling. However, the mule death in the former scene is an accident; the animal slips and falls, while the mule deaths in the latter scene are caused maliciously by the scalphunters; the men push the beasts off of the pass. McCarthy's western texts also have scenes of bovine death, and both *The Crossing* and *Cities of the Plain* include passages that allude directly to bovine death.

For instance, in *The Crossing*, the second text of the trilogy, two passages, quite early in the text, provide scenes of bovine death. The first is narrated with informative purpose:

> The wolves in that country had been killing cattle for a long time but the ignorance of the animals was a puzzle to them. The cows bellowing and stumbling through the mountain meadows with their shovel feet and their confusion, bawling and floundering through the fences and dragging posts and wires behind. The ranchers said they [wolves] brutalized the cattle in a way they did not the wild game. As if the cows evoked in them some anger. As if they were offended by some violation of an old order. Old ceremonies. Old protocols [25].

This passage begins through the narrator, and then reads the wolf's mind, and also includes the rancher's point of focalization, before returning to the narrator's optic. In this instance, the cows are seen by the wolves as stupid beasts, beasts clumsy and incapable of learning and evolving. This passage also conjoins the ancient with the modern, a common McCarthy interassociation. McCarthy's old ceremonies and old protocols refer to the pre-historic hunt of the wolf and the pre-domesticated bovine, a hunt five thousand to twenty thousand years prior to the text's contemporary present. The wolves are offended by the bovines' passive domesticity, and as such, the wolves desecrate the bovines. McCarthy's portrait of the bovines is unflattering on many levels; the cattle are stupid, beyond the point of learning; as well, the cows are so passive that the beasts subjugate themselves to man's control; as well, the animals are killed and desecrated by the ancient predators, the wolves. Only pages later, McCarthy conjoins the ancient history of the wolf to the existence of Billy Parham and includes a brief passage regarding the she-wolf's killing of a heifer: "He picked up her track again and followed it across the open country and onto the benchland above Cloverdale Draw ... and here she'd killed a two year old heifer at the edge of the tree" (32). Again, McCarthy has used the death of a stock bovine for effect, and the death of the heifer produces urgency in the story. But as a rule, in the other two texts of the Border Trilogy, bovines exist in the periphery of the narrative action.

In *All the Pretty Horses* and *Cities of the Plain,* the texts which frame the trilogy, McCarthy includes the mention of cattle in passing, and the cattle pass in and out of scenes quite quickly, akin to horsemen who pass by on their horses. At the open of section two of the former text, McCarthy's narrator describes Don Héctor Rocha y Villareal's vast Coahuila ranch: "La Purísima was one of very few ranches in that part of Mexico retaining the full complement of six square leagues of land allotted by the colonizing legislation of eighteen twenty-four ... land which had been in his family for one hundred and seventy years.... He ran upwards of a thousand head of cattle on this land" (97). The history of the land is the history of the family, and the vehicle for the success of this landed familial enterprise is the stock bovine. In an era dominated by the Mexican national government's socialist controls, controls motivated by American capitalist interest and investment in Mexico, Don Héctor's Hacienda is a working cattle ranch, a ranch with a history dating back to about seventeen eighty. Consequently, the history of cattle runs through the text, but *All the Pretty Horses* is a horse text, not a cattle story, and as such, McCarthy does not keep the bovine close to the narrative action.

In this regard, *Cities of the Plain* is similar to *All the Pretty Horses.* While the latter text is set on Mac McGovern's working ranch in New Mexico, cattle do not feature prominently in the text. However there is one passage where bovines are prominent. In the first scene, a dialogue between the elder statesman of the ranch and Cole, Mr. Johnson tells Cole of previous cattle drives. In the first tale he tells, Mr. Johnson tells of a massive flock of geese that flew overhead one night, but did not spook the herd; Johnson then tells of a cat on fire, which was thrown into a herd of cattle, which stampeded the herd (124–5). When asked by Cole about what happened to the fellow who threw the cat into the herd, Mr. Johnson replies, "Oh. Best I remember he didn't make out too well" (125). Here, the cattle associated levity is understated yet obvious; the fellow who caused the stampede was probably killed via vigilante justice. Of course, as this is the fiction of McCarthy, death can produce levity. In the second scene of the passage, a dialogue between Cole and Billy, Cole meets Parham after speaking with Mr. Johnson and this brief, but comical, exchange occurs:

What was he [Johnson] talking about?
Just stuff.
What did he say?
I guess he said cattle could tell the difference between a flight of geese and a cat on fire [127].

This timely dialogue exists as an inside joke between Cole and the narrator and the reader. Billy has no idea that Cole's response is appropriate to the question, but when Cole's response is read with the former scene, it is apparent that in this scene, the response is adroit and witty. Here, stock bovines and levity are found, even though the cattle are peripheral to the primary story within the text.

As seen, McCarthy often uses stock mules and cattle in specific textual situations and in specific manner. Mules fall and disappear from the text, while bovines die and are used in situations of levity. *Child of God* is the seminal text for McCarthy's manner of using the stock beasts in this way, for *Child of God* contains scenes of bovine death and abuse, which are quite humorous, and further, the text also contains a scene of a mule team falling and disappearing, a scene which ends on a note of levity. *Child of God*, for all of the novel's gruesomeness, is a work that is perhaps McCarthy's funniest. Lester Ballard's murder and necrophilia is juxtaposed with scenes of outright levity and humor. Ballard's interactions with the domestic, stock and wild animals of the text prove that Lester is as ill adept with animals as he is with human beings. Further, the levity associated with the stock animals, cows, oxen, and a team of mules, illustrates man's ceaseless desire to control the animals that populate the world around him. John Lang argues that the violent acts orchestrated in *Child of God* point to "the pervasive tendency to violence in human nature" (94), and that the text offers the argument of "the potential for violence inherent in all human beings" (94). Lang's thesis is correct, because murder and necrophilia are violent acts of the most ultimate control; person A kills person B, and the former has *taken* the latter's life. Gary M. Ciuba concurs with Lang's premise that men are inherently violent, and argues that the text offers that men, "all are mean-hearted children of Adam and kin to Lester Ballard" (81); as such, *all* men are violent. Further, *Child of God* is a text that argues man's obsession with control of the fauna — stock, domestic and wild — that surrounds him. And as all men are violent, all men are obsessed with control of the natural world. Consequently, of the four scenes of bovine and mule levity in the text, only two include Lester, but all four include broken stock animals, that is, animals under the domination of man.

In the first scene of bovine levity, told in the third person by McCarthy's narrator, Lester is on the hunt for food; here is the scene in its entirety:

> In late summer there were bass in the creek. Ballard went from pool to pool on the downsun side peeking through the bushes. He'd been on a diet of stolen fieldcorn and summer garden stuff for weeks save for the few frogs he'd shot. He knelt in the high grass and spoke to the fish where they stood in the clear water on wimpling fins. Ain't you a fine fat son of a bitch, he said.
>
> He fairly loped toward the house. When he came back he had the rifle. He made his way along the creek and eased himself through the sedge and briers. He checked the sun to see it would not be in his eyes, making his way on all fours, the rifle cocked. He peered over the bank. Then he raised up on his knees. Then he stood up. Upstream below the ford Waldrop's cattle stood belly deep in the creek.
>
> You sons of bitches, croaked Ballard. The creek was thick red with mud. He brought the rifle up and leveled it and fired. The cattle veered and surged in the red water, their eyes white. One of them made its way toward the bank holding its head at an odd angle. At the bank it slipped and fell and rose again. Ballard watched it with his jaw knotted. Oh shit, he said [3–4].

This three-paragraph scene is exquisite in its balance and narration.

In the first paragraph, the narrator sets scene, time of year, and issue at hand — Ballard's hunger. It is late in the summer, after the harvest of home gardens, and Lester needs meat, or fish, for a diet of fieldcorn and stolen vegetables and frogs are not enough to sustain a man. Lester, presented as a voyeur, kneels in the grass, concealed, and he peers at and salivates over the bounty — live bass, decent dinner. Also note that Lester has been shooting frogs when the amphibians are readily available, so Lester kills and eats what he can. In this first paragraph, the bass are readily available, and Lester has purpose. In the second paragraph, the hinge paragraph, Lester runs to his shack to gather his rifle, his one "totemic" (Ciuba 77) possession; interestingly, this is one of the few instances in the text when Lester does not have his rifle at hand, at the ready, and subsequently, he loses his intended kill, but kills, nonetheless. After gathering his rifle, Lester seeks proper placement for killing. He chooses a position without direct, vision obscuring, sunlight, and shows he is an adept pre-hunter. Then McCarthy writes Lester's actions in a staccato series of three brief sentences of action; Lester peers over the bank; he rises to his knees; he stands. Lester's standing is an important act because, in standing, the hunter exposes himself to his prey; thus, he scares away the prey. But Lester, as a wizened hunter, stands because he knows the fish hunt is over. But, the bovine hunt has just begun. As the paragraph closes, it is revealed to the reader that Waldrop's cattle — the cattle of Lester's landlord — have wandered into the stream. The reader can picture the image of the stupid beasts standing immobile in the stream, chewing their cuds. These two paragraphs illustrate an example of bovine levity, but because the text is *Child of God* and the protagonist is Lester Ballard, McCarthy includes a third paragraph to conclude the scene.

In the third paragraph, in anger, Lester loses his self-control, and as a result, he takes control through the impulse act of shooting into the herd. The third paragraph is full of the rhetoric of death. When he sees the cattle in the stream, Lester croaks, a verb used usually to describe the call of a frog, an animal that Lester has killed and eaten, and controlled. As well, croak is slang for the act of dying, so, to croak is to die. Additionally, the water is red, the color of blood. This use of the language of death is a methodology McCarthy uses often, and as death and Lester Ballard are conjoined twins, a bovine must die, and one does. So, as Lester shoots into the herd, a bovine is shot. As one, the herd lurches in fear, aroused by the gunfire. The mortally wounded animal has its head at an odd angle, not unlike Lester (9), and it stumbles and dies. Oh shit, is Lester's reply. In this scene, McCarthy uses the first two paragraphs to create the scene, for the first two paragraphs could stand alone as the scene, and the bovine levity is still apparent and laughable. But, with the inclusion of the third paragraph — through Lester's reply —

comes an exponential leap in levity, and the death, of course, of the cow. In this three-paragraph scene, McCarthy proves that Lester can be a vehicle for humor. In the second scene of bovine levity, McCarthy again uses Lester as vehicle to affix humor and bovine death.

In the second scene of bovine levity, McCarthy uses an interpolated first person account to summon humor from the gruesome text:

> I'll tell ye another thing he [Lester] done one time. He had this old cow to balk on him, couldn't get her to do nothin. He pushed and pulled and beat on her till she'd wore him out. He went and borry'd Squire Helton's tractor and went back over there and thowed a rope over the old cow's head and took off on the tractor hard as he could go. When it took up the slack it like to of jerked her head plumb off. Broke her neck and killed her where she stood. Ast Floyd if he didn't [35].

This brief paragraph opens in the middle of the action. More than one Lester Ballard story has already been told, and the audience is one that is being narrated to, for the purpose of telling Ballard stories. The story is told by an individual who states that he will tell the audience [ye] yet *another* story of the absurd exploits of Lester Ballard. In this story, the storyteller tells of a separate incident of Ballard-induced bovine death. It is worth mention that the second and the third scenes of bovine levity directly follow the first scene of bovine levity. As such, the three scenes of levity occur on three continuous pages, pages thirty-four, thirty-five and thirty-six. In this scene, Lester is trying to control an already controlled animal, the stock cow, but the animal, stubborn and stupid, and facing death unaware, refuses Lester's prompts, up to the point when Lester beats the animal until he is the one who becomes exhausted from the effort of swinging the lash; the roles have become inverse, and Lester is the beast who is working. Lester, typically human, seeks control of an animal, and he resorts to violence when the abject animal refuses to be controlled. For the abject get tired of the abject position and sometimes refuse to obey the commands of the controller, but the human remains human and resorts to human nature — increasing the act of control through increasing the acts of violence. Lester, again through impulse, borrows a tractor to even the battle of wills, and he then applies his equalizer to the cow. Of course simple common sense should allow that pulling a cow with a rope by the neck with the full torque of a tractor would lead to injury of the bovine, but when he is angry, Lester seems to lack any type of common or intellectual sense. As a result of this cognitive lapse, Lester follows his impulse driven plan to tragicomic result—tragic for the cow but comic for the reader. For the tractor and lasso setup nearly decapitates the bovine, and the beast's neck is broken, and she dies at the point of her stand. The narrator closes the story with an act of confirmation and witness, "Ast Floyd" (35). Apparently Floyd was there, too. Obviously, the stubborn beast had had enough abuse at Lester's hand, and in the McCarthy, an animal not controlled is an animal soon dead. For if a man cannot control an animal, he will injure the beast to the point of mortality, and in this scene, a comical one, the beast is mortally injured. In the third scene of bovine levity, the bovines do not die, and the beasts exact some measure of revenge against a human antagonist.

The third and final scene of bovine levity in *Child of God* is one in which McCarthy utilizes the ancient stock beast, and former Egyptian deity, the ox, to humorously present a bit of bovine revenge; again, this scene seems to be narrated by the first person narrator from the preceding scene of bovine levity:

> That reminds me of that Trantham boy had them oldtimey oxes over at the fair here a year or two back. They sulled up on him and wouldn't go till finally he took and built a fire in underneath of em. The old oxes looked down and seen it and took about five steps and quit again. Trantham boy looked and there set the fire directly in under his wagon. He hollered and crawled up under the wagon and commenced a beatin at the fire with his hat and about that time them old oxes took off again. Drug the wagon over him and like to broke both his legs. You never seen more contrary beasts than them was [36].

In this example, the boy's youth can stand as an excuse for his stupidity. The man telling the story identifies the Trantham boy as a boy by not stating the boy's first name; men are named, even idiots such as Lester, but boys are referred to by the term, boy. That narrator also dates the oxen as "oldtimey"—ancient—animals, so that the animals seem more aged than the boy. And, as hearsay suggests, with age comes wisdom, so even at the beginning of the story, the oxen have an advantage over the boy. Here, as with the previous scene of bovine levity, the issue between the human and the bovine is one of control. The human seeks to control the stock bovine, but the stubborn beast will not cooperate in submission. Thus, man, so very predictable, resorts to force and violence. In this example, the Trantham boy lights a fire underneath the team of oxen. The oxen move all right, but in a measured and considered act, the beasts, wizened and belligerent with age, move forward only a number of feet. This exacting movement results in the placement of the wagon, a valued commodity and practical tool, directly over the fire. The beasts mutiny, and the oxen mutiny is ironically humorous, as is the following action of the boy. The Trantham boy — devolving — hollers like an animal, forgets the focus of his anger and attempts to save the wagon by oxygenating the fire with his hat. In doing so, the soon to be injured oxenteer crawls under the wagon, and into the wheel path of the oxen controlled vehicle. The wagon, which must be stout and heavy as it is driven by oxen not mules, is driverless but is not directionless, and the astute oxen direct the wagon forward and over their young comic foil, injuring both of the young man's legs. Again, McCarthy concludes the scene with a comical summary comment: oxen are very, very contrary beasts. This comical passage argues that Lester is not alone in his impulsive and violent response to animal stubbornness, for even young humans react violently when control is taken from them. And, for the third time in three pages, McCarthy uses bovines to produce levity in the text, for all three bovine scenes are funny, despite the fact that the rhetoric on man and violence, and control of the natural world, is not. McCarthy closes the text with a third person narrated passage of the like, but in the final passage of stock animal levity, the author chooses an equine beast of burden to produce both the textual levity and the rhetoric of man's control, the mule.

In this last freestanding passage, McCarthy includes a scene of animal levity, a scene where a team of mules becomes a device for disappearance and discovery:

> In April of that same year a man named Arthur Ogle was plowing an upland field one evening when the plow was snatched from his hands. He looked in time to see his span of mules disappear into the earth taking the plow with them. He crawled with caution to the place where the ground had swallowed them but all was darkness there. A cool wind was coming from inside the earth and far below he could hear water running.
> ... They never found the mules [195].

This scene of mule levity is quite similar to the previous three scenes of bovine levity. The animal in question is again a stock animal, this time, specifically a hybrid, an animal bred by man for labor under man's control. As such, the mule team pulls Ogle's plow under the farmer's control, and while these mules are not as belligerent and uncooperative as Ballard's and the Trantham boy's bovines, their controller is an adult working man and not a murderous ghoul or a dimwitted boy. Likely,

Ogle is past the point in his life where he is outwitted by stock animals, but in this situation, the natural world takes from man, rather than the inverse. For during spring plowing, Mr. Ogle, while plowing upland, that is, up a hill, loses his mule team to a spontaneous sinkhole. Of course, sinkholes are natural occurrences in areas with both hills and underground catacombs, and the farmer does not seem very shocked at the turn of events, which he shows by crawling to the edge of the hole for a listen. He hears nothing but the sound of flowing water. Notice McCarthy's verb to describe what happens to the mules; the mules *disappear* from the face of the Earth, and fall from sight, or are swallowed, into the bowels of Mother Earth, and in this inverse act, the natural world takes from man, as he has so often from her. Here, the mules disappear and fall, something that occurs as well in *Blood Meridian*. Additionally, as in the latter text, the mules are either dead or soon to be dead, for if the fall, while hitched to the plow-rig, does not kill the team, lack of sustenance in the catacombs will. Therefore, it can be concluded that McCarthy's motif of the mule falling, disappearing and dying was created with the above-cited passage from *Child of God*. However, unlike in *Blood Meridian*, in this text, McCarthy concludes the scene of mule death with light levity, "They never found the mules" (195). Those mules are forever gone. This fourth example of stock-driven levity has something else in common with the previous three examples of bovine levity. In each of the four examples of levity, man controls or attempts to control the stock animal at hand, be the animal cow, ox or mule, and in each example, the animal (or animals) suffers or dies under man's control. Additionally though, even in scenes of death and injury, there are passages of great levity and humor, and explication of the paradox of death and humor is one which the young McCarthy is quite comfortable with and successful at. Nonetheless, the author does include in *Child of God* a number of other scenes of animal associated levity, not all of which are yoked to death.

Lester Ballard is ill adept with man and beast, and even the animals seem to be aware of this fact. Consequently, even animals realize Ballard is not quite right, not quite normal. Early in the text, McCarthy offers a junkyard cat's assessment of the ghoulish gnome. As Lester walks through a junkyard, "an assortment of cats taking the weak sun watched him go. Ballard pointed the rifle at a large mottled tom and said bang. The cat looked at him without interest. It seemed to think him not too bright" (26). Lester catches the attention of the collection of junkyard cats, which notice a freak when one walks by, but Lester, in return, turns his attention to an individual adult, unneutered male cat. In an attempt at passive control, Lester takes his power totem, his rifle, and points it at the male cat, but the cat will not surrender power and react to Ballard's challenge. The cat is uninterested, not because he is afraid of Ballard, but because he thinks Ballard is an idiot, for in the last two cited sentences, McCarthy elevates the feline above the human, and the cat is the subject of the sentence, while Ballard is the direct object of the cat's intellectual disdain and physical ambivalence. McCarthy writes this brief but funny scene as a few seconds of textual time, but when the scene is considered with the other scenes of animal levity and human control, the reader can ascertain that McCarthy utilizes the uses of animal levity to juxtapose the overwhelming textual brutality produced by man, brutality man uses against man and woman and animal. What is more, cats are not the only nonhuman animals who disavow Lester, for later in the text, a stray dog enters, and exits, Lester's life.

In another scene constructed around the junkyard, Lester ambles down a quarry road after exiting the dump, when a lost, tired, hungry, weak, stray dog discovers a potential master: "A dog followed him out the quarry road. Ballard gave a little dry whistle and snapped his fingers and the dog sniffed at his cuff. They went on up the road" (38). The dog and Lester meet, and the animal accompanies Lester up the road. McCarthy uses a plural pronoun, they, as the subject of the final sentence of the cited passage. This would seem to imply that the dog and Lester are now a pair, but this pair is not to be, because the reader remembers that previously, Lester has beaten a dog to death (24). Accordingly, the stray dog divorces itself from Lester; while in the quarry, Lester "called the dog, his voice relaying from rock to rock and back again" (39), but the canine neither answers nor comes to the caller. After returning to the road, Lester "looked around.... He called the dog once more and he waited and then he went on" (39). This passage is pathetic because Lester is truly alone, and yet the passage is also humorous because even a stray dog chooses a life against the elements over a life with the warped Ballard. Cats and dogs know to ignore or avoid Lester, and the effect is both comic and pathetic. However, quite briefly within the action of the text, McCarthy does allow Lester some levity of his own.

McCarthy allows Lester a laugh and two grins in *Child of God,* and all three very short passages of Lester's levity involve animals and human control. In the first passage of Lester levity, the passage of Lester laughing, Lester actually plays in the new snow and catches a small robin: "He entered a glade and a robin flew. Another ... A group of them were huddled under a cedar tree ... At his approach they set forth ... and Ballard ran after them ... He fell and rose and ran laughing. He caught and held one" (75–6). Lester laughs in fun. Of course, Lester's fun will lead to the control and death of the little robin. Lester captures, and thus controls the little bird, and later in the text, Lester gives the bird to an idiot child, while the idiot's sister comments: "He'll kill it, the girl said. Ballard grinned at her. It's hisn to kill if he wants to, he said" (77). Here, Lester grins at the girl because she does not understand that, according to Lester's law, the human in possession of an animal has the right to do with the animal as he [the human] sees fit. If the idiot wants to kill the bird, so be it. And, of course, the idiot mortally injures the robin: "He's done chewed its legs off, the girl said. Ballard grinned uneasily. He wanted it to where it couldn't run off, he said" (79). Ballard grins in empathy, for all of Ballard's loves, up to this point, have escaped him: his mother by familial desertion; his father by suicide; and his adopted dog by abandonment. Ballard empathizes with the idiot child's desire to keep the bird near him; the idiot wants to keep and control the bird, so he maims the animal in an act of control. Here, the reader's repulsion is Ballard's levity, and again McCarthy has shown his ability to perpetuate the inverse. What horrifies the reader pleases Ballard, and the idiot's violent act of control is one that produces levity, but this time, it is Ballard who grins and not the reader.

In *Child of God*, Cormac McCarthy effectively juxtaposes Lester Ballard's gruesome actions with scenes of animal levity. Quite often in the text, the humor is produced when a character attempts to control the actions of a stock animal, most often a bovine — two cows and a team of oxen. The result of man's attempt at control is the killing or injuring of the controlled stock bovines. As such, McCarthy adroitly hitches levity to death, for if man cannot control an animal, he will then resort to violent attempts at control, and if violence fails, man's subsequent impulsive actions will often doom or injure the bovine, or comically, sometimes the human involved. At the close of the text, McCarthy again juxtaposes levity and death with the scene of the disappearing mules. The mules fall and disappear and die, and this comic scene precedes the narration describing the semi-decomposed remains of Lester's catacombed victims. Further, in this text, McCarthy includes a number of passages which produce levity in the reader and levity in Lester Ballard. In the former passages, Lester is rejected by both cats and dogs, and in the latter passages, Lester's levity is the levity of bloody human bondage and control. In any case, *Child of God* is, paradoxically, McCarthy's most gruesome and funny text.

Cormac McCarthy's fourth published novel, the plotless epic *Suttree,* is also grotesque and humorous, for Gene Harrogate, AKA, the country mouse and the city rat, comically kills fauna without Lester Ballard's murderous maliciousness. Harrogate, who lives under a bridge span, is adept at killing animals that fly, and as winged flight is the greatest natural freedom, Harrogate's killing of birds and bats is a bold statement of human control over the natural world. Chapter 5 will examine man's attempt at control of the natural world, via man's— Harrogate's— killing of the birds and bats which surround him, for while Harrogate is an idiot, he is also a success at controlling the flying pigeons and bats which co-populate McAnally Flats, Tennessee.

5

Birds and Bats in *Suttree*

In *Suttree,* the author's fourth published novel, Cormac McCarthy further expands his textual argument that man seeks to control the natural world, with the emphasis in this text on the control of flying animals, specifically, birds and bats. As flying is the ultimate natural act of freedom, and killing is the ultimate act of control — for to take something's life is to assert absolute control — man sees freedom via flight as an insult. Subsequently, man is motivated to kill and control animals that fly. In *Suttree,* McCarthy offers the character of Gene Harrogate, metaphorically an animal himself as the country mouse and city rat, as a vehicle to argue man's desire for control over avians — pigeons — and bats. Harrogate, a master of misdirected schemes, takes the lives of pigeons and bats in separate schemes, for separate reasons. Harrogate seeks pigeons for sustenance, and he seeks bats for bounty. In the first paragraph of the text, McCarthy introduces the bridge-pigeons (7) that Harrogate is to kill, and references to these pigeons are scattered through the length of the text. The pigeons become easy fodder for Harrogate by their very omnipresence in the text and their availability in McAnally Flats, for the pigeons live on the bridge-span of the bridge, under which Harrogate also lives. From early in the text, Harrogate watches birds and then specifically pigeons, and he watches them, and he watches them. Clearly, while jailed, Harrogate longs for the freedom possessed by the flying birds, but as the text commences, Harrogate's focus turns to pigeons, and he eventually devises a number of plots to kill the avians. Harrogate's first plot to kill the pigeons is one that utilizes grain as bait and rat traps as killing devices; the city rat's next plan to kill the birds involves the use of electricity and the electrocution of the pigeons. Trapped like rats or zapped like the judicially condemned of the era (1951–5), the pigeons are equally deceased, and as such, equally and completely controlled. Bats also fall prey to Harrogate's methodology of control through killing. Alerted by Suttree of a bat bounty, but ignorant of the fact that only rabid bats constitute bounty, Harrogate devises a number of manners by which he can kill the little flying beasts, *en masse,* in order to collect a substantial bounty. After a failed attempt to kill the bats with a slingshot, and after a night of "heavy thinking" (212), Harrogate chooses poison by strychnine as his tool of execution, and he puts his plan into action. Harrogate's plan results in the deaths of a bag full of bats, as the bats rain from the sky, each dead bat an animal ultimately controlled at the hand of man. McCarthy presents bats as part of the catalog of the natural world, and except for the Harrogate scene, rarely insults or kills off the little creatures, but of course, Harrogate is out of harmony with the natural world. However, through the course of the text, many avians other than pigeons are killed, and avian death is often alluded to: Chickens exist to be slaughtered and eaten; Suttree dreams of "a hawk nailed to a barn door" (86), and additionally, Suttree and Harrogate dine on turkey at Walgreen's on Thanksgiving Day (171–2). It is bad to be a bird in *Suttree,* and in this work, Harrogate's attempts at controlling birds and bats are but the two most evident examples of man's desire and ability to control flying animals by executing them, for whatever reason. Moreover, with a bit of ironic humor, McCarthy labels Harrogate the city rat, and of course, in the vernacular, both bats and pigeons are popularly referred to as flying rats.

The placement of pigeons and bats in literature is not a construction of McCarthy's creation, and much literary and historical precedent can be found for either animal. Aristotle (384–322 BC), in his *History of Animals,* writes of pigeons' proclivity to retain their eggs during times of duress: "Pigeons have the faculty of holding back the egg at the very moment of parturition; if a hen pigeon be put about by any one, for instance if it be disturbed on its nest, or have a feather plucked out, or sustain any other annoyance or disturbance, then even though she had made up her mind to lay she can keep the egg back in abeyance" (Book VI. Part 2). This passage of pre–Christian Aristotelian science seems to evidence man's more than two millennia long interassociation with and control of pigeons. And while *Suttree* contains no scenes of egg laying pigeons—perhaps because many of the pigeons in the text are under duress—the text does contain one brief passage which directly alludes to pigeon eggs: "A cat regarded him [Harrogate] dreamily from the domed roof of the coach, belly weighted with pigeon eggs" (92). No doubt, according to Aristotelian science, that McCarthy's pigeons did not realize that danger—in the form of the predatory cat—was about. But, since danger is always about in McCarthy's fiction, perhaps the pigeons have evolved to the point where they can lay eggs under duress and the threat of death. Regardless, Aristotle's writings show that man and the pigeon are historically paired, in real life and in literature.

Bats, like pigeons, have precedent in literature, legend and lore, and often the bat is demonized as evil or supernaturally adept, as in Bram Stoker's classic tale, *Dracula: or the Undead* (1897). In Stoker's work, Count Dracula is able to transmute himself into a variety of animals, one of which is the bat. In Guyana, on the South American continent, a bat is close enough to the bloodsucker of literature to merit the name, vampire—a blatantly pejorative and pragmatic name:

> Some years ago I went to the river Paumaron with a Scotch gentleman by name Tarbet. We hung our hammocks in the thatched loft of a planter's house. Next morning I heard this gentleman muttering in his hammock ..."What is the matter, Sir?" said I, softly ..."What's the matter!" answered he surlily; "why, the vampires have been sucking me to death." As soon as there was light enough, I went to his hammock, and saw it much stained with blood [Waterton 102].

A bat that visits and draws sustenance and escapes, unnoticed, has visited the Scottish gentleman, and one can see the potential for vilification of the flying mammal, for this excerpt, published in 1839, is one which is emotionally driven, not scientifically motivated, and as such, the narrator relies on the emotion of the victim to promote the pathos of the situation. Further, the bitten one identifies the creature as a vampire, not a vampire bat, as is proper, and this identification lends a supernatural aspect to the animal. Waterton continues, "'There,' said he, thrusting his foot out of the hammock, 'see how those infernal imps have been drawing my life's blood.' On examining his foot, I found the vampire had tapped his great toe ... the blood was still oozing from it" (269). The bat-stricken man labels the animal an imp, a small demon, and in doing so, the gentleman again pejoratively identifies the little bloodsucker, and this time, he demonizes the beast as well. In using two proto-modern terms, vampire and imp, to identify the bat, the passage above indicates and identifies the long negative association of the flying animal in natural historical literature; the bat is identified as a stealthy bloodsucker, which it is, and a demon, which it is not. This passage calls to mind the scene in *Blood Meridian* in which the wounded filibuster Sproule is fed upon, while sleeping, by a vampire bat (65–6); Sproule, however, awakens during the bloodletting: "He woke, put up a hand. He shrieked and the bloodbat flailed and sat back upon his chest and righted itself again and hissed and clicked its teeth" (66). McCarthy's scene is more urgent in tone and action than the former passage, but perhaps the calmness in the former passage can be explained by the fact that the first person narrator of the first passage is not the one who has been bitten by the vampire bat. Finally, of course, the identification of the bat as a primary carrier of the rabies virus also serves to ostracize the little flying beast.

In *Outer Dark,* McCarthy includes bats briefly in the bleak text. In a three paragraph, italicized section — the last italicized passage of the text — McCarthy offers the tinker, the child, bats, and in the third paragraph of the passage, the appearance of the murderous trio, The Three. As the passage begins, the ever-wandering tinker settles on a campsite for the night: *"In the clearing he set down his cart and circled the remains of a fire out of which rose a slender stem of smoke ... his thin nose constricted and eyes wary. Shapes of risen sleepers lay in the pressed and poison grass. He set out the child and gathered wood and built back the fire"* (229). Here, the tinker, with Culla and Rinthy's child, settles at a previously, very recently used campsite. For the fire remnants still burn, but the question begs, who previously occupied the site? A hint is in the phrase "shapes of risen sleepers." At first thought, the line could seem to allude to nocturnal hunters rising for the night's hunt. What follows the cited passage also seems to conclude this premise: *"Dark fell and bats came to hunt the glade, crossing above the figure sulking there on his gaunt shanks like little voiceless souls"* (229). The bats come to hunt at the glade, and as these bats hunt on the wing, the little beasts hunt and move in their nocturnal search for prey. As such, it seems that the bats in this scene serve merely as a part of the natural world, and McCarthy does not dishonor the little beasts by presenting them as bloodsucking fiends or rodent-faced flying rats. Instead, in a brief incorporation of the bats into the text, McCarthy uses the bats in two ways. First, the bats, as little voiceless souls, are associated with the Holme child, a voiceless soul if ever one existed. This association of bat and human is unMcCarthy-like in its relation of bat and human, for this conjunction seems to be a positive not a pejorative simile. But, conversely, the bats serve as harbingers of human death, the deaths of the tinker and the child at the hands of The Three: "*Then they went away. A fox stopped barking... . The three men when they came might have risen from the ground*" (229). Now it becomes clear that the risen sleepers from the above first cited passage are The Three, not the wild nocturnal hunting animals. Additionally, concurrently in the scene, the bats fly away and the fox stops barking; these acts are the harbinger acts, which notify the reader that death, always close in *Outer Dark,* is at hand, and the tinker and the child are doomed. In this scene, McCarthy uses bats in two ways; he interassociates the little voiceless souls with the child, in a manner not pejorative, for the bats are not drawn in a pejorative manner; they hunt, and then they leave the glade. As well, the author uses the bats as harbingers of human death, and in this sense, the bats' departure is triggered by the appearance of The Three. Neither of these uses seems to indicate the idea of man controlling the natural world, but in *Blood Meridian,* the author's first novel of the Border Southwest, McCarthy does utilize the thesis of man's control of the natural world, here, via Judge Holden's control of bats.

Blood Meridian is a text dominated by the controlling actions of man, and both men and animals are controlled and killed in the text. But in a particular scene, one told retrospectively by Tobin the ex-priest to the kid, the judge seeks and gains control of bat via control and use of the animals' guano. While on the run from Apaches, and out of gunpowder, Glanton and his gang of killers come upon the judge, who sits upon a great boulder in the Mexican desert. Told of the gang's situation, the judge and the gang head into the cave-laden, volcanic mountains that surround the desert. As the gang waits, Tobin narrates, the judge sits up all night, "Watchin the bats" (126). The judge directs the course of the gang through the mountains, as he follows the bats: "As soon as it was dusk and the bats was about the judge altered our course again, ridin along holdin onto his hat, lookin up at the little animals" (127). But why is the judge following the bats? Because the judge is going to use the bats' guano, along with nitre, crystal saltpeter, sulphur, coal, and urine to fashion crude but effective gunpowder, with which the gang will fight off the Apaches. The gang leads the Indians on a forty eight hour chase, while "in those two days the judge leached out the guano with creekwater and woodash and precipitated it out and he built a clay kiln and burned charcoal in it, doused the fire by day and fired it again come dark" (128). The judge refines the guano until it is readily firable for the gunpowder. In this act of using the guano for his desires and needs, the judge controls the by-product of the bat, and while this act of control is not as ultimate as killing the bat, nonetheless, the processing of the guano is an act of nonlethal control. Additionally, these bats are harbingers of human death, the Apaches', but only the judge is aware that the bats preface the Apaches' deaths. So as in *Outer Dark*, McCarthy uses bats in two manners. First, the bats—when they appear in the text and the judge becomes aware of them —are harbingers of human death, and second, the bats are animals of the natural world controlled by man, in this example, controlled via their refined guano. Control of flying animals is human tendency, if the tendency is to be defined through McCarthy's other texts, and many examples of man controlling the natural world through the control of birds are to be found in McCarthy's *oeuvre.*

Looking back to *The Orchard Keeper,* one scene stands as an example of man's successful attempts at control of the flying birds of the natural world. In an italicized back-story scene, McCarthy narrates of the time when John Wesley Rattner and Warn Pulliam met, and of a curiosity bound by the neck:

> *He met Warn Pulliam that summer ... when he saw the buzzard circling low over Tipton's field and noticed there was a string looping down from its leg ... and there was Warn holding the other end of the string while the buzzard soared with lazy unconcern above his head.*
> *Howdy, Warn said.*
> *Howdy ... What you doin?*
> *Ah, jest flying the buzzard some* [133–4].

This bird, though flying, is under Warn's control, and has been since capture; Rattner asks, "*Where'd you get him*" (134), and Warn replies, "*Caught him in a steel trap*" (134). Evidently, the bird was drawn to the trap by raw meat and subsequently imprisoned and controlled by Pulliam. The theme of control continues as Warn asks Rattner if he wants to see the bird up-close, and John Wesley, of course, replies in the affirmative: "*He pulled the bird out of the sky by main force, heaving on the cord against the huge and ungiving expanse of wing, lowering him circle by circle until he brought him to earth ... Here, don't get too close or he'll puke on ye ... I like him cause he's about a mean son of a bitch*" (134). This scene is full of control of the bird by Pulliam, but the bird does not submit willingly, for it refuses to fly down to the hand until forced, and in retaliation, he pukes on his controllers when he can. However, this buzzard is an example of man's thirst for control of the flying animals of the natural world; the bird was enticed, caught, bound, and controlled, and through Pullium's love of control of the buzzard, McCarthy indicates that the flying beast will never fly freely again. At least Pulliam does not maim and mortally wound the bird, as does the idiot child in *Child of God* (79), for the baby robin in that text is fated to shortly die, but its death is unseen in the text, as is a hawk's death at the hand of man in *The Crossing.*

In *The Crossing,* the second text of the Border Trilogy, flawed protagonist Billy Parham, out of spite and anger, shoots at and mortally wounds a flying hawk:

> ... in the mountains a hawk passed before the sun and its shadow ran so quick in the grass before them that it caused the horse to shy and the boy looked up where the bird turned high above them and he took the bow from his shoulder and nocked and loosed an arrow and watched it rise ... and watched it turning and arcing and the hawk wheeling and then flaring suddenly with the arrow locked in its pale breast [129].

Here, Parham, wandering the mountains of Mexico after he has killed the she-wolf through action and idealism, kills the hawk because he has the opportunity to do so. He is not killing for sustenance, nor is he killing in self-defense. He appears to be killing for spite, and for control. In a typically human act, Billy, infuriated at himself, acts out in impulse and in rage, and kills the noble hawk. For a hawk is noble, and as a master predator, the hawk is usually presented in a positive light by the author. Although in McCarthy's drama, *The Stonemason,* Soldier Telfair is a member of a street-gang whose moniker is the Nighthawks, but it can be ascertained that the young men chose the name Nighthawks because of the hawk's predatory reputation and ability to hunt in the day or, in this case, in the night. In *The Crossing,* though, the hawk is a victim of the ultimate human control, control through killing, and an honorable character commits a dishonorable act. As well, in *Blood Meridian,* the judge also controls birds through killing the flying beasts.

As the gang of scalphunters rides through the Border Southwest, killing Apaches and others, Judge Holden makes continual studies of the flora and the fauna he comes across, and as the judge is the consummate killer of all things living, he includes birds in his menagerie of death:

> The judge had taken to riding ahead with one of the Delawares and he carried his rifle loaded with the small hard seeds of the nopal fruit and in the evening he would dress expertly the colorful birds he'd shot, rubbing

the skins with gunpowder and stuffing them with balls of dried grass and packing them away in his wallets [198].

The judge controls the birds on multiple levels. He kills the animals, which is the ultimate act of control, and then he expertly dresses the animals, keeping the birds true to their living forms, but dead. Additionally, the judge fills his journals with information regarding the birds he kills, and he keeps the carcasses contained in his panniers, for permanent confinement and control. These acts are acts of human control on an exponential level, and when he is asked about his acts of conquer and control upon the birds, the judge replies, "Whatever exists ... Whatever in creation exists without my knowledge exists without my consent ... the freedom of birds is an insult to me" (198, 199). This statement is the apex of the rhetoric of man's control over the natural world; the role of the judge is the role of man as god, and as god, man has the power to take life when man chooses to. The judge is insulted by the bird's ultimate freedom — the freedom to fly, and subsequently he kills the birds, and contains, even after death, the mortal bodies of the avians. As such, the judge controls the birds in life, in death and even after death. In *Suttree,* a text which precedes *Blood Meridian* and *The Crossing,* Gene Harrogate also controls and kills the flying creatures around him, but Harrogate, unlike the judge, is a buffoon, not a suzerain, and as such, he kills and controls for sustenance and bounty, not godliness and taxidermy.

Suttree, McCarthy's fourth published novel, is a departure from the first three rurally situated texts in that most of the action takes place in McAnally Flats, a run-down section of Knoxville, given birth by the Tennessee River. However, what is constant in the text is man's desire to control the natural world — with emphasis here on pigeons and bats, for the text is filled with narrative references to all manner of birds, and as well, a significant portion of Gene Harrogate's scheming involves the control of avians and bats. Harrogate, according to Thomas D. Young, Jr., exists in the text as "the amoral, acquisitive center of the human animal, prior to the development of a socially expedient moral sensibility" (113). That is, Harrogate is a collector without moral compass, and of course, to collect is to control, and to control in this example is to kill. As such, Harrogate, in "tireless stratagems" (Young 111), collects all manner of animals for various reasons, and he collects and controls, not to be a suzerain, but to exist another day, and for this reason, he collects pigeons, for to collect and control pigeons is to eat.

Vereen M. Bell argues that McCarthy's characters have a "fascination with wild animals" (15), and it is not only the characters that are fascinated with wild animals, for the author's Naturalist narrator is fixated on the natural world and the animals of that world, as well. From the opening of the text, the junction of man's world and the natural world, here via the presence of flying fauna of all sorts and allusion to Harrogate, is McCarthy's focus: "Under the high cool arches and dark keeps of the span's undercarriage where pigeons babble and the hollow flap of their wings echoes in stark applause" (7). This punctuated sentence is McCarthy's first mention of the pigeons, and it is taken from the first page of the text proper. The bridge-pigeons are to play a prominent role in the text, and additionally, this passage offers a prominent McCarthy and *Suttree* theme, the collision between man and the natural world. Unknown to the reader at this point is the fact that Gene Harrogate is also to live under the bridge-span. And of course, Harrogate and the pigeons are to collide. As the text continues, the narrator refers to the bridge-pigeons as an omnipresent matter of fact, "Arched sumac fronds quivered in the noon warmth and pigeons squabbled and crooned in the bridge's ribbed spandrels" (11). The pigeons are as omnipresent as is the heat of the day and the span of bridge, and again the wild and the man-made are conjoined in one sentence. Later in the text, pigeons are again found in the same sentence with a man-made architectural structure: "Pigeons bobbed and preened in the high barbicans or shat from the blackened parapets [of the markethouse]" (67). For a third time, McCarthy fastens the pigeons to man, and of course, man controls the animals that are in proximity, so these conjunctions do not bode well for the pigeons.

Early in the text, McCarthy's narrator shows that Gene Harrogate is fixated with flying animals. As a gravity bound and imprisoned animal, Harrogate envies the freedom of birds' flight; from the interior of the workhouse bus, "Harrogate watched two birds come out of the colorless heavens and alight upon a wire and look down into the truck and fly again" (45). Harrogate's envy is obvious; he envies the unimpeded freedom of the birds, and he envies the flight of the birds. The narrator even has the birds condescendingly look down upon the bus and Harrogate. Later in the text, a freed Harrogate sets up house under the bridge-span in which the pigeons live, and in hunger, he watches the birds with a plan brewing in his animal mind: "Fat birds the color of slate crooned among the concrete trusses overhead" (97). Notice that in all of the bridge scenes, the pigeons are constantly making noise, and of course, loud prey becomes dead prey, because there is no stealth in noise. Also, the relaxed but noisy manner of the birds indicates that the pigeons do not exist in fear of predators. Also notice that the bridge-pigeons are fat; that is, plump and ready to eat. As the text continues, Harrogate watches the birds and devises the first of two pigeon killing plans: "He watched the pigeons come and go up under the high arches..." (116). Harrogate's hunger and the availability of the pigeons evolve into a scheme, which is realized in a scene with Harrogate and Suttree:

> Overhead in the arches there was a dull snap and a violent flapping of wings.
> Hot damn, said Harrogate, slapping his thigh.
> A pigeon fluttered down brokenly and landed in the dust and wobbled and flopped. It had a rat trap about its neck.
> That makes three, said Harrogate, scurrying to secure the bird.
> ... Harrogate removed the trap and climbed up into the vaulted under-carriage of the viaduct and reset it, scooping up scattered grain ... Boy ... them sons of bitches is really dumb [117].

When asked by Suttree what he plans to do with the dead pigeons, Harrogate replies, "I got two in the pot yonder stewin up with some taters and stuff" (117). Harrogate's is a slick plan, no doubt, but one cringes when one thinks of eating urban pigeons. Harrogate sees his pigeon scheme as ingenious, and he also understands the pragmatism involved; the pigeons eat the grain, and the rat traps catch and mortally wound the pigeons, and he eats the pigeons. He is quite proud of himself, but for some reason, perhaps American greed, the city rat evolves (devolves?) his rat trap plan to one which utilizes electricity.

Harrogate's second pigeon killing plan is one that electrocutes the animals, while Gene and Suttree watch:

> They sat in purloined lawn chairs and watched a pigeon ringing down ... while his pink pettysingles reached to grasp the pole and then like the Dove itself descending the bird limned in blue flame and a hot crackle of burnt feathers and the thing pitching backward to fall blackened to the ground in a plume of acrid smoke [137].

Suttree looks on, amused. "Slick aint it?" (137) Harrogate offers. Suttree asks, "What have you got that pole wired to?" (137) and Harrogate proudly informs him that the pole is wired to the above-ground wires that carry electricity to the city: "What I done, I got me some copper wire and wired it and tied one end to a rock and thowed it..." (137).

Of course, Gene does not think about what would happen if a human touched the pole or wire, but such is life for Harrogate, and he is more concerned with controlling — killing and eating — the pigeons. Remember, Harrogate's goal in his pigeon-killing scheme is to gain sustenance, and he is not one who could articulate the rhetoric of man's control over the natural world, but his actions are his — and McCarthy's — rhetoric of control. Harrogate controls the pigeons through killing and then eating the birds, and to eat what one kills is a pragmatic act for a hungry man. To take an animal's life is to commit the ultimate act of control, and Harrogate is quite efficient in the killing and controlling of pigeons. Harrogate kills because he is hungry, but McCarthy is the suzerain of the text, and as such, it is he who is the rhetorician and creator of Harrogate's methods and motivations. Nonetheless, Harrogate is a strong model for the rhetoric of man's control over the natural world, because he kills and controls other animals, too; he steals and kills chickens when available, and as previously noted, Harrogate makes a mess of a young pig. Additionally, he is very adept at killing, and thus, controlling, bats, but in this situation, Harrogate kills and controls for bounty, not sustenance.

As it is commonly known, bats — like all mammals — are carriers of rabies, and perhaps this is one of the reasons bats are feared by human beings. What is more, bats that hunt and feed on the wing are not gravity bound, as are other mammalian carriers of rabies, such as raccoons and skunks, and human beings and dogs. Bats are feared because they come from the sky, and the little beasts escape to the sky, and so are difficult to catch. As McCarthy's narrator dictates, bats are "life forms meant for other mediums than the earth and having no affinity for it" (14). That is, bats are animals that exist in a different sphere than ground beasts, and are foreign in nature to human beings. Further, when bitten by a bat, because the animal has probably not been caught, a human of Harrogate's era must undergo dreaded series of rabies shots to the abdomen (a shot schedule and technique no longer used). So, in Knoxville, Tennessee, in the early nineteen fifties, a rabid bat was a serious and scary matter to the board of health and the enlightened public, which of course, does not include Gene Harrogate, bat bounty hunter.

Except for Harrogate's bat hunting scene, McCarthy's narrator only refers to bats briefly in *Suttree,* and when he does, bats are mentioned only in passing. In addition to the cited passage above, only two other brief mentions of the flying creatures are readily evident. One is very early in the text, when Suttree walks through Knoxville: "He walked up Front Street ... the western sky before him still a deep cyanic blue shot through with the shapes of bats crossing blind and spastic like spores on a slide" (21). What is being described here of course are bats on the hunt in the evening, and the narrator uses an ironic simile, ironic because bats on the hunt are anything but undirected spores. The bat hunt is a complex, sonar driven dance, a predatory ballet rather than an aimless spasm. Another brief reference to the bats occurs later in the text, and again, the evening scene involves bats hunting on the wing, this time, while Harrogate watches: "He watched the insects rise and wheel there [at a street lamp]. A hunting bat cut through the cone of light and sucked them scattering. They reformed slowly. Soon two bats.... "Harrogate awonder at how they did not collide" (102). McCarthy has linked the bats and Harrogate, for future textual reference, and furthermore, Harrogate is unaware of the bats' sonar abilities, so the reader is enlightened to the fact that Harrogate, already identified as a kooky schemer, knows very little about zoology. In the scene where Harrogate attempts to kill the bats *en masse*, the young man seeks control of the little flying animals for material gain, and he ignores the stated warnings regarding safe handling of the potentially rabid animals.

In the bat bounty scene, Harrogate, with society's permission via the posted bat bounty, seeks to kill and gather as many bats as possible in order to receive the posted bounty of one dollar per bat. Consequently, Harrogate is controlling the flying mammals through extermination of the *anima* — the life force — of the beasts. By doing so, Harrogate is taking away the beasts ability to fly — their ultimate natural freedom — in addition to taking their lives. So, as with the pigeons previously killed, the bats are controlled by man on more than one level. And as in the pigeon-controlling scene, Harrogate devises more than one way to kill the bats. The scene opens with a rabid man running into McAnally flats and evolves from there: "How a madman came down from the town and through the steep and vacant lots above the river ... plunging past in a drunken run ... until he was capsized by a clotheswire ... the man screamed ... then he turned and ran again" (207). The gentleman is rabid, and the board of health is concerned, and so is Harrogate: "A few dead bats or dying appeared in the streets. Roving bands of unclaimed dogs were herded off to the gas chamber. Harrogate kept himself attuned, somehow fearing that he might be next" (207). With a dose of levity, McCarthy informs the reader of the potential epidemic and of Harrogate's less than fine-tuned mental machinations. When informed by Sut-tree of the bat bounty, Harrogate inquires, "Why would anybody want to give a dollar for an old dead bat?" (207), and Suttree replies, "They think they've got rabies ... Harrogate had already started out the door" (207), and like that, a plan is conceived and put into action.

Harrogate first confirms the bounty by turning in a single found bat for a dollar. With delusions of grandeur, Harrogate begins to devise his first bat-killing plot: "Already schemes were clambering through his head" (208). First, Harrogate needs a boat, so he makes one out of two car hoods, which he welds together, and he seals with tar. After testing the boat for floatability (it floats barely and unsteadily), Harrogate sets to the hunt, and as such sets out to control the natural world: "By late afternoon he was up and about, flexing his sling with its new red rub-bers and firing a few flat stones through the lightwires where they car-omed and sang enormous lyrenotes in the budding tranquility of evening" (211–2). Harrogate is going to hunt the bats with a slingshot, shooting stolen rat poison pellets into the air. Even a daft idiot would be able to ascertain that shooting pellets into the air with a slingshot, in order to get the bats to ingest the poison, is a near impossibility, but Harrogate attempts the absurd hunting technique nonetheless. He takes his unstable boat out onto the river, and he embarks on a bat hunt, an attempted act at control:

> Coming about on the placid evening calm and easing back the oars alongside and taking up his sling. Pinching up the leather in his fingers. Pouring the pellets. One flew. And there. A goatsucker wheeled and croaked. He hove back on the sling bands nearly to the floor and let go. And again ... across the watered sky the bats crossed and checked and flared. Dark fell but that was all ... he laid down the sling and took up the oars and came back.
> It was a night of heavy thinking [212].

Harrogate's first bat hunting scheme is an abject failure, for bats know the difference between flying insects and flying pellets. With tongue in cheek, McCarthy narrates that a bat croaks, and to croak, of course is to die or to make a noise; obviously, in this scene to croak is not to die, but to express one's self verbally, for nothing falls but the darkness of night. In defeat, the bat hunter takes his slingshot and his odd boat home, and he commences to spend the night in deep thought; he is aware that he needs a better plan, and he devises one, for the bats are yet in control.

Harrogate's second plan, not a bad plan and actually a very effective one, also involves poison — strychnine this time — and a catapult. After a failed attempt to purchase the strychnine — the pharmacist is no idiot, and he states, "I can't sell strychnine to minors ... nor to folk of other than right mind" (213) — the city rat cajoles his friend Suttree into purchasing the poison. With his plan in motion, Harrogate sets about controlling the bats: "He had a pieplate with a piece of high and wormy hog's liver in it and he was cutting this up in small gobbets with his pocketknife. Suttree came through the weeds hot and perspiring and squatted on the bank and drew a small package from the hippocket of his jeans. Here, you crazy son of a bitch, he said" (214). Harrogate, like a smart rat, evolves, and he realizes that meat is the hook with which to poison the bats and subsequently gain the bounty. Control over the bats will be attained through lobbing the poison packet hog's liver up and into the air with the crude catapult: "Unwiring himself from the land he took up his makeshift oars and feathered gently into the current and away" (214). The hunt is on, and Harrogate is the hunter, in absolute control:

> Suttree muttered to himself. He'd not muttered long before a bat came boring crazily askew out of the sky and fell with a plop onto the surface of the river and fluttered briefly and was still... . Bats had begun to drop everywhere from the heavens. Little leatherwinged creatures struggling in the river. Harrogate oaring among them. One dropped with a mild and vesperal bong on the tin of Suttree's roof. Another close by in the water. Lying there on the dark current it seemed surprised and pitiful [214].

First, Harrogate controls the bats by taking the flying ability from the beasts, and then, he controls the animals by taking their lives. And he is not killing the bats one at a time, as he was with the pigeons. Harrogate is killing and controlling a great number of the little beasts, "a plague of bats" (215) fell from the sky that night, "and by dark he had a half a boatload ... [he] waited for the last of the crawling pile of bats to die. When they had done so he loaded them in his sack and staggered home" (215). The hunt has been an absolute success, the inverse of the first bat hunt. The bats are controlled and conquered, and man is the victor over the natural world. Unfortunately for Harrogate, though, he gains no bounty for his hunting mastery, for the bounty is only for rabid bats, and Harrogate's bats, while unquestionably dead, are not rabid. As such, the bat killing is a profitless task, but, when considered in the context of man's desire to control the natural world via the killing of the object of desired control, the hunt is an unmitigated statement of man's control over the animals of the natural world; the bats lose their power of flight, and then the bats lose their lives. The animals are absolutely controlled by man, a flawed man at that.

In *Suttree,* man's ceaseless desire to control the natural world, through the control of the animals of the natural world, is evidenced most explicitly through the actions of Gene Harrogate and his successful attempts to control the flying animals of the natural world, namely pigeons and bats. In successfully controlling the pigeons, Harrogate gains sustenance and, as such, he gains life. In successfully controlling the bats, Harrogate believes that he will gain monetary bounty, and as such, he will gain material possessions and stature. In either case, Harrogate is controlling the flying freedom of the animals involved, and he is controlling the animals by taking their lives, on both a small and a grand scale. On a broader plane, Harrogate's successful control of the avians and bats in the text is a positive rhetorical act, one that symbolizes man's ceaseless desire to control the natural world. For flying is the ultimate act of animal freedom, and man cannot tolerate arrogant acts of freedom by animals; as such, the flying animals must be controlled, and killing is the ultimate act of control. And even though the animal controller and killer in *Suttree* is a clown, the clown is nonetheless a very effective killer of avians and bats.

In *Blood Meridian,* his historiographic, first novel of the Border Southwest, McCarthy returns to animal hierarchy, this time positing the domestic canine through the canine's master. The canine lives a life analogous to its master. Thus, a deterministic warrior master will own a deterministic warrior canine. Or a doctor who is in charge of a ferry crossing will own a dog of some like stature. Further, a circus buffoon will own a performing buffoonish dog. And finally, a peasant dogvendor will own a pair of doomed mutt puppies. In *Blood Meridian,* the analogy is clear; one is as one's master, and as such, canines with deterministic masters are themselves vehicles for determinism.

6

Canine Hierarchy in
Blood Meridian

In the historiographic masterpiece, *Blood Meridian, or The Evening Redness in the West,* McCarthy's fifth published novel and his first novel of the Border Southwest, Cormac McCarthy again uses an animal hierarchy to posit genus sub-species in a systematic order. In this text, canines are the creatures in the animal hierarchy. Unlike the feline hierarchy in *The Orchard Keeper,* a hierarchy that includes wild, feral and domestic felines, the canine hierarchy in *Blood Meridian* is entirely organized and structured around domestic dogs, and further, this canine hierarchy is one structured on a canine and human analogy. Each canine is analogous to the human being who possesses that specific canine. McCarthy shows that canines are reflections of their masters, in behavior, in emotion, in social status, in life and in death, or manner of death. For example, a puppy doomed to be snuffed out in a deterministic world is possessed by a child whose chances at a long life are dubious. As well, a warrior canine is possessed by a warrior human. In between the abject and the apex canines are performing buffoons that mirror their owner and a half-mastiff that is immolated with its master.

Specifically, in order of abject to apex, the dogs in the lowest slot are town curs, the least of which are the wretched specimens found in the primitive pueblos south of the Rio Bravo River. The most obvious example of this lowly canine's position in the hierarchy is a pair of puppies owned by an urchin "dogvendor" (192); the puppies are fated to die secondary to the whims of Judge Holden, as are many Mexican and

Indian children. And while this particular ragged urchin is not to die at the hand of the judge, the child is as doomed as the puppies, for the reader is well aware of the judge's murderous abilities. So, in McCarthy's deterministic world, the town dog, like the town child, is endangered and abject. Next in the canine hierarchy is a pair of performing Chihuahuas that perform with a troop of traveling Mexican *bufones*. These pirouetting, dancing dogs possess neither pride nor intelligence beyond their training, and the animals are unkindly drawn as well, resembling their underfed, underweight, undersized owners, in both appearance and action. The reader can easily wonder why Glanton does not kill off the entire traveling lot, but to do so would endanger the scalphunting bounty so coveted by Glanton and his bloodletting gang. As such, both the Chihuahuas and the magicians survive, but the point is made; one is as one's master is, so buffoon humans own buffoon dogs, and each species has evolved to the same position in history and the world.

Third in the hierarchy, and slotted far above the two lower castes of dogs, is Dr. Lincoln's "half-mastiff" (253). Prior to the arrival of Glanton's gang at the Yuma crossing on the Colorado River, Dr. Lincoln was the ferrymaster at the crossing, and he had a nice syndicate with the Yumas, which provided riches for both the Indians and the good doctor. Lincoln is at an elevated position in McCarthy's chain of being, and as such, he has a dog of elevated status, for the dog is neither a wretched puppy, nor an undernourished Chihuahua; the beast is at least fifty percent mastiff, and as such, is quite a sizable beast, one that possesses a threatening quality, regardless of temperament, and one that Dr. Lincoln would, no doubt, use as a device of threat. As well, both Lincoln and his dog die together; determinism strikes once, yet kills both.

At the pinnacle of the canine hierarchy is Glanton's dog, one described only as "large and vicious" (149). Here, McCarthy lets the reader decide what constitutes large and vicious. Captain John Joel Glanton, a vicious determinist warrior if ever there was one, possesses a vicious warrior dog. Subsequently, Glanton treats the dog, which attends massacres and is wounded, with respect as it lives and fights and dies with the captain. Further, this unnamed dog incorporates into the gang of scalphunters and is the most prominently featured domestic canine in the text. And, as with the examples above, this canine beast lives a life analogous to its human master. Strong humans, who are consciously deterministic, dominate weak and apathetic humans, and domestic canines owned by strong humans fare better, at least while alive, than weak and cartoonish canines. This is how the domestic canine hierarchy in *Blood Meridian* is ordered.

Man has long domesticated the canine, and the line of oldest continuous breed, the Greyhound, can be traced back more than six thousand years (Greyhounds 0–2:00). Dogs were originally bred for the hunt — a topic to be covered in Chapter 9. Equally important to the hunt is the dogs' place as a companion to man and a performer for man, both subjects that McCarthy covers extensively in *Blood Meridian*. So of course, McCarthy is following and setting precedent, as is his habit. Historically, then, dogs have a rich tradition in literature and the performing arts. As Montaigne notes, "We must not forget what Plutarch says he saw a dog doing at Rome with the emperor Vespasian (the elder) in the theatre of Marcellus. This dog served a comic who was performing a play with several scenes and several parts, and it had a role ... it had to play dead ... after eating a certain drug" (26). This entertaining dog, one trained by man to perform on the stage, bears a striking resemblance to the *bufones'* bat-eared Chihuahuas. Moreover, this ancient scene takes place in a society where animal sport, bloody as well as not, was a popular spectator event, and as evidenced by Plutarch's affirmation in literature, dogs as stage performers were forced to perform ridiculous stunts two millennia prior to the creation of the McCarthy text.

In *The Two Gentlemen of Verona*, the Bard had something to say regarding the behavior of dog and master, and the analogy between the two: "'O, 'tis a foul thing, when a cur cannot keep himself in all companies! I would have, as one should say, one that takes upon him to be a dog indeed, to be, as it were, a dog at all things ... [as] the company of three or four gentleman-like dogs under the duke's table'" (Shakespeare 4.4.10–3, 17–8). The speaker is Launce, servant to Proteus — one of the title characters, and the dog he is referring to, the dog that does not behave like a gentleman's dog, is his own, Crab, for Crab has urinated under the feast table during dinner. As such, the servant's cur has behaved in an unpleasant, uncouth manner, much as a servant would in a class and caste based society. Conversely, the duke's dogs behave and rest under the dinner table, at the duke's feet. The implication and analogy are quite clear in this brief passage; the dog of a servant is a lower beast, as is a servant, and the dog of a duke is a gentle-animal, as a duke is a gentleman. The canine mirrors the master.

In addition to Shakespeare, Voltaire has something to write regarding the kinship and analogous position between man and canine. The extremely prolific French essayist, poet, philosopher, scientist, wrote in 1764 that man should not perform vivisection on the dog because the canine is so close to man in anatomy:

> Barbarians seize this dog who so prodigiously surpasses man in friendship. They nail him to a table and dissect him alive to show you the mesenteric veins. You discover in him all the same organs of feeling that you possess. Answer me, mechanist, has nature arranged all the springs of feeling in this animal in order that he should not feel? ["Bêtes: Animals"]

Man and dog are mammals, but Voltaire also includes the emotional power of the canine to surpass man in friendship. In doing so, Voltaire elevates the canine, while he denigrates mankind, so that, in this passage, it is man who is the animal, the barbarian, the beast. Of course, Voltaire is utilizing double entendre through the passage. The references to organs of feeling can refer to both the organs of the beast as well as the emotional ability of the canine, and the author's rhetoric indicates that he believes the canine to be a sentient animal. Voltaire also argues that a dog shows "him [his master] his [the dog's] joy by the tenderness of cries, by his leaps, by his caresses" ("Animals"). The author uses the pronouns, him and his, to refer to both the master and the dog. In doing so, Voltaire makes the two analogous. By naming neither, Voltaire also equalizes the status of each. Voltaire's feeling regarding the canine is clear, and he sees the dog as an emotional, loving animal, loyal to man, and analogous to man. Moving on to the middle nineteenth century and the era of expansion west of the Mississippi River and south of the Rio Bravo, George Frederick Ruxton and Samuel E. Chamberlain also write of dogs, but the nobility of the animal fails to make the record.

Long established by John E. Sepich and others is the fact that *Blood Meridian* is a historically based text. While McCarthy's story does not follow a single historical thread, many of the characters and actions within the text are historically documented and documentable. What is more, McCarthy's use of canines in the text of *Blood Meridian* is historically documented. George Frederick Ruxton, in his account of adventuring in the Border Southwest during the middle nineteenth century, *Adventures in Mexico and the Rocky Mountains* (1855), writes of the people and dogs of war-torn Vera Cruz, Mexico:

> The aspect of the interior of the town is dreary and desolate beyond description ... scarcely a human being is to be met, and the few seen are sallow and lank, and skulk through the streets as if fearing ... the dread vomito [cholera]....

> The very natives and Negroes are a cadaverous stunted race; and the
> dogs, which contend in the streets with the sopilotes (sic) [turkeybuz-
> zards—zopilotes] for carrion are the most miserable of the genus cur. Just
> before my window one of these curs lay expiring in the middle of the
> street [24–5].

This unflattering portrait of the citizenry and the canine populace of
Vera Cruz offers precedent for McCarthy, for, as it shall be seen,
McCarthy devalues the town cur to the point where the animal has no
life-value. In the scene above, Ruxton first notes the dreariness of the
town, a town worn by both a cholera epidemic and a constant state of
war; then he alludes to the citizen population, one that is ill and malnourished. Finally, Ruxton mentions the canines, in a passage longer
than the passages which describe the town and the people, for the scene
continues, and the cur beneath Ruxton's window is quickly living carrion: "As the wretched animal quivered in the last gasp, a sopilote flew
down ... [and] commenced its feast. It was soon joined by several others, and in five minutes the carcass was devoured" (25). This unattrac-
tive illustration of the town cur and its unpleasant demise is one that
places the cur in the abject position of the scene.

Samuel E. Chamberlain also has something negative to write about
the Mexican border town dogs of the era. In a portrait not unlike that
of Ruxton's, Chamberlain writes in *My Confession: Recollections of a
Rogue* of entering the (1846) Mexican "town of Presidio del Rio Grande
el Norte" (57):

> We marched through the Town next day.... It was a miserable tumble
> down place, built of adoba, or unburnt brick, all seem to be about to
> return to their original material, the mud that filled the streets. The Pre-
> sidio, or Soldiers quarters, an old Church, with its clumsy tower cracked
> and threatening to fall on the dirty "greassers" (sic) who crowded its huge
> doors ... and about one hundred hovels made up the Town.... We passed
> through droves of Donkeys, Pigs, Goats, no-haired Dogs... [57].

Here, Chamberlain, in a manner similar to Ruxton, writes first of the
town, then of the people, then of the animal life — with a slight pejorative emphasis on the town curs. Chamberlain, one who traveled with
the Glanton gang up to the Yuma massacre, which historically occurred
on 21 April (Sepich 130) or 23 April (Sepich 132), 1850, writes of what
he observes on his adventures, and what he observes here is a war-torn
town, claimed by both the Mexican and American federal governments.
In condescending tone, Chamberlain notes the mud-constructed build-

ings and sacrilegiously describes the falling-down church tower and the "greassers" who gather round the church. He labels the houses, hovels, and proceeds to the town's animal life. Note that Chamberlain uses no adjectives when naming the town's animals, until he comes to the town dogs, which he derogatorily labels, no-haired. And it need not be said, but here, a hairless dog is an ugly dog. It does bear note, though, that in *Blood Meridian,* McCarthy describes the town curs of Gallego as "wretched hairless dogs" (165). One can assume that both Chamberlian's and McCarthy's hairless dogs are hairless secondary to malnutrition, and not breed specifics, for the animals are not identified as hairless by breeding. What is clear in both the Ruxton passage and the Chamberlain passage is that the town dogs of Mexico's border towns and pueblos of the middle nineteenth century are an ugly, wretched lot — hungry, abused, beaten, barely or not surviving — as are the inhabitants of the towns; in this way, the wretched humans and the wretched dogs are analogous in existence and suffering. And in texts other than *Blood Meridian,* McCarthy presents dogs as analogous to humans in their existence and dying; as well, McCarthy also draws many, many scenes of downtrodden dogs, dogs abused and killed at the hand of man.

As McCarthy's literary world is a violently determinist one, animals are very often abused by the characters in the texts. One of the primary animals abused by man, because of its proximity to man, is the domestic dog or hound. From McCarthy's first published novel *The Orchard Keeper* to his ninth, dogs bear much of the violence that man perpetuates, and in the first novel, the character Earl Legwater, ironically the Knox or Sevier county humane officer, is "known throughout the county for cruelty to animals" (Kirves 307). In the first scene where Legwater kills canines, the killing action is narrated retrospectively, while the contemporary action occurs in Mr. Eller's general store, a locus for the local society of older gentlemen. Legwater exits the store after drinking a dope: " ... but no one paid him any attention. Most of the old men had been there the day he shot two dogs behind the store with a .22 rifle, one of them seven times, it screaming and dragging itself along the fence in the field below the forks while a cluster of children stood watching until they too began screaming" (116–7). Even in prohibition era agrarian Appalachia, a violent time and a violent place, Legwater's acts of cruel violence against the two, probably stray, dogs leave a lasting negative impression in the minds of the old men and the children, and as such, Legwater is ostracized within his own community. Legwater's ostracization is interesting because in McCarthy's texts violence by man against animals is very often applauded within the story, but as the classic cinematic advice goes, "Just don't shoot the dog." That is, kill any human character, but do spare the pooch. Since Legwater has committed a barbarity, as Voltaire would attest, Legwater must be communally punished, but he seems ambivalent and still kills dogs, for in the second scene of Legwater's killing of a canine, he kills Ather Ownby's beloved hound, Scout, but only after attempting to do so three times.

As the homeless, blind, starving hound approaches Legwater, who is digging at the sight of Kenneth Rattner's composting and immolation looking for a platinum plate from Rattner's head, Legwater first bears his shotgun in order to kill the geriatric hound, but the hound exits (237). Later in the scene, the hound returns after dark, and Legwater again draws his shotgun to kill the hound, and again the hound exits (239). Finally, the next day, Legwater again spies the hound as he and Gifford walk down the road to the ash pit, and this time, Legwater finishes his killing business: " ... and when he [Gifford] turned it was in time only to see Legwater recoil under the shotgun... . He spun and saw the dog lurch forward, still holding up its head, slew sideways and fold up in the dust of the road" (242). Legwater kills the aged hound for pleasure.

Lester Ballard, the necrophilic murderer from McCarthy's third published text, *Child of God*, also kills a dog, but he does so in anger. On a night when Lester is trying to get some sleep in his decrepit cabin, a string of foxhounds runs an unidentified creature through the airy shack; the hounds follow the critter through the shack and invoke Lester's rage: "He kicked one as it passed and stove his bare toes on its bony rump ... a final hound entered the room. He fell upon it and seized its hind leg. It set up a piteous howling. Ballard flailed blindly at it with his fist, great drumlike thumps that echoed in the near empty room among the desperate oaths and wailings" (24). The thumps will continue after the howls cease. And as Lester is very proficient at killing all manner of things, one can reasonably assume that the dog dies at Lester's hand. What both Legwater and Lester have in common is a lack of conscience. Neither man ever shows an iota of sympathy towards the dead or dying canines. And in each man's situation, sympathy is bad for business. Legwater obviously likes to kill dogs, and Lester obviously likes to kill as well, and in this scene Lester kills secondary to anger. Either way, the hound or hounds are dead at the hand of man. Neither Legwater, nor Lester is a sympathetic character, and both exist in an oppositional dyad with the canines they kill. However, in later works, McCarthy creates an analogous nexus with man and canine.

In McCarthy's drama, *The Stonemason*, where the death of the trade of stonemasonry is a metaphor for the death of the family Telfair's way of life, as well as the deaths of both elder and younger members of the Telfair family, the dominant theme in the text is death. And even though the text ends on a hopeful note — the last twenty lines of Ben Telfair's narrative to the fourth wall — death hovers around the Telfair family. By the close of the text, the family patriarch Papaw Telfair, a master stonemason, is dead of advanced age; Ben's father Big Ben Telfair, a journeyman stonemason and the owner of the family stonemasonry business, is dead of suicide; and Ben's nephew Soldier, a gang member and petty criminal, is dead of an intravenous overdose. As well, the family business dies — the motivation behind Big Ben's suicide, the family structure collapses, and the Telfairs must vacate their home. As Act five, scene one, opens, in the empty kitchen of the now abandoned Telfair home, Ben addresses the fourth wall, the audience: "The big elm tree died. The dog died. Things that you can touch go away forever. I dont know what that means. I dont know what it means that things exist and then exist no more. Trees. Dogs. People" (104). At the low point of his life, after the deaths of his father and of his beloved grandfather, Ben laments on death, and as the theme of the text is death, Ben refers to other familial deaths, while in his late father's bedroom. The big elm tree that dominated their yard has died; strong, timeless trees die, too. And the family dog has died. The dog of course is a member of the Telfair family, and can be found in previous scenes which take place in the Telfair kitchen, a familial meeting place, and as such, the dog is included in the family dynamic. After the deaths, the Telfair family home is unoccupied and the windows boarded up, and Ben is in abject loneliness. Nonetheless, when philosophizing upon death, he refers to the beloved dog and to the fact that the dog done died. The dog is analogous to the Telfair family and to the deceased patriarchal members of the family; the theme of the text is the death of the family, and as such, as a member of the family, after the dog dies, he deserves and gains post-mortem recognition.

Neil Campbell argues that Cormac McCarthy's bloody west is a locus where "Death is the only law and what counts is feeling life asserted against the risk of being at the very edge of existence itself" (220). While

Campbell is writing in regard to McCarthy's characters, as the canines
in the canine hierarchy in *Blood Meridian* are analogous to the humans
who own them, Campbell's argument can be applied to the canines in
the bloody text. Death is the only law in *Blood Meridian,* and it is a
purely deterministic law at that. As such, the characters in the text, man
and canine, are marked by a continual "movement towards death ... the
individual struggles of people [and canines] against the starkness of life
and the inevitability of death" (Campbell 225). But in their individual
movements towards death inevitable, not all canines are equal in life and
in struggle. As such, the canines in the text exist in a hierarchy analogous to their human owners, and the lowest and least in the hierarchical slotting are the Mexican town curs, canines which are analogous to
their poverty-stricken peasant owners, and the war-torn pueblos they
inhabit.

McCarthy describes the Mexican town cur in the most pejorative
of terms— stool-eating (155), wretched (165), hairless (165), mutant
(239), to name a few, while he also conjoins the cur to the Mexican peasant. In doing so, the author gives both the town cur and the peasant very
little life value. The town curs are "naked dogs that seemed composed
of bone entirely" (73), while the peasants are fodder to be beaten and
shot by Glanton's scalphunters. Just as canines in the text exist in roles
analogous to the human beings who own the canines, town curs are too
beaten and shot by the gang, and by Glanton. The most abject example
of the abject town cur is the pair of puppies in Jesús María, Mexico,
puppies for sale by an urchin of a dogvendor: "It was gray and raining,
leaves were blowing down. A ragged stripling stepped from a doorway
by a wooden rainspout and tugged at the judge's elbow. He had two pups
in his shirtfront and these he offered for sale, dragging one forth by the
neck" (191–2). Notice McCarthy's use of the weather in enhancing the
pejorative description of the boy. Leaves are blowing down in the wind
and rain, and the boy is a ragged stripling, a sliver or branch of a larger
tree replanted to grow on its own. The leaves blown from the trees by
the rain will never grow, and the boy, born from an older male, is unlikely
to thrive, as well. For the boy lives in a poverty-stricken town in a time
of nearly perpetual war and violence, and as such, is destined to neither
survive, nor thrive. And as the reader is aware, any child near the judge
is a child in mortal danger, for at the same time, "A little girl was missing and parties of citizens had turned out to search the mineshafts" (191).
Meanwhile, the judge continues his business: "The judge was looking

off up the street. When he looked down at the boy the boy hauled forth the other dog" (192). Now the judge and the peasant boy are in business, but unaware to the boy, the business is the killing business. As the judge, here, does not kill the child, it is the puppies that are fated and determined to die. The judge gives the boy a coin for the dogs, and he commences to his business: "... the judge had set forth, dogs dangling. He crossed upon the stone bridge and he looked down into the swollen waters and raised the dogs and pitched them in.... The dogs disappeared in the foam. They swept one and the next down a broad green race over sheets of polished rock into the pool below" (192–3). The judge, in evil disguise, purchases the doomed puppies from the probably short-lived urchin dogvendor, and throws the curs into the river, without hesitation, as is his way. It bears mention that the sight of this dog-throwing is a locale mentioned by John Woodhouse Audubon in *Audubon's Western Journal: 1849–1850*, but there are no dog killings in the passage, only reference to the streams in Jesús María: "We came to the extraordinary little town of Jesús María, situated at the junction of two little torrents of clear, beautiful water, tumbling in noisy, joyous splashing from rock to basin" (120–1). Audubon's tone and subject are pleasant, happy even. Conversely, immediately prior to the attempted puppy drowning, the judge murders a peasant girl (191); then he throws the puppies to their watery deaths. And while the judge attempts to drown the puppies, it is Bathcat, the Vandiemenlander, who shoots the curs out of mercy: "The pistol bucked in his hand and one of the dogs leaped in the water and he cocked it again and fired again and a pink stain diffused. He cocked and fired the pistol a third time and the other dog also blossomed and sank" (193). Again, McCarthy uses botanical rhetoric to describe loss of life; the puppy blossoms, but unlike a flower, the puppy dies in bloom. This botanical rhetoric is symbolic of the child dogvendor's determined death and short life. The maltreatment of these particular puppies, after the death of a peasant child, clearly identifies the canine/human analogy. Even though the judge does not kill the ragged urchin dogvendor, the boy's life is determined to be an unpleasant and short one. The unnamed child lives among death, and his death is as inevitable as the deaths of the puppies. A peasant boy owns two peasant dogs, and the dogs die, so will the child, as did the little girl. Here, death takes the very young, and the cur and peasant analogy is clear. As such, the town cur, here in its most abject form and conjoined to the town urchin, takes the abject position in the canine hierarchy in *Blood Meridian*. Next in the canine hierarchy, and if not so abject but more clownish, is the performing circus canine — a dog sans pride, owned by humans sans pride.

In a scene with historically verifiable human and canine performers (Audubon 100), the second position in the canine hierarchy is slotted when Glanton's gang meets and escorts a traveling troupe of *bufones*—buffoons and magicians—from Corralitos to Janos, Mexico. Glanton asks the patriarch of the small clan of magicians if they are "a show?" (89), and the gentleman does not reply. But, when Glanton asks if they are buffoons, the man and canine analogy is presented and performed: "The man's face brightened. Sí, he said. Sí, bufones. Todo. He turned to the boy. Casimero! Los perros!" (89). Translated: "Yes, buffoons. All of us. Casimero! Get the dogs!" As such, the patriarch identifies each in the entire troop, man and animal, as buffoons. This nexus of canine and man is an illustration of the argument that in this text, each canine is as is his master. The scene continues with a bit of contemporaneous canine and human performance:

> The boy ran to one of the burros and began to tug among the packings. He came up with a pair of bald and bat-eared animals slightly larger than rats and pale in color and he pitched them into the air and caught them on the palms of his hands where they began to pirouette mindlessly.
>
> Mire, mire! Called the man. He was fishing about in his pockets and soon he was juggling four small wooden balls in front of Glanton's horse ... and Glanton leaned over the saddle and spat.... .
>
> The man was juggling and calling back over his shoulder to the women and the dogs were dancing and the women were turning to in preparation of something when Glanton spoke to the man [89–90].

Clearly, this scene is one of clown canines possessed by clown human beings, and the leader of the gang, as his expectoration indicates, holds both canine buffoon and human buffoon in contempt. Here, the patriarch orders the troupe to perform, and they do. Additionally, the patriarch joins in, as if on cue. What is funny here is that the humans keep their performing canines packed like juggling balls or other performing paraphernalia, which the dogs are. The little canines are not even accorded the dignity of existing in the free air. McCarthy's pejorative description of the dogs also bears attention. The canines are bat-eared and pale and mindless. Bat-eared, refers to the dogs' ugliness and over-sized ears, ill fitted for their heads. Pale, of course, is a generalized symptom for illness, and finally, mindless, infers that the beasts, while trained, cannot think for themselves. Notice how the man and then the other members of the troop immediately begin to perform after the dogs begin to pirouette mindlessly. The implication here is that the human performers are also mindless, and as such, perform their tricks mindlessly. In this scene, mindless is as mindless does, and mindless humans own mindless dogs. What is more, these canines and these performing humans do so without dignity. In McCarthy's literature, mindless physical movement is acceptable, if the action is one with strength or honor; for example, shooting someone or gouging someone in the eye with a bottle are acceptable actions. But clownish, goofy, mindless juggling and dancing — by canines and humans — are disdainful acts, beneath contempt — as Glanton's reaction indicates. But, apparently, the silly canines are not killing material, for no one harms the little prideless dogs, and unlike the child peasants in the former scene, the humans in this scene seem adept at surviving in an unforgiving, dangerous environment, and their buffoonish performing is their life-value. As such, both the dogs and the humans survive the scene and continue on after parting ways with Glanton and his gang of killers. And survivability immediately places the performing Chihuahuas above the purchased, loosed, wetted, shot puppies of the former scene. In the former scene, the child puppy vendor and the murdered girl do not know how to live, how to survive, and in the case of the puppy vendor, he makes a profit for all in the town to see, and as such, he places himself at risk of murder and robbery. So, in the latter scene, both the canine circus performer and the human buffoon exist and seem adept at survival, but in the previous scene, neither the puppies, nor the puppy vendor, are long for terra firma. But, dying is not necessarily a limiting qualifier in the canine hierarchy, for both of the canines that exist at the upper end of the canine hierarchy are dead by the close of the text, as are their masters, but both canines, and both masters, lived determinist lives of conquer and control.

Both of the canines at the top of the canine hierarchy are dogs that die at the Yuma massacre (275), as do their masters. Again, as with parts of the previous two scenes, the Yuma massacre scene has historical precedent — the literary scene mirrors a historical event that occurred at a ferry crossing on the Colorado River on 21 or 23 April, 1850 (Sepich 130, 132). The third canine in the *Blood Meridian* canine hierarchy is found at the ferry crossing on the Colorado, and the canine is the ferry master's half-mastiff:

> The ferryman was a doctor from New York state named Lincoln. He was supervising the loading, the travelers stepping aboard and squatting along the rails of the scow with their parcels and looking out uncertainly at the

broad water. A half-mastiff dog sat on the bank watching. At Glanton's
approach it stood bristling [253].

The half-mastiff is not unwise to bristle at the killer Glanton, for the scalphunter is now, so to speak, the top dog. But until Glanton's arrival at
the crossing, Dr. Lincoln is top dog, and so is his half-mastiff, for to own
the ferry franchise on the Colorado, the last water crossing between Arizona territory and California, is to own a gold mine without the prob-
ability of the strike running dry. All westerly bound migrants have to
cross the river to get to their geographic goal, and all migrants have to
pay to cross, so, the ferryman is a powerful and rich man, a man able
to take something from everyone whom he meets and ferries. Subsequently, as canine and owner are analogous in the canine hierarchy found
in *Blood Meridian*, the half-mastiff has an elevated position in the hierarchy. The half-mastiff's fate is not to drown and be shot as a puppy, as
were the puppies of Jesús María, nor is it the half-mastiff's duty to sub-
missively perform indignities under the hand of man. No, it appears that
the half-mastiff's duty is to have a presence as a guard dog, for Dr. Lincoln is a man who is wealthy, so he needs a bodyguard. And for most
greedy pilgrims, the appearance of a large and threatening dog — even
a half-mastiff, still a very large dog, no doubt — at the hand of the ferryman would be sufficient threat to inhibit robbery, for people are scared
of large dogs. Additionally, McCarthy allows the guard dog a dominant
breed, mastiff, for a guard cur or a guard Chihuahua would not suffice
in the literature, and the threat of a smaller canine would be naught.
What is more, the half-mastiff is not intimidated by Glanton, as are
many beasts, so the reader is aware that the half-mastiff does possess
courage, and the sense to know that Glanton threatens its master. So this
canine does possess some deterministic power, in size, in breed, in sense,
in temperament, and this canine is a superior beast when measured
against the two canines which exist below it in the canine hierarchy, the
town cur puppy and the performing circus Chihuahua.

Turning to the half-mastiff's owner, note that Lincoln the ferryman
is a medical doctor, from New York state, no less. To be a doctor, in
almost any era, is to be a person of elevated social, intellectual and financial status. And to be a doctor in 1850 is no different; a doctor at the
time could expect a very good living and some deal of respect and elevated status within his community. So, one must wonder why the good
doctor became a ferryman profiteer. Historically, and literarily, the
answer is not clear, but what is clear is that at the time a profiteering

ferryman could make much more money stealing from pilgrims than he could from treating patients, and so, the good doctor becomes the rich ferryman, and subsequently, he is much more powerful and wealthy than any medical doctor.

Regardless of the canine's and the ferryman's elevated status in the text, however, both are to die at the hands of the Yuma Indians in what is historically known as the Yuma massacre: "The first quarters they entered were Lincoln's. When they emerged a few minutes later one of them carried the doctor's dripping head by the hair and others were dragging behind them the doctor's dog, bound at the muzzle, jerking and bucking across the dry clay of the concourse" (274). For the third time in the text and in the canine hierarchy, dog and owner are analogous in life, and here, eventually in death, for in the canine hierarchy, even the mighty eventually fall: "The doctor's torso was dragged up by the heels and raised and flung onto the pyre and the doctor's mastiff also was committed to the flames. It slid struggling down the far side and ... it began to crawl charred and blind and smoking from the fire and was flung back with a shovel" (275). Immolated together, the mastiff and Lincoln exist together, in death as in life, and regardless of situation of death, the half-mastiff and Lincoln existed in explicit determinism, and died in the like. At the apex of the canine hierarchy in *Blood Meridian* is Glanton's dog, a warrior dog for a warrior man.

Captain John Joel Glanton's dog is, not coincidentally, the apex canine in the hierarchy as well as the most cited canine in the text, for Glanton's dog is present in at least fourteen situations, beginning in Chapter XI, in the scene titled, "Glanton on the management of animals." In this scene, Glanton and the gang ride into an abandoned Apache village, a collection of hovels in a valley, where Glanton finds the apex canine, the warrior canine:

> The last one [hovel] they entered was defended by a large and vicious dog. Brown drew his pistol but Glanton stopped him. He dropped to one knee and spoke to the animal. It crouched against the rear wall of the Hogan and bared its teeth and swung its head from side to side, the ears flattened alongside its skull.
> He crouched, talking to the dog. The dog watched him.
> ... the dog was looking about uneasily. When they rode west out of the canyon it was trotting with a slight limp at the heels of Glanton's horse [149].

This warrior canine is not encumbered with a specific breed, as was the mastiff, for this canine was once an Apache canine, and the narrator's description of the dog as large and vicious suffices. At the open of the passage, the dog is guarding its home territory, but by the end of the passage, the dog trots with Glanton, at the feet of his horse. Captain Glanton has sought and gained another warrior recruit, but this time the warrior is a dog, not a man. And this dog becomes assimilated into the gang, riding where the gang rides, marauding where the gang marauds: "Glanton's dog trotted beneath the horse's belly, its footfalls stitched precisely among the hooves" (152). The dog is now referred to by the narrator as Glanton's dog, and the dog is bound to Glanton in a symmetry of step, life and death — others' deaths, as well as their own. The dog has assimilated Glanton's personality, habit and lifestyle. Later, after the slaughter of the Gileños, Glanton looks for his dog, a warrior missing in action; he asks the judge, "You aint seen my dog have ye?" (160), and the judge replies in the negative. But the dog catches up, a wounded warrior: "They rode all day with Glanton bringing up the rear of the column. Toward noon the dog caught them up. His chest was dark with blood and Glanton carried him on the pommel of the saddle until he could recruit himself. In the long afternoon he trotted in the shadow of the horse ..." (160–1). Glanton longs for the dog, and when the wounded beast catches up with the gang, Glanton physically aids the dog, something he never does with any of his men.

The men ride on and on and on, moving westerly, killing along the way, and always present is Glanton's dog. In Nacori, the dog, upon seeing a pack of town curs, "rose up bristling" (177), ready to fight. And as the gang moves on, "Glanton's dog trotted moaning among the endlessly articulating legs of the horses" (188). Later, as they approach a church, "His dog heeled to the horse and they approached cautiously the sagging walls ..." (224). Here, Glanton and the dog are a pair united in stealth, wary and alert for danger and death. Even before a potential battle with the Chiricahua Apaches, the dog can sense the danger, "Glanton's dog was quartering back and forth nervously ..." (228). The dog, like a good veteran warrior, senses the danger about, and his hyperactive movement indicates this, as would the nervous movements of one of the human gang members. The gang moves west, eventually arriving at the ferry crossing on the Colorado River, where Glanton usurps the ferryman position from Lincoln, a more mighty determinist he, and subsequently places himself in charge of the perpetual gold mine and all of its riches: "He sat his horse and looked down at the river who was keeper of the crossroads of all that world and his dog came to him and nuzzled his foot in the stirrup" (272). In this bucolic scene, man and canine, master and dog, exist at peace together, but as this is McCarthy, their peace is short-lived, for in the Yuma massacre is but a dawn away, and in the massacre, Glanton and his beloved warrior dog receive rather than give: "When they entered Glanton's chamber he lurched upright and glared wildly about him ... Glanton spat ... Hack away you mean red nigger, he said" (274–5), and the Yuma did. And, as it has been shown, in this text, canine and man are analogous in life and in death, so with Glanton goes the dog: "The savages built a bonfire on the hill ... and they raised up Glanton's body and bore it aloft in the manner of a slain champion and hurled it onto the flames. They'd tied his dog to his corpse and it was snatched after in howling suttee to disappear crackling in the rolling greenwood smoke" (275). The death of the warrior Glanton and the death of the warrior dog close the canine hierarchy at its apex, for no human and animal pairing in the text could be more deterministic than these two— unless of course, the judge had a dog, but he does not.

In *Blood Meridian*, McCarthy posits canines in the canine hierarchy according to their deterministic value and the deterministic value of each canine's human owner. McCarthy repeatedly conjoins canine and man in a manner that emphasizes the similarities of the canine to the man; the canine reflects the master. As such, in the abject position of the hierarchy is the doomed town cur, owned by a malnourished, short-lived urchin peasant. Next in the canine hierarchy are performing circus Chihuahuas, canines that manage to stay alive, as do their buffoon owners. Situated above these lowly canines and their lowly masters are canines of power and status. The first of these upper echelon canines is Dr. Lincoln's half-mastiff, a dog superior to all dogs at the ferry crossing, and a dog owned by the ferryman. Glanton and his warrior canine assume the dominant position at the ferry crossing, while Glanton's dog takes the top place in the canine hierarchy. For both Glanton and his dog are warriors, and as such, the analogous position between the two and the actions exhibited by the two posit Glanton's dog at the apex of canines in *Blood Meridian*. McCarthy's emphasis on this tandem relationship between canine and man does two things. First, the relationship calls attention to the canine's status as a social and behavioral reflection of its master. Second, this proximal relationship posits the canine on a hierarchical, deterministic scale. But, in McCarthy's works, dogs are not the only warrior animals, for in *All the Pretty Horses*, horses are also portrayed as warriors.

In McCarthy's sixth novel, *All the Pretty Horses,* the author argues the horse as a warrior, and the horse is not merely a warrior animal but is an animal that is at one with war and the existence of life as a warrior. The horse is ideally suited for existence in a deterministic world, and consequently, the author presents the horse in a number of different societies and cultures in order to prove this thesis, for the horse is conjoined to pre-modern Comanche culture and early modern Spanish culture, and to high-modern Mexican culture and late-modern Anglo culture. The effect of McCarthy's rhetoric is the calling of the horse as a deterministic, warrior animal.

7

Horses as Warriors in
All the Pretty Horses

In the first text of the Border Trilogy, *All the Pretty Horses*, Cormac McCarthy presents horses as warriors. Additionally, the text is a lament for the end of the horse's role as warrior, for by the period in which the action occurs, the fall of 1949 through the spring of 1951 (J. Bell 2–6), the horse's role as a cavalry warrior has been reduced to one where the noble equine is working cattle and racing. Moreover, McCarthy argues that the horse is not merely a warrior but is an animal that is at one with war and the existence of life as a warrior. So, the horse is ideally suited for existence in a deterministic world. For this reason, McCarthy presents the warrior animal in a number of different societies and cultures in order to prove his thesis, for the horse is conjoined to the pre-modern Indian culture and early-modern Spanish culture, and to high-modern Mexican culture and late-modern Anglo-American culture.

In *All the Pretty Horses*, the horse exists as a warrior, as is narrated in John Grady Cole's opening horse-ride of the text, where the ghosts of The People — the Comanche — and their ponies, all painted for war, haunt the passage with their historic and bloody presence. The passage links the consummate twentieth century horseman, John Grady Cole, with the greatest warrior horsemen of the nineteenth century, the Comanche, a group of people who were at one with their warrior horses. The Indian past and the mythic past of the horse are personified through the actions of Cole, a twentieth century American horseman. Further, the warrior horse, like a human ally captured and imprisoned, is worth rescue, regardless of the mortal danger the rescue entails. On more than one occasion in the story, Cole risks his life in order to repatriate a horse. In the first example, Cole, Lacey Rawlins and Jimmy Blevins risk their lives to steal back Blevins' unnamed horse from its Mexican captors. In the second example, Cole, now a rider alone, risks his life again to re-steal Blevins' horse and as well, Rawlins' beloved horse, Junior, and his own purloined equine, Redbo. The rhetoric is clear; a horse is an ally worth dying for, and one worth rescuing, no matter the inherent danger, and as such, in the text, men kill and are killed over the warrior equines. McCarthy's focus on the horse as a warrior animal is articulated through the character of Luis, a Mexican vaquero at La Purísima and a veteran of the Mexican Revolution. Luis argues the horse's common love for war and communal soul. Moreover, Luis argues that horse's souls mirror men's souls, and that the greatest ballet between man and horse is the ballet of the cavalry. However, by the middle of the twentieth century, in Mexico and in the United States, the horse has been reduced, for the most part, to a metaphoric role of warrior, that of cattle herding equine, and the only war that exists for the horse is the war of being broken by man for cattle work. As such, the warrior animal has been de-elevated from warrior to work animal. But, as the text is McCarthy's, his young protagonist John Grady Cole is forced, coerced and self-volunteered into a number of battle situations where the horse and the man must act as warriors under fire in order to survive, and the failure of the warrior horse under fire will result in the man's demise and the horse's capture. Also it bears mention that, but for a hound or two, horses are the only named animals in the novels of the Border Southwest. Warrior horses are befitting of names, as are warrior hounds, and except for the hunting hound, the only other animal that coexists in honor with man is the horse, the warrior equine.

The horse has long been used by man as an aid in war, and as such, the horse can be found in myth, legend, literature, and history, for the warrior animal has helped man conquer man, and man and horse have for centuries been partners in work and in war. As Joel Berger notes:

> More than forty-five thousand books have been written about horses—probably more than have been published on any other mammal except for man and dog. Not only are horses ubiquitous, but their appearance in historical writings, mythology, and art, and their use in exploration, war, sports, leisure, farming, and other work, are testimony to their enduring popularity [101].

Clearly then, the horse has long been present in literature, and the animal has been popular outside of literature because of its many practical roles in assisting man:

> It is not clear where horses were first domesticated, but it is well known that they played an important role in ancient times. Horses were revered in early Greece and Rome as animals of beauty, strength, and valor, and were frequently depicted in sculpture. They were used to pull chariots and became part of sporting events, and they played prominent roles in Greek and Roman militias; it is even said that Philip of Macedon seized twenty thousand horses from the Scythians, most probably for military purposes [Berger 103].

Berger points out that historically horses have been appreciated by man for multiple reasons. Horses are noble, beautiful, strong animals that can serve man in a variety of roles beyond the aesthetic. As such, the horse has practical value to man, while the animal also has aesthetic value to man. The result is an animal that is documented in literature, sculpture, lore, and history, as Berger observes:

> Since horses were so important in early European and Middle Eastern cultures, it is not surprising that they were highly regarded and well represented in western mythology and art. Throughout history, horses were granted divine status and became symbols of the gods ... Paintings and sculpture from many periods of European history depict kings, warriors, and other important people astride their horses ... it is clear that in western mythology and art, the horse generally has been portrayed very favorably [104].

Berger makes the point that the horse is an animal that has never fallen out of favor. As well, he notes that leaders ancient and pre-modern used the horse as a prop to elevate themselves, and as such, the leaders and warriors have concurrently elevated the warrior animal. And not only are horses associated with warriors and kings, but horses are also symbolic of the divine. When a leader associates himself with a horse, that leader is associating himself with the divine. Thus, he is elevating himself above earthly men. So, historically, in addition to being a practical animal, and an animal of aesthetic beauty, the horse is also an animal deified by man and used by man for self-deification. But it is not only the ancient Macedonians, Greeks and Romans, and pre-modern European rulers, who revered and idolized the horse, the noble equine can be found in the Bible as well.

As M. Oldfield Howey states in *The Horse in Magic and Myth*, "Perhaps courage was the quality of the horse that most appealed to early peoples, and we frequently find the steed used as an emblem of this virtue ... [and] in Christian art the horse is the emblem of ... courage" (161). In the Book of Job, the horse can be found in the role of courageous warrior, a willing courageous warrior at that:

> Do you give the horse his strength or clothe his neck with a flowing mane?
> Do you make him leap like a locust, striking terror with his proud snorting?
> He paws fiercely, rejoicing in his strength, and charges into the fray.
> He laughs at fear, afraid of nothing; he does not shy away from the sword.
> The quiver rattles against his side, along with the flashing spear and lance.
> In frenzied excitement he eats up the ground; he cannot stand still when the trumpet sounds.
> At the blast of the trumpet he snorts, 'Aha!' He catches the scent of battle from afar, the shout of commanders and the battle cry [39.19–25].

The horse is this passage, metonymous for the body of horses that honorably and willingly go to battle, is one that is self-aware of its own strengths and power. The horse is given strength by God, and the animal is not afraid when he goes to meet the armed men in battle, for this horse is a warrior horse, one who is in its glory during battle. This glorious warrior equine is one that can be found in McCarthy's literature — a willing warrior, who understands and enjoys battle. As Howey notes, "The Hebrews ... used the horse only for military riding ... [and] noted how 'the horse rusheth into battle' (Jer. viii 6)" (166, 167). As well, "Searching ancient Assyrian and Babylonian records that were written about five thousand years ago, we find no mention or representation of horses being used as beasts of burden. The ox and the ass were the labourers, but the horse was regarded only as a warrior, and is frequently described as 'glorious in war'" (Howey 167). So, it can be seen that in the ancient East and in the ancient West, the horse was regarded as a great and noble warrior, an animal above menial labors, and that the horse was a gift from the deity — or deities — to man. What is more, the horse is an animal that works well with man, in a sort of team precision, as Charles Darwin points out.

In *The Voyage of the Beagle*, Darwin observes that the horse is indeed a beast of burden, but yet is a beast of burden that works very well under the control of man:

In the course of the day I was amused by the dexterity with which a Gaucho forced a restive horse to swim a river. He stripped off his clothes, and jumping on its back, rode into the water till it was out of its depth; then slipping off over the crupper, he caught hold of the tail, and as often as the horse turned round, the man frightened it back by splashing water in its face. As soon as the horse touched the bottom on the other side, the man pulled himself on, and was firmly seated, bridle in hand, before the horse gained the bank. A naked man on a naked horse is a fine spectacle; I had no idea how well the two animals suited each other [156].

In this passage, the horse is forced into the water, literally under man, and Darwin is amazed that the man and the horse could work so well together, to cross a river "of a length at least 600 yards" (156). But, regardless of the fact that the horse struggles under the hand of man, the man and the horse work together to swim across the water. For without the gaucho pushing the horse across the river, and the horse pulling the man across the river, neither might be able to cross on his own. Six hundred yards is a long way to swim, for the man and for the horse, but in tandem, the pair fords the obstacle.

This conjugation of man and horse is something that can occur only after the horse is trained and broken under the hand of man, something that Anna Sewell empathetically points out in *Black Beauty*, from the point of view of the horse:

Everyone may not know what breaking in is, therefore I will describe it. It means to teach a horse to wear a saddle and bridle and to carry on his back a man, woman, or child; to go just the way they wish, and to go quietly ... and he must go fast or slow, just as his driver wishes. He must never start at what he sees, nor speak to other horses, nor bite, nor kick, nor have any will of his own; but always do his master's will, even though he may be very tired or hungry; but the worst of all is, when his harness in once on, he may neither jump for joy not lie down for weariness. So you see this breaking in is a great thing [10–1].

This literary portrait of what it takes to permanently control a horse is the inverse of the willing warrior of the ancient times, and this portrait also deglorifies Darwin's man and horse ballet, but nonetheless, the ancient view of the horse as courageous warrior and Darwin's of the horse as teammate to man are also factually correct, for the horse is all of the above; the horse is a warrior, and the horse is a partner to man in labor, and the horse is also a broken animal, broken by man, not by choice. So, the horse in its relationship with man is in a complex role and relationship. As Joel Berger argues, "For many centuries horses have been lauded and esteemed. These animals have aided humans in their varied conquests; horses have been celebrated in many different cultures, and have formed the economic basis for entire societies. I suspect that most people still view horses as noble beasts that symbolize glamour, beauty, and freedom" (111). In fact, John Grady Cole and ranch patriarch Don Héctor Rocha Villareal discuss a text on horses and the American culture, "*The Horse of America*, by Wallace" (116). And let us not forget war, for in *Outer Dark*, a horse on a ferry declares war against Culla Holme, and like many others in the text, attempts to kill the incestuous nomad.

In his novels of the South, because the horse and man nexus is not as prominent as in the Border Southwest, McCarthy rarely includes horses in the texts, but in *Outer Dark*, the author does include one scene where a panicked horse declares war upon Culla Holme and attempts to kill the wandering miscreant. In this scene, as a thunder and lightning storm gains momentum and a river rises, Holme is forced to seek passage on a ferry in order to cross the river: "When the road reached the river it went right on into the water and he could see the water was up" (157). When he is approached by the ferryman, Holme is told that because of financial restraints he cannot cross alone: "So anyway you still cain't cross till I get a horse.... People is just a dime. Horses is four bits" (159). As the ferryman and Holme wait in the dusk, the river rises ominously: "With the dark the river grew louder and Holme wondered if the water was rising or if it was just the dark" (161). As Holme and the ferryman converse, the ferryman foreshadows the coming scene: "Cable busted once and killed a horse ... it knocked the horse plumb in the river...." (162). In this scene, the cable on which the ferry runs is also to part. While the river rises and the rains commence, and after a horse and man appear, the four load the ferry and embark on their river crossing, "with the water beginning to boil against the hull" (164). The river rages, and the rider is lost, and the cable parts, and the ferryman is washed away, and the only living beings on the ferry are Culla and the insane horse, a horse that takes deadly aim upon Culla: "Something reared up out of the dark before him with a strangled cry and he fell to the deck, scrabbling backwards as the hoofs sliced past him and burst against the planking" (165). Here, the mad horse's hooves are weapons, blades to slice Culla up if given the opportunity, and as well, the hooves burst like bombs; the horse is at war: " ... the horse pounded past and crashed in the bow ... he [Culla] heard it coming again. He clawed at the darkness before him, cursing, throwing himself to the deck again while the horse went past with a sound like pistolfire" (165–6). Again, McCarthy uses a warlike term, pistolfire, to describe the horse's actions. And as the horse's war comes to a close, McCarthy again uses the rhetoric of war to describe the horse's attack: "When the horse came at him a third time ... the horse reared before him black and screaming, the hoofs exploding on the planks ... [then] there was an enormous concussion of water and then nothing" (166). Repeatedly, McCarthy uses the rhetoric of combat to explicate the violent scene, and it seems that the horse has declared war upon Culla because he is the only remaining human on the ferry, and as such, he represents all humans. The horse slices and explodes and concusses when it crashes into the water and into death — a war casualty. The horse declares war against the species that placed him in burden, and as such, Culla is the only target available, yet the horse, as is often the case with those hasty in war, is the one that dies. But in *Blood Meridian*, McCarthy offers the horse as warrior in unison with man, something he also does extensively in *All the Pretty Horses*.

In *Blood Meridian*, the horse gets many, many chances to participate in bloody acts of war, and the horse most commonly focused upon is Captain John Joel Glanton's warrior animal. As shown previously, Captain Glanton's dog is clearly a warrior canine, and his horse is fit for battle, as well. For in scene after scene, Glanton the warrior is shown with his horse, and thereby the nexus is created. Glanton is a warrior; Glanton's horse is a warrior, as are the horses of the other warrior scalphunters. In a scene where the gang comes upon a snake-bitten and dying horse, one of the gang's horses attacks the weakened and wounded animal:

> The American horses began to mill and separate along the wall at its [the wounded horse] approach and it swung after them blindly. There was a flurry of thumps and kicks and the horses began to circle the compound. A small mottled stallion belonging to one of the Delawares came out of the remuda and struck at the thing twice and then turned and buried its teeth in its neck [115].

Here, even the wounded and dying horse is a warrior and it strikes out at the American horses, but the gang's horses do not take insult well, as one might suspect, and one aggressively attacks the weakened equine, sinking its teeth into the neck of the dying beast. The effect is obvious; the horses are warriors and exist in a state of war, and even the dying commit to battle. Additionally, in a scene where the gang exits Chihuahua city for a final time, the warriors and their warrior equines are again conjoined: "They rode out on the north road as would parties bound for El Paso but before they were even quite out of sight of the city they had turned their tragic mounts to the west and they rode infatuate and half fond toward the red demise of that day..." (185). The men, who carry tragedy among them, and their horses, who also carry tragedy among them, ride away from one bloody scene to the next, and they do so in unison, warrior man upon warrior horse, within warrior gang. McCarthy's litany of the phrases, they rode out, they rode on, they rode, they rode up, and they rode along (71, 79, 86, 88, 90, 104, 105, 107, 111, 112, 113, 119, 120, et al), indicates the role of the men as mounted cavalry, men who would cease to be warriors without their mounts. Consequently, the warrior pairing of man and horse creates the effective scalphunter.

As well, through the course of the text, the specific nexus between the warrior Glanton and his warrior horse is created. On a stormy night, his "horse put its long wet face in at the door and Glanton looked up and spoke to it and it lifted its head and curled its lip and withdrew into the rain and night" (117). This scene, one where Glanton coaxes the beast back into the rainy night, is just one of many scenes where Glanton and the horse are in conjunction. Later, during a battle with the Apache, Glanton again calms his warring horse through verbal communication: "He [Tate] swiveled both barrels and fired the second charge and it [the Apache chief's horse] plowed to the ground. The Apaches reined with shrill cries. Glanton leaned forward and spoke into the horse's ear" (158). Glanton sooths his horse after the killing of another horse, for as it will be shown, horses have a communal soul, and the killing of one warrior horse affects other warrior horses. As such, Glanton, one at kin with animals, speaks to his equine to calm the warring beast. Even in scenes where Glanton is alone, the horse is with him: "He rode alone on the desert and sat the horse and he and the horse ... looked out across the rolling scrubland ..." (172). Here, Glanton is a man alone, but for his horse. And even when he is a warrior king among men and ruler of the Colorado River ferry, Glanton remains alone, on top of his horse: "Glanton returned to Yuma alone, his men had gone to the gold fields... . He sat the horse and looked down at the river who was keeper of the crossroads of all that world ..." (272). Again, Glanton is a man who rules, yet he is alone but for his horse, and warrior man and warrior horse exist in conjunction, waiting for the next war. While McCarthy does not explicate the horse's status as warrior in *Blood Meridian,* the author does so in *All the Pretty Horses,* and from the onset of the first text of the Border Trilogy, McCarthy's rhetoric clearly indicates the horse's status as warrior equine.

Barcley Owens notes that in *All the Pretty Horses,* after humans have turned their backs on him, "John Grady will return to his love of horses, as they prove more reliable and less complicated than other dreams. His love for horses marks him as a traditional cowboy hero, in love with the cowboy's wandering, rustic life ... [and] horses represent his hope for a meaningful life ... the life of his grandfather who pioneered Comanche country" (72–3). Owens' overly romantic assessment of Cole's romantic notions is partially correct, for in scene after scene, Cole is left disappointed by human beings, but horses, most often in travel, and in work and in battle, support him. Additionally, from the onset of the text, McCarthy secures Cole to the Comanche Indian past, and thus, posits the horse in the slot of warrior, for the Comanche were history's greatest warrior horsemen, and their horses, too, were warriors. Further, the text is a lament on the passing of the horse's status as warrior, for as the Comanche have been annihilated and relocated by the late nineteenth century, by the mid-twentieth century, the horse-riding cowboy is exceedingly rare, even in Texas. Cole is a man out of time, and his romantic idealism promotes the past and his love of horses over men. As such, McCarthy frames the text with scenes that evoke the Indian past and present, scenes that include Cole and his warrior equine, Redbo.

In the first scene that invokes the Comanche past and calls to the reader's attention the role of the horse as warrior, Cole and Redbo ride the soon-to-be-sold Grady ranch, and Cole seeks out an old Comanche travel route:

> At the hour he'd always choose when the shadows were long and the ancient road was shaped before him in the rose and canted light like a dream of the past where the painted ponies and the riders of that lost nation came down out of the north with their faces chalked and their long hair plaited and each armed for war which was their life and the women and children and women with children at their breasts all of them pledged in blood and redeemable in blood only. When the wind was in the north you could hear them, the horses and the breath of the horses and the horses' hooves that were shod in rawhide and the rattle of lances and the constant drag of the travois poles in the sand like the passing of some enormous serpent and the young boys naked on wild horses jaunty as

circus riders and hazing wild horses before them and the dogs trotting
with their tongues aloll and footslaves following half naked and sorely
burdened and above all the low chant of their traveling song which the
riders sang as they rode, nation and ghost of nation passing in a soft
chorale across that mineral waste to darkness bearing lost to all history
and all remembrance like a grail the sum of their secular and transitory
and violent lives [5].

This dreamy two-sentence passage serves a number of rhetorical purposes. First, the passage is a lament on an ancient nation of people whose
way of life is now extinct, the Comanche. For as the Anglo settled Texas,
and land was parceled off, the Comanche were overwhelmed by the sheer
numbers of settlers and the U. S. Cavalry and were unable to stop the
onslaught of civilization upon their ancient lands. Analogously, in
autumn of 1949, the cowboy way of life is also becoming extinct. With
reference to Cole, as his mother is going to sell the Grady homestead,
his specific cowboy life is coming to a close. Notice as well, the Comanche
are riding south, and as Cole is conjoined in this passage with the Indians and the Indian past, their ghostly visitation is an invitation and a
foreshadowing of Cole's imminent journey south into Mexico— to Cole,
unchartered, uncivilized warrior territory. Of course, the Comanche
men are armed and ready for war, "which was their life." For these people are a warrior race, and all debts are redeemable "in blood only."
Moreover, even the women and breast-suckling infants are "pledged in
blood." As such, one can safely assume the whole of the Comanche nation
exists in a unified and constant state of war, and from birth, the
Comanche children are trained and taught the manners of battle and
the skills of war. The presence of footslaves indicates the Comanche
determinism to conquer and kill or capture all whom they encounter.
And of course, as members of the Comanche nation, the horses of the
warriors are themselves warriors.

M. Oldfield Howey indicates that in times prior to the onslaught
of the Anglo, when horses were plenty, "the Comanches, in Texas [would]
kill and bury the horses of their dead comrades, so that the dead may
ride them to the Happy Hunting-grounds ... [and] the manes and tails
of the horses of the tribe are cut off as a testimony of grief" (201). This
death ritual indicates that a warrior and a warrior horse should be
together in death as well as in life, and the McCarthy passage also shows
a particular warrior kinship between horse and man, for the warriors
are chalked and painted for war, as are the ponies. This duality of war

decoration unites the warrior human with the warrior equine, and the bond is one that will exist in the afterlife. A Comanche warrior and his warrior pony will live and wage war, in life and in death, and the Indian warrior is spiritually shackled to his warrior horse. Clearly, McCarthy is arguing the horse as a warrior animal, a warrior whose time is passing and soon to be past. And clearly, McCarthy is hitching Cole and Redbo to the Comanche and his warrior pony; as Cole's father states, "We're like the Comanches was two hundred years ago. We don't know what's goin to show up here come daylight" (25–6). That is, the times are changing, and we are unable to stop the onslaught of change, just as the Comanche were unable to stop the onslaught of Anglo driven change. Conjoining Cole and Redbo to the Comanche past, and their extinct way of life, is an attempt to show that the warrior equine — whose role now is cattle horse in Texas— will soon be absolutely extinct in the United States, regardless of the animal's deterministic abilities. But before extinction, the warrior horse and his rider travel to old Mexico, where a warrior equine is a handy partner in a cowboy's survival. As such, Redbo proves himself a warrior under fire, and further, one of McCarthy's characters specifically articulates the horse's position as warrior animal.

One of the defining characteristics of a warrior is that a captured warrior is worth the life risk of rescuing, and on more than one occasion in the text, a captured horse, or horses, are rescued — or re-stolen — by Cole and his compatriots Lacey Rawlins and Jimmy Blevins. In the first example, Blevins loses his fine bay horse in a lightning storm, and Cole, Rawlins and Blevins, at much risk, rescue the captured warrior, who is being held in the Mexican pueblo of Encantada. Prior to the rescue, Redbo anticipates the battle, "John Grady leaned forward and spoke to the horse and put his hand on the horse's shoulder. The horse had begun to step nervously and it was not a nervous horse" (82). The horse, as a warrior and no longer a cow horse, can sense that battle is about to be waged, and he is right, for Blevins re-steals his horse, and the three boy warriors and their three warrior horses must make a hasty retreat from the town:

> Rawlins pulled his horse around and the horse stamped and trotted and he whacked it across the rump with the barrel of the gun ... and Blevins in his underwear atop the big bay horse ... exploded into the road ... and there were three pistol shots from somewhere in the dark ... [and] before they reached the turn at the top of the hill there were three more shots from the road behind them [83].

The horses three have passed their first trial by fire, but the boys are the ones who will eventually pay for this battle — Blevins with his life and Rawlins and Cole with their blood and innocence. But at this point in the text, all three warrior horses are united in their first successful battle and their courage under fire, and the author has shown that in Mexico, the horse remains a warrior.

Much later in the text, after Blevins is dead and Rawlins is back in San Angelo, Texas, Cole again re-steals Blevins' horse, and in this example, he re-steals Rawlins' horse, Junior, as well as his own animal, Redbo. As Cole justifies to himself, "The hell with it ... I aint leavin my horse down here" (257). So again, McCarthy argues the horse's status as a warrior worth rescuing, no matter the risk to the rescuing warrior, and so again, Cole rides into Encantada to rescue the captured prisoners of war. And again, the warrior horses prove themselves under fire. After gathering the three horses, and the Captain who killed Blevins and raped Rawlins, Cole is shot as he attempts to exit the pueblo, but the horses do not panic under fire: "Redbo and Junior stood trembling in the shadow of the stable wall with their legs slightly spread and their eyes rolling ... they all waited... . He talked to Redbo while the charro saddled and bridled him. Blevins' horse was breathing with slow regularity ..." (265–6). Obviously, Redbo and Junior are afraid, yet the two warrior equines do not panic preceding or under fire. Analogously, even human warriors are afraid in battle, but the stout warrior does not panic, even though he is afraid. As well, McCarthy uses the plural pronoun, they, to unite the human warrior Cole with the equine warriors; as such, they are a team of warriors united in battle and in survival. And all exhibit Hemingway's courage — grace under pressure. What is more, the warrior Cole again speaks to Redbo to calm the warrior horse, not unlike how the warrior John Joel Glanton speaks to his warrior equine in *Blood Meridian*. Here, McCarthy is following his own warrior defining precedent, but in the latter text, the rider and the horses survive and escape, eventually to exit Mexico and regain Texas (286), where Cole returns the warrior Junior to Rawlins (298) and unsuccessfully attempts to find the true home of Blevins' warrior steed (287–98). So, on two very different occasions in the text, McCarthy shows the horse to be a warrior worth rescuing, no matter the cost involved to the rescuing warrior, and in both situations, the warrior horses involved prove themselves under fire, thus the animals enhance their warrior status. As such, in their actions, the horses in the text prove themselves worthy of the designation of warrior, and additionally, McCarthy provides a character in the text to articulate, and further enhance, the horse's status as warrior.

At the opening of Part Two of the text, when Cole and Rawlins, now separated from Blevins, come upon Don Héctor Rocha y Villareal's cattle and horse ranch, La Hacienda de Nuestra Señora de la Purísima Concepción, the two enter a world of Spanish and Mexican history, horses and men, a world where warrior status for men is gained from the breaking and working of horses. Consequently, when Cole, aided by Rawlins, breaks the herd of sixteen three-year-old quarter horses (103–8), both Cole and Rawlins are afforded respect from the vaqueros who inhabit and work the ranch, and as well, both are accepted and invited into the closed community which exists on the ranch. As a result, Cole and Rawlins are given more responsibility and duties, one of which is to head into the mountains to gather more wild horses to break.

On their trip into the mountains, the two are accompanied by an old *mozo* named Luis, who tells the boys of the warring history of the horse in Mexico. The narrator has this to say regarding Luis: "He'd loved horses all his life and he and his father and two brothers had fought in the cavalry and his father and two brothers had died in the cavalry but they'd all despised Vitoriano Huerta above all other men and the deeds of Huerta above all other visited evils" (110). This brief description of Luis alerts the reader that Luis has ethical credibility through experience with horses, and as such, when Luis speaks of horses, he knows of that which he is speaking, for Luis has seen the horse as warrior, and he has lived the warring life upon the backs of horses. And after a life spent at war, Luis is exceptionally fit to speak on the topic of war and on the topic of warrior horses. On the topic of war, Luis has this to say: "He said that war had destroyed the country and that men believe the cure for war is war" (110–11). Luis well knows the destructive power of war, but war is not all bad. There resides in war some nobility, and that nobility comes in the form of the warrior horse, an animal born for war:

> He spoke of his campaigns in the deserts of Mexico and he told them of horses killed under him and he said that the souls of horses mirror the souls of men more closely than men suppose and that horses love war. Men say they only learn this but he said that no creature can learn that which his heart has no shape to hold. His own father said that no man who has not gone to war on horseback can ever truly understand the horse and he said that he supposed he wished this were not so but that it was so [111].

From the position of his own experience with warrior horses, Luis argues that horses love war. This statement clearly indicates that horses are naturally disposed to battle, and that the horse cannot be taught to love battle, because he is born loving battle. As such, the horse is a born warrior, not a tutored and taught warrior. And regardless of the fact that two world wars have come and gone, Luis, from his father's wisdom, still believes that the ultimate form of war is fought from the back of a warrior horse, and that true knowledge of the horse comes from waging war with the horse. This passage is the in-story rhetorical support for the status of the horse as warrior, and McCarthy uses this passage in conjunction with the in-text actions of Redbo and Junior and Blevins' horse under fire to elevate the equine to a position of deterministic warrior. Further, Luis speaks of the common soul of the horse, " ... the horse shares a common soul and its separate life only forms it out of all horses and makes it mortal" (111). If this is so, that horses share a common soul, then horses are warriors by breed and birth and place on earth, and further, horses are warriors before, during and after life on terra firma. Interestingly, Luis' line of thought is more in line with the pre-modern Comanche way of thinking than of the modern Mexican Catholic, and so again, McCarthy links the contemporary present of the text with the Indian past, but the existence of the Indian warrior horseman and the warrior horse and, as well, the American cowboy, is a way of life that is short lived by 1950, and as *All the Pretty Horses* is a lament on passing ways of life, the text closes on a lamentable note as the horseman rides west into the sunset.

At the close of the text, and after experiencing numerous battles in Mexico with Redbo, John Grady Cole, a man out of time and out of place, rides because he knows of nothing else. As Cole rides west, he crosses the fields scarred with steel pumpjacks, and he sees Indians camped out, but these Indians are not warriors; they are broken peoples: "At that time there were still indians camped out on the western plains and late in the day he passed in his riding a scattered group of their wickiups propped upon that scoured and trembling waste" (301). While historically inaccurate, this image of the Indians camped out on the plains is an effective one. The day is passing, and so is the era of the warrior, be he Indian, cowboy or horse. And all involved are aware of this passing era: "They stood and watched him pass and watched him vanish upon that landscape solely because he was passing. Solely because he would vanish" (301). In the middle twentieth century, even in Texas, the cowboy has no place, and as such, the horse has no place. And as the final position of the horse as warrior is cattle horse, even this limited role is a role passing in time. But, for a brief period in history, in deep Mexico, Cole and his horse, Redbo, fought and lived as warriors do, and as warriors should.

From the onset of the text of *All the Pretty Horses,* Cormac McCarthy defines the horse as a warrior animal, one born for war and at one with war. Additionally, McCarthy conjoins John Grady Cole with the Comanche past in order to show that while the era of the warrior Indian pony has passed, the role of the horse as warrior has not. As such, McCarthy allows Cole and Rawlins and Blevins to be warriors, in concert with their horses, without whom, the three boys would be absolutely ill-adept at their brief but violent attempts at war. McCarthy even elevates the warrior horses to the status of prisoners of war in order to show the animals' warrior value; subsequently, the boys must re-capture their equine comrades in arms. As such, McCarthy shows that the value of the warrior horses is such that the three boys, and even Cole alone, risk their lives in order to rescue and re-rescue the prisoner horses. Not coincidentally, Cole's father was a prisoner of war during World War Two, and he was not rescued, but was freed at the end of the war. This illustrates the value of the warrior equine, and perhaps even places the warrior horse above the warrior human. Additionally, McCarthy presents scenes of battle where Redbo and Junior and Blevins' horse perform honorably under battle. This cements the status of the horses as warrior animals. Finally, if the battle sequences were not enough, McCarthy includes a battle-tested cavalryman, Luis, to explicate the intrinsic warrior soul of the horse; as such, the horse is defined as a warrior, before, during and after life on earth, and as all horses possess one communal soul, all horses are warriors, without exception. But, as the text is set in the middle of the twentieth century, not the middle of the nineteenth century, the time of the warrior horse in Texas is over. As the text closes, so does the era of the warrior horse, and regardless of the warrior horse's deterministic instincts, there are no more battles left to fight. McCarthy's second novel of the Border Trilogy, *The Crossing,* also looks upon a warrior animal of honor whose time has passed, the wolf.

In *The Crossing,* though, the wolf is a warrior animal of honor that is McCarthy's metaphor for man's appetite for control over the natural world. Consequently, in the text, the absence of the wolf from New

Mexico signals the presence of man. As such, the wolf is a negative analogy for man's control over the natural world. Subsequently, in the text, the presence of man leads to the absence of wildlife, especially predatory wildlife that preys upon man's valued stock commodities. And the wolf, unlike the carrion scavenging coyote, is the bane of stock cattle, so the wolf must be annihilated. Man's desire to rid southern New Mexico of the wolf grants the wolf bounty-value, and as such, the wolf, previous to the chronology of the text, is exterminated from the southwestern United States. Man seeks to control the natural world, and in the case of the wolf, man succeeds in his quest for control. This is why Billy Parham is so infatuated with the she-wolf that appears in Hidalgo County in the winter of 1940–41 (J. Bell 40). This is why Billy futilely attempts to save the she-wolf. But in his attempt to save the animal, he actually dooms the animal. Of course, had Billy not initially caught and taken control over the wild animal, the she-wolf perhaps would have returned to the Animas Peaks and survived and birthed her litter, thus perpetuating her species, but man controls or kills that which exists freely in the natural world, and the absence of the wolf from New Mexico is the direct result of the acts of man. In McCarthy's fiction, even honorable acts of control by man over beast, such as Billy's, most often have disastrous consequences.

8

Wolves as Metaphor in
The Crossing

In *The Crossing*, the hinge of the Border Trilogy and Cormac McCarthy's seventh novel, the wolf is a warrior animal of honor, and its absence from the New Mexico of the novel signals man's presence there and becomes a negative metaphor for man's ceaseless appetite for control over the natural world. Man controls or kills that which exists freely in the natural world, and in *The Crossing*, the absence of the wolf from southern New Mexico is the direct result of the acts and desires of man, for the wolf is a livestock predator and as such, must be eradicated.

In order to better understand Cormac McCarthy's use of the wolf in *The Crossing*, historical context of European man's views on the wolf must be addressed. Fear and loathing of the wolf have long been custom in Europe, and as Barry Lopez, the author of the comprehensive text *Of Wolves and Men*, notes, the Lascaux caves in Dordogne, France, feature pictographs—drawn circa 13,000 b.c.—of prey animals and highlight the ancient rivalry between wolf and man (88, 96). Further, the prehistoric competition between man and wolf for game and territory was the dominant predatory rivalry of its day, and that competition for prey created a natural oppositional dyad between man and beast (Lopez 88). Because of this rivalry, the wolf was both vilified by peoples of European descent well into twentieth century and mythologized by many indigenous peoples in the western hemisphere. For the Europeans, the wolf was an enemy in the fight of survival, but the wolf played an important role in the religious ceremony of many non–Christian and pre–Christian peoples, and "native human hunters ascribed to wolves many positive qualities such as intelligence, boldness, and skill" (Klinghammer 80).

The importance of the wolf in the life of pre-modern, pre–Christian man can best be evidenced by the legend of the founding of Rome, which, according to Roman mythology, would have been impossible without the aid of a benevolent she-wolf. Romulus and Remus, the twin sons of the god Mars and the Vestal Virgin, Rea Silvia, were cast into the Tiber River in a basket by Amulius, Rea Silvia's father; after the basket floated to shore, the infants "were suckled by a she-wolf" (Tripp 514–5), an animal sacred to their father. Eventually, Romulus, determined to found a new city, did so, naming it after himself (Tripp 514–6). The pre–Roman she-wolf is not the rival of man, but is the savior of Rome and is a sacred animal worthy of veneration. In an image that McCarthy exploits in *The Crossing*, the she-wolf is maternalized as well, becoming a surrogate mother to the infants (Tripp 516). Clearly, the she-wolf of classical Roman mythology is, in a manner of speaking, the mother of Rome, and she is neither feared nor loathed.

However, in Greek mythology, the pejorative legend of the werewolf was created (Klinghammer 79), and the werewolf legend threaded through history and became intertwined with Christianity. With the advent of Christianity and the dawning of the Dark Ages, the wolf once again became a villain. The wolf was vilified in medieval Europe primarily because the Roman church, the dominant cultural and religious force of the day, "exploited the sinister image of the wolves" (Lopez 208) in order to control the people through fear, and subsequently, thousands of people were tried and then executed as werewolves. The Church's use of the lycanthropic image was so effective because "in medieval Europe ... the wolf had become a widespread symbol of evil" (Klinghammer 79), and to equate a person — man, woman or child — with a wolf was to equate that person with evil incarnate. Through both propaganda and prosecution, the ruthless Church hegemony contributed to the common perception of the wolf and wolf-likeness as evil. The result was a sort of mass hysteria, which lasted for seven centuries of the second millennia.

The second great medieval European influence contributing to the wolf's vilification was the advent of early modern agricultural and ranching practices. In early modern Europe, with the domestication of sheep and cattle, farmers viewed the wolf as a threat to their existence and sustenance. As Erich Klinghammer notes, wolves and agriculturists have long been at odds:

> Early European pastoralists and farmers probably knew very little about
> the ways of the wolves with which they shared a common habitat, other
> than that wolves killed their livestock. The wolf thus became hated as a
> raider and an enemy, and to this day ranchers chiefly see what (to them) is
> the bad side of the wolf—its predatory nature [80].

Clearly, the farmer of early Europe and the wolf were at fatal odds, and
the medieval farmer rightly feared the wolf's ability to prey upon stock,
but his image of the wolf was "embellished, exaggerated, distorted, or
twisted to fit an image based not on careful observation but on imagination, myth, and anthropomorphic projections of human characteristics onto the wolf" (Klinghammer 78).

Interestingly, the wolf remains vilified through the second millennia and into the third. And regardless of where European settlers landed
in the Western Hemisphere, they perpetuated their phobia and hatred
of the wolf. As Klinghammer notes, people's hatreds and prejudices
migrate with them: "European immigrants to North America brought
along their negative attitudes toward the wolf, and this resulted in efforts
to destroy wolves wherever they were found" (88). In the early 1600s,
William Penn "established possibly the first governmental wolf bounty"
(Robisch 289) in the new world; the wolf suddenly had bounty-value
and thus was worth more dead than it is alive. Klinghammer also points
out that "as the continent was settled during the westward migration,
the wolf and one of its prey species, the American bison, had to give
way" (88). Consequently, wolves "did take their share of livestock, especially when human activities displaced or destroyed their natural prey"
(Klinghammer 81). And as the wolves' prey diminished during the last
half of the nineteenth century, secondary to man's hunting and land
clearing and not the wolves' natural predator role, the wolves sought sustenance by attacking easy fodder — the domestic animals owned by westerly moving settlers. As the wolves attacked more and more livestock,
their increasing bounty-value occasioned a bounty system created to
eradicate them and to appease and compensate the livestock owners who
were settling the American West and Southwest (Klinghammer 81). The
bounty system in New Mexico continued through the turn of the twentieth century and into the late nineteen twenties, when it was led by J.
Stokely Ligon, "who oversaw the New Mexico district of the Bureau of
Biological Survey [and] made heroes of the trappers on the payroll"
(Robisch 289). The result of the centuries-old battle against the wolf in
the United States is obvious: the wolf has very nearly been eradicated

from North America. But, as the twentieth century closed, the federal government again has gone to work, this time in an attempt to save the wolf:

> Two pairs of endangered Mexican gray wolves were placed in holding pens Thursday on the Gila Wilderness as a preamble to their eventual release into the wild. Ranchers, including one not far from the release site, accepted the news philosophically, but said they were opposed to it ... [and] are surprised that the Bush administration permits the program to continue [Associated Press B15].

Even at the dawn of the twenty-first century, old animosities persist, and ranchers continue to hate and to fear the wolf, and as the Associated Press has reported, "the livestock industry continues to try to sabotage the [wolf release] program" (B15). Even one wolf near livestock is one too many, as will be evidenced in *The Crossing*, and to some extent, in all three texts of the Border Trilogy.

In McCarthy's Naturalist world, man — as a separate and unequal member of nature — controls the animals he can, and he kills those animals he cannot. Ranchers and their families need grazing and farming land, so their presence leads to the absence of wildlife, particularly predatory wildlife, which man eradicates to protect his valued livestock commodities. This is not to say that capitalism caused the demise of the wolf; European man's hatred of the wolf is much older than is New World capitalism. But the wolf, unlike the carrion-scavenging coyote, is the bane of stock cattle, so the wolf has to be annihilated. The rancher's desire to rid southern New Mexico of the wolf made the wolf bounty lucrative, so the wolf had already been nearly exterminated from the southwestern United States prior to the chronology of *The Crossing*. In this example of control through eradication, man succeeds in his quest, and the loss of the wolf is a motif in all three texts of the Border Trilogy.

It is in this period of lobo-phobia and wolf eradication that McCarthy situates *The Crossing*, and the wolf's absence from southern New Mexico is why the she-wolf's presence in Hidalgo County is so exciting to Billy Parham. By the opening of the text proper, which James Bell identifies as 1941 (40), the wolf has been banished from the area of action, but in a brief scene of pre-chronology, set in 1931, a six-year-old Billy watches the last of the New Mexico–based Mexican Gray Wolves run antelope in the winter moonlight (3–5); the ethereal scene of these master predators is one Billy will never see again, for the wolf is gone from New Mexico by Billy's sixteenth year. But through Part I of *The Crossing*, McCarthy promotes wolves collectively and the she-wolf individually, and elevates the beast above popular mythology while concurrently acknowledging its doom as an indigenous species of the southwestern United States. In so doing, McCarthy also argues the unquenchable desire of man to control the natural world and the animals within it. In this example, the wolf is hunted to the point of extinction because man has justified the killing by his commercial needs — the propagation of sustenance livestock and the commercial livestock industry. And in the midst of this wolf eradication frenzy, Billy commits a shortsighted, but seemingly noble and honorable act: he attempts to return the captured she-wolf to Sonora, Mexico. But after the she-wolf is trapped, she suffers a series of indignities. In addition to being captured by an adolescent, the she-wolf, pregnant and forever separated from her deceased life-mate, is dragged by Billy's horse, muzzled, attacked by ranch dogs, tied up, force-fed cold rabbit (a humiliation to the master predator), nearly drowned while bound, stolen from Billy, poked and spit upon by Mexican rabble, forced to fight for show until death, and finally, shot by Billy out of mercy. Of course, had Billy not initially caught and taken control over the wild animal — an utterly human act in McCarthy's world — the she-wolf perhaps would have returned to Mexico on her own and survived and birthed her litter, thus perpetuating her species. But the she-wolf is most likely doomed from the instant a rancher discovers her first local kill, a "veal calf" (15) — a valued commodity. Nonetheless, Billy's misdirected attempts at honor do allow the doomed she-wolf some honor prior to her demise, as she does fight ferociously and violently against the dogs. Nonetheless, the she-wolf is just as dead as she would have been if some rancher had shot her while she was caught in a trap. The calculus remains the same: man controls, often through killing, that which exists freely in the natural world, and in *The Crossing*, the absence of the wolf from southern New Mexico is the direct result of the acts and desires of man, for the wolf is a livestock and game animal predator and as such, must be controlled, that is, killed-off and hunted to the point of extinction.

Conversely, in *Blood Meridian*, the bloody predators are mythologized and granted warrior status, akin to the scalphunters they shadow through the mountains and deserts of Chihuahua and Sonora states, Mexico. In "The Trapper Mystic: Werewolves in *The Crossing*," S. K. Robisch addresses the issue of the mythology of the trapper, the wolf and the hunt. Robisch argues that in *The Crossing*, the trapper (the *wer-wulf* / the man-wolf) is in a cosmic dyad with the wolf, whereby both are mystified and mythologized: "McCarthy has given us opportunities to romanticize and mystify the wolf, but he has also loaded his narrative with the blood and darkness that ensue when we seize those opportunities—that is, when we trap the wolf. Four particular moments in the novel assure us that McCarthy is spiritualizing the trapper's occupation" (290). These four moments of trapper spiritualization begin with the scene of Billy and Will Parham's visit to Echols's apothecaryesque cabin (17–18), specifically the long paragraph on page 17 in which McCarthy catalogs the master trapper's vials of ground organs and the contents of the cabin. Robisch points out that the scene, sans the material presence of Echols the man, is one that implies that "the success of the trapper results in his own extinction as well as his prey's" (290). The trapper and the wolf are in a blood covenant, the result of which is loss of trapper and loss of wolf, and perhaps the ancient rituals of blood between man and wolf are part of the collective unconscious of each, and of both. Therefore, as ordained, the hunt must run its course. The second moment of trapper mystification is the scene in which Will Parham attempts to teach Billy how to dig and set a wolf trap (22–3). Parham attempts to set and anchor the traps by cosmic feel. According to Robisch, Parham's "effort to fix himself in the cosmos, tying an arc or cord to, possibly around, space, is consistent with a motif common to many wolf stories—the wide open region, whether tundra, desert, or sky, and by whom that space is given a boundary or fitted with an anchor" (290). Robisch calls attention to the motif of man, anchored trap and open space, to show that in previous literature and in life, the hunt cosmically transcends the tools and animals of the hunt. Robisch's third mystical scene (291) is the scene of Billy's visit to the Mexican master trapper Don Arnulfo (42–7), who tells Billy that the traps must be set where earth and fire meet. Don Arnulfo also warns Billy that trapping a wolf sets the wolf towards incorporeality, for one can neither possess nor know a wolf. Billy sets the traps as instructed, and he traps the she-wolf and himself. Robisch's final mystification of the trapper, of the wolf and "of the hunt is found in McCarthy's indication that the she-wolf is caught in Billy's trap the day his parents are killed" (292). Death begets death, and "there is no mechanical trap without its astral counterpart" (Robisch 292).

Robisch effectively shows the mystification and mythologizing of the wolf in *The Crossing*, but McCarthy mythologizes the wolf in other texts as well. In Cormac McCarthy's first four novels of the Border Southwest, the presence of wolves in the text decreases as the dating of the action of the texts moves forward approximately one hundred years. In the Border Southwest of 1848–49, wolves actively inhabit the region and the text and are quite often present with McCarthy's historical gang of scalphunters. *Blood Meridian* has McCarthy first defining the mythic qualities of the wolf, while the text also lends a ghost-like quality to the animal — as if the animals are haunting the scalphunters: "They [the scalphunters] set forth with first light while wolves ... dissolved in the fog of the streets" (61). The wolves, who trail the scalphunters in shadowy fashion, disappear when the killing is in temporary reprieve; the wolves reappear when killing occurs to dine on gore "pudding" (60), but McCarthy uses a verb with mythic, mystical and magical connotation — *dissolve*— to label the animals' exit from the streets. These wolves do not lope into the bushes; they become incorporeal. In using such a verb, McCarthy's narrator implies that wolves are not bound by material limits, and wolves can thus appear, disappear and reappear at will. Later in the text, the wolf's supernatural powers are further alluded to when the kid and Sproule are afoot and come upon a band of Mexican bandits; the lead bandit says to the Anglo pair, "When the lamb is lost in the mountain... . They is cry. Sometime come the mother. Sometime the wolf" (65). This explicit warning utilizes the legend of the wolf's predatory prowess to suggest that the Anglo pair is lucky the Mexicans are in a benevolent frame of mind. But read more closely, the passage suggests the wolf is such a tremendous predator that the animal's auditory sense is so acute that it is finer than the hearing of the lamb's mother, that the wolf's predatory senses are in effect more powerful than the bond between mother and child. Consequently, the wolf can halt the life cycle. This interpretation also hints at the wolf as the bane of commercial or sustenance livestock owners of the early and middle twentieth century. In *Blood Meridian*, McCarthy yet again promotes the mythos of the wolf through the articulations of Tobin the ex-priest, the second most educated and learned scalphunter, to show that the mythological power of the wolf supercedes the reason of even an enlightened man: "we come upon a band of wolves. They scattered and come back, not a sound out of them no more than smoke... . Bold as brass ... I would never shoot a wolf and I know other men of the same sentiments" (129). In this passage, McCarthy again alludes to the wolves' power to mesmerize and mystify; the wolves are silent as smoke — soundless ... and weightless, as floating smoke is lighter than air. McCarthy implies that the wolves are ethereal, not physical. These wolves are also animals of courage, and the wolves do not cower in fear of the scalphunters, but close in around the human predators. Moreover, Tobin implicitly argues that it is a karmic mistake to kill a wolf, and for effect, Tobin includes the assertion that other men feel about wolves as he does. Even the judge, master predator among the predatory, seems somewhat in awe of wolves: "Wolves cull themselves, man. What other creature could?"(146). Tobin and the judge and the others, men who live and kill and die on a daily basis, fear and admire wolves for their legendary and factual powers.

Perhaps these superstitious fears are part of what contributed to the demise of the wolf in the Border Southwest. By the opening of *All the Pretty Horses,* wolves are all but extinct in Texas, the border regions of Mexico and the southwestern United States. In *All the Pretty Horses,* McCarthy has stepped forward a century, and in late March of 1950 (J. Bell 3), John Grady Cole, Lacey Rawlins and Jimmy Blevins exit Texas, U.S.A., and enter Mexico. In doing so, the trio enters a world unknown to them, and part of this unknown world is the fauna of Mexico, specifically, the wolf. On a night spent on the run from a posse from the pueblo of Encantada, the trio settles for the evening and hears a sound heretofore unheard by their twentieth century Texans' ears:

> At just dark they benched out on a gravel shelf and made their camp and that night they heard what they'd none heard before, three long howls to the southwest and all afterwards a silence.
> You hear that? Said Rawlins.
> Yeah.
> It's a wolf, ain't it?
> Yeah.
> ... He [Cole] sat a long time listening to the others ... while he contemplated the wildness about him ... [59–60].

In this brief dialogue, Rawlins and Cole comment upon the three howls of the lone wolf, and it is readily apparent that neither has heard the call of a wolf before, for McCarthy presents Texas in 1950 as a place where the wolf is extinct. Rawlins seeks a second in his opinion that the three howls are those of a wolf, and Cole responds in the affirmative. The presence of the wolf symbolizes that the three are no longer in the civilized confines of the forty-eight United States and that they are now in a wild, savage country. The howling wolf, now no longer merely a legend to the boys, has the power to capture the boys' minds and conversation. Interestingly, in this scene the wolf is heard, but is not seen. In presenting the animal as a sound in the dark, McCarthy further elevates the mystical and supernatural value of the wolf. The power of the wolf's howl resonates in Cole's mind; up until this moment in his life, Cole, growing up in a land where wolves have been displaced by cattle and cattle ranches, knows only the legend of wolves.

In *Cities of the Plain,* McCarthy uses the character of the aged rancher, Mr. Johnson, as a conduit to the era between *Blood Meridian* and the Border Trilogy, and through him, explains the disappearance of the wolf from the Border Southwest while further reinforcing the mystical qualities of the master canine. Mr. Johnson, McCarthy's vehicle to the vanished past, tells of man's ignoble treatment of the noble, but problematic, master predator:

> ... it's just that when things are gone they're gone... .
> The day after my fiftieth birthday in March of nineteen and seventeen I rode into the old headquarters at the Wilde well and there was six dead wolves hanging on the fence. I rode along the fence and ran my hand along em. I looked in their eyes. A government trapper had brought em in the night before. They'd been killed with poison baits. Strychnine. Whatever. Up in the Sacramentos. A week later he brought in four more. I aint heard a wolf in this country since. I suppose that's a good thing. They can be hell on stock. But I guess I was always what you might call superstitious. I know I damn sure wasnt religious. And it had always seemed to me that something can live and die but that the kind of thing that they were was always there. I didn't know you could poison that. I aint heard a wolf howl in thirty years. I don't know where you'd go to hear one. There may not be any such place [126].

Mr. Johnson shows that the wolves' time in that country has passed, secondary to man's ability to effectively poison and eradicate the predators. Wolves kill stock, so the wolves must be banished from the country. And as usual in McCarthy's universe, through blood or poison, the stronger, better, more effective predator defeats the able, but lesser skilled predator. And as Mr. Johnson indicates, not only is the wolf gone from the area, but also the aura of the wolf has been poisoned and has disappeared. Clearly, Mr. Johnson's lament is meant to bridge the chronological gap between the close of *Blood Meridian,* 1878, and the opening of *All the Pretty Horses* and *The Crossing,* 1949 and 1941, respectively. Note also that the passage alludes to the federal government's wolf eradication program and hints at the bounty-value of the dead wolf; to man, to the rancher, to the hunter, to the federal government, the wolf is an animal worth more dead than alive. In this brief but telling passage, the sad history of the eradication of the wolf from the southwestern United States is redacted. The wolf was not allowed to survive. Hence, McCarthy throws a wolf into a wolfless world, and hence Billy Parham begins his ill-fated quest.

In the influential essay, "The Vanishing World of Cormac McCarthy's Border Trilogy," Dianne C. Luce argues that Billy Parham becomes externally and internally hardened by death and brutality, "because he has learned not to feel so deeply his pain at the extermination of the Mexican wolf in the Southwest, the incursion of technology and government into the terrain of his youth, the vanishing of the cowboy and his way of life — or to acknowledge it consciously" (121). Ecologically, emotionally and psychically, Billy has been most affected by the loss of the she-wolf, and Luce maintains "the ecological vision of the Border Trilogy" (121) is at its most "explicit" in Part I of *The Crossing* and situates upon "the ecological and spiritual concerns of Billy Parham, whose totem is the wolf (the predator who must remain wild if she is to exist at all)" (122). The Border Trilogy, "an elegy for the evanescent world of the Southwest" (123), considers the "relationship of wildness to domesticity, the predatory nature of man and his drive for civilization" (Luce 122). The "world of the Border Trilogy is a vanishing world" (Luce 122); cowboys, wolves, Indians, deer, are all vanishing (to be out of sight) to the point of disappearing (to be gone forever), and the "great terror and beauty manifested in the world's creatures are evanescent, while the world itself endures" (Luce 122). Thus, when the animal is eradicated, the aura, the authenticity, the "essence" (Luce 124) of that animal dissipates like vapor and is forever gone from the Earth, which always remains. Luce points out that "the core image of the vanishing world in the trilogy is the vanishing *loba*—the Mexican gray wolf... . In McCarthy's hands she comes to represent not only the material world of nature destroyed by man, but the very spirit of wildness and of the external world itself, a swift huntress that the world cannot lose ... an indispensable manifestation of the world itself" (125,130). But Billy and the world do lose the Mexican gray wolf, and as Luce adroitly shows, the centrality of this loss exists in Part I of *The Crossing*.

In *The Crossing*, McCarthy uses the wolf as a metaphor for man's ceaseless quest to control the natural world. The absence of the wolf from the southwestern United States— with emphasis here on Hidalgo

County, New Mexico, in the winter and spring of 1941—indicates the presence and encroachment of Western man upon the wolf's historical territories. To meet his own agricultural needs, man must displace the wolf. However, in a scene set a decade before the primary action of the text, McCarthy shows that the eradication of the wolf from the area is a fairly recent thing, while the author also mythologizes the ancient hunters:

> On a winter's night that first year he [Billy Parham] woke to hear wolves in the low hills to the west of the house and he knew that they would be coming out onto the plain in the new snow to run the antelope in the moonlight... .
>
> They were running on the plain harrying the antelope and the antelope moved like phantoms in the snow and circled and wheeled and the dry powder blew about them in the cold moonlight ... and the wolves twisted and turned and leapt in a silence such that they seemed of another world entire. They moved down the valley and turned and moved far out on the plain until they were the smallest of figures in that dim whiteness and then they disappeared [3, 4].

The prehistoric action of this moonlight hunt is a window into the past, not only Billy's childhood past, but the pre-human past. McCarthy is allowing the reader, as well as Billy, to see that which occurred prior to the encroachment of man upon the territories of the wolf. This ancient ritual, taking place in 1931, is McCarthy's statement of the wolf's mythic timelessness; time will pass, and the wolf will be eradicated, but the wolf's essence — its social and predatory skills — will exist so long as one wolf exists in the wild. The scene takes place during the first winter the Parham family spends in Hidalgo County. The family is representative of many, many families encroaching upon the wolf's territory at the time. Additionally, the family's home is located on the fringe of the wilderness. Aided by proximity, Billy is allowed to field study the wolf pack on the hunt to the west of the house. This direction indicates the Wild West, that is, the uncivilized and untamed west, the west of the wolf. Of course, the proximity of wolf to agricultural man is a negative thing for the wolf, because those who raise livestock see the wolf as the bane of commercial and sustenance livestock.

In this passage early in the novel, McCarthy turns the hunt into an ethereal ballet, and the wolves and their prey leap and dance, seemingly at play. But as "they" enter onto the plain, that is, as the wolves and antelope collectively race onto the plain, the killing will occur, outside the textual action. Because McCarthy presents the scene from Billy's point of view, the narrator does not follow the hunt to its climax. Instead, McCarthy waits with Billy until the wolves, sans antelope, return moving south and west:

> He was very cold ... and he waited a long time. Then he saw them coming. Loping and twisting. Dancing. Tunneling their noses in the snow. Loping and running and rising by twos in a standing dance and running on again.
>
> There were seven of them and they passed within twenty feet of where he lay. He could see their almond eyes in the moonlight. He could hear their breath. He could feel the presence of their knowing that was electric in the air. They bunched and nuzzled and licked one another. Then they stopped. They stood with their ears cocked. Some with one forefoot raised to their chest. They were looking at him. He did not breathe. They did not breathe. They stood. Then they turned and quietly trotted on.... . He never told anybody [4–5].

As six-year-old Billy waits for the return of the hunters, he notices the cold, but as the wolves approach, he is transfixed as the animals socialize in collective joy. Notice that in this scene, McCarthy does not perpetuate any negative mythology of the wolf, but he shows a prehistoric action that is eventually extinguished by civilized man. What makes this hunt even more unique is that it is a pack-on-herd hunt, not a hunt between individual animals. This group-on-group hunt emphasizes the destructive power of man upon the natural world, for by 1941, the year the text proper begins, no wolf packs or antelope herds exist in Hidalgo County. Another facet reinforcing the hunt's mystical quality is the fact that Billy never tells anyone about what he saw and experienced on this night, and as readers of the third text in the Border Trilogy are aware, Billy lives quite a long life.

A recent Associated Press piece concerning the reintroduction of the wolf into the southwestern United States notes that the Mexican gray wolf "was hunted to the brink of extinction by the 1950s" (B15). As previously noted, the federal government's methodical wolf-eradication program was based on the bounty-value of a dead wolf whereby man controlled the natural world through killing the animal in question. And quite obviously nearly every human character in Part I of *The Crossing* is hostile to the she-wolf, or to any wolf. Interestingly, Billy learns of the presence of the she-wolf in Hidalgo County at the dinner table, when the Parham family is dining on beefsteak:

> You all set down, their mother said. She set a platter of fried steaks on the table. A bowl of beans. When they'd said grace she handed the platter

to their father and he forked one of the steaks onto his plate and passed it
on to Billy.

Pap says there's a wolf on the range, she said.

Billy sat holding the platter, his knife aloft.

A wolf? Boyd said.

His father nodded. She pulled down a pretty good sized veal calf up at
the head of Foster Draw.

When? said Billy.

Been a week or more.... She come up out of Mexico [15–6].

This ironic scene identifies the absolutely important role of the beef in
the lives of the Parham family; beef is sustenance and life. For without
beef, there is little meat on which to survive. Twice in this brief passage,
McCarthy identifies the bovine with human consumption. The family
dines on fried beefsteak, while the family discusses the presence and
damage caused by a lone wolf. Of course, the wolf has killed a calf, and
not merely a calf, but a veal calf — a calf specifically bred for commercial production and human consumption. So, obvious to reader and
character alike, the wolf must be eradicated by whatever means necessary, for one marauding wolf in Hidalgo County is one wolf too many:

What do you aim to do? Said Billy.

Well, I reckon we better catch her. Don't you?

Yessir.

... If Mr Echols was here he'd catch her.

Yes he would. But he aint [16].

The hunt is on, but when Billy traps the she-wolf, he is faced with a
dilemma, one in which even honorable acts go horribly awry.

While McCarthy honors and promotes the mythos of the wolf in
The Crossing, he also demonstrates man's urge to control the natural
world in a series of human-driven indignities the she-wolf is forced to
undergo prior to her death. Ironically, all of these indignities occur only
because Billy attempts to help the she-wolf. As is true with many of
McCarthy's other works, the noble act is punished. Although noble,
Billy's mission to return the captured she-wolf to Mexico is abjectly
flawed. It is based on human control over the natural world; Billy first
captures and controls the she-wolf through trickery and force (52). He
then binds and muzzles the animal and drags her back to Mexico (74).
Thus Billy's noble mission is nothing more than a man violently controlling a wild animal through the guise of pseudo-nobility, and Billy's
mission is just another of many McCarthy examples of man overwhelming the fauna and flora of the natural world.

In *The Crossing,* not only do Anglos seek dominion over the natural world, but Mexicans do as well, and McCarthy shows that the thirst to control the natural world is not limited by race or nationality. In a telling scene, a scene that incorporates the Mexican citizen into the slaughter of the wolf, McCarthy's narrator describes the situation for the she-wolf on the Mexican side of the border:

> She carried a scabbedover wound on her hip where her mate had bitten her two weeks before somewhere in the mountains of Sonora. He'd bitten her because she would not leave him. Standing with one forefoot in the jaws of a steeltrap and snarling at her to drive her off where she lay just beyond the reach of the chain. She'd flattened her ears and whined and she would not leave. In the morning they came on horses. She watched from a slope a hundred yards away as he stood up to meet them.
> She wandered the eastern slopes of the Sierra de la Madera for a week. Her ancestors had hunted camels and primitive toy horses on these grounds. She found little to eat. Most of the game was slaughtered out of the country. Most of the forest cut to feed the boilers of the stampmills of the mines [24–5].

Here, the she-wolf is witness to man's controlling hand, and the she-wolf is also astute enough to move from the area as man approaches. Of course, the wolf hunters are to kill the trapped male wolf. In doing so, the trappers kill the progenitor of the she-wolf's unborn litter (25) and the social and biological mate of the she-wolf. In essence, killing the alpha member of this pack of two is killing the entire genetic line, for the fetal pups die after the she-wolf is killed and buried (129). Consequently, the pair and all of their offspring and potential offspring are eradicated in the single snapping shut of a trap. The passage above indicates that northern Mexico is devoid of wolves, too, and that man's encroachment upon the natural world — in this case the industry is mining — in either Mexico or the United States leads to devastation of the wolf. Notable, too, is the fact that hunting, ranching, farming, mining, and lumbering are all commercial ventures where man seeks to control or dominate the natural world. Also, all of the above devastate the wolf's natural habitat. And as in the southwestern United States, Sonora state, Mexico, is devoid of prey animals for the wolf, for man in Mexico has also killed off the wolf's natural prey. The result for a wolf is the same in both Mexico and New Mexico. On both sides of the border, man is attempting to eradicate the wolf, so the Mexicans' delight in seeing the wolf do blood-battle with the hounds is somewhat understandable. But, of course, the she-wolf would not have ended up in the gladiatorial arena if Billy had not trapped, muzzled and bound her in the first place.

Billy's trapping and capture of the she-wolf are the actions that ultimately destroy the she-wolf. Billy is representative of man, and his actions are representative of man's encroachment upon the natural world. Billy traps and captures the she-wolf because she is encroaching upon ranching man's world, a world where cattle are both highly valued commercial property and a primary source of sustenance. Billy therefore knows that his father or another rancher will kill the she-wolf without hesitation. Also, it is Billy's capture of the she-wolf that is analogous to all the previous captures and killings of wolves that were committed by man: "She was caught by the right forefoot [like her mate]. The drag had caught in a cholla less than a hundred feet from the fire and there she stood. He patted the horse and spoke to it and reached down and unfastened the buckle on the saddlescabbard and slid the rifle free and stepped down and dropped the reins. The wolf crouched slightly" (52). In a scene foreshadowing the she-wolf's death, Billy pulls his rifle from its scabbard and considers shooting the she-wolf, as his father had advised, but he does not. In "no way prepared for what he beheld" (53), Billy remounts his horse and begins to ride away. However, he decides to return to the she-wolf, and in a mildly brutal scene, he successfully muzzles and lassoes and secures the she-wolf. "It aint no use to fight it" (56), Billy says to the wolf. As well, it is no use for the wolf to fight the encroachment of man, for man overwhelms the natural world. And once the she-wolf is captured, or any wolf for that matter, the wolf is doomed. Billy's binding and muzzling of the she-wolf is a very human act in McCarthy's world, and a rare one in middle twentieth century New Mexico, for a passing old man — a character type similar to Mr. Johnson — is McCarthy's vehicle into the present and the past:

> I guess you'll collect the bounty. Sell the hide.
> Yessir.
> ... When we used to bring up cattle from the valley from down around Ciénega Springs... . And you could hear em all across the valley. Them first warm nights. You'd nearly always hear em in that part of the valley. I aint heard one in years [60].

The old gentleman, a former cowboy, notes that the wolves heard once are to be heard no longer, because the lupine predator became a bounty animal, and subsequently, the animal was hunted to regional extinction.

Additionally, this passage indicates a change in the natural world that was brought on by man's will, wishes and actions. And when Billy decides to take the she-wolf to Mexico, his decision only hastens the inevitable death of the animal.

Billy decides to take the she-wolf into Mexico (63), but his decision is not necessarily the decision that kills the she-wolf, for the she-wolf as negative metaphor for man's encroachment upon, and destruction of, the natural world, must die. The day following the capture, the ill-fated pair enters Sonora state, Mexico. But in Mexico, as has previously been noted, the wolf is also a bounty animal, and as well, the wolf is a rare sight. Subsequently, Billy is arrested and the she-wolf is confiscated, and Billy's dream of returning the she-wolf to the Pilares Teras comes to its necessary end, and the she-wolf is to be engaged in combat to the death against paired teams of hunting, hounding and fighting dogs. The she-wolf battles nobly, and to save the she-wolf from being torn apart, Billy first argues for the wolf's life, and then shoots the she-wolf: "He said that the tracks of the wolf had led out of Mexico. He said the wolf knew nothing of boundaries. The young don nodded as if in agreement but what he said was that whatever the wolf knew was irrelevant and that if the wolf had crossed that boundary it was perhaps so much the worse for the wolf but the boundary stood without regard" (119). That is, the wolf dies in battle, for boundaries and borders are manmade entities, but, regardless, man rules either side of any boundary or border. Billy and the she-wolf are encamped on the wrong side of the boundary, but, on either side of any manmade boundary, the wolf will die, so both sides are the wrong side for the she-wolf — and the wolf, because man occupies both sides. In an act of submission and an attempt to save the she-wolf from further humiliation and suffering, Billy finishes off the beast: "He ... levered a shell into the chamber of the rifle and halted ten feet from her and raised the rifle to his shoulder and took aim at the bloodied head and fired" (122). Billy returns the she-wolf to the earth, but McCarthy does not entirely remove the wolf from the text, for Billy dreams of wolves as the text continues.

Interestingly, the text is devoid of wolves after Part I, but Billy does manifestly dream of wolves two times (295–6, 325–6). The first of Billy's two dreams is of more importance to the thesis of the wolf as negative metaphor for man's encroachment upon the natural world:

> He'd trudged in his dream through a deep snow along a ridge toward a darkened house and the wolves had followed him as far as the fence. They

ran their lean mouths against each other's flanks and they flowed about his
knees and furrowed the snow with their noses and tossed their heads and
in the cold their pooled breath made a cauldron about him and the snow
lay so blue in the moonlight and those eyes were palest topaz where they
crouched and whined and tucked their tales and they fawned and shud-
dered as they drew close to the house and their teeth shone that were so
white and their red tongues lolled. At the gate they would go no further.
They looked back toward the dark shapes of the mountains ... and then
they turned and wheeled away and loped off through the snow and vanished smoking into the winter night [295].

The dreamscape is similar in tone and atmosphere to the opening hunting passage of the text, but here, the wolves follow Billy. However, he is
followed only up to the point where he enters the world of civilized man,
the fence. Of course, in the old west, the gated fence was symbolic of
man corralling or capturing a measured and surveyed section of the natural world. In this dream, the wolves refuse to enter the world of civilized man, even though the wolves do follow Billy part way. For to enter
the gated area is to enter a world of imminent death and destruction,
because the gated fence is also representative of man as cattle rancher,
and cattle ranchers are the bane of the wolf. The wolves let Billy enter
the gated area, while they also look and then run toward the mountains,
a possible avenue to freedom from man. Of course, as the reader is well
aware, the mountains, be they in Mexico or New Mexico, cannot hide
the wolf from man, and in this dream scene, the narrator, the reader,
and perhaps even Billy, can read the explicit symbolism of the wolves'
refusal to enter the gated area of the homestead. Wolf and man cannot
coexist, and before the wolves, is the gate, the fence, man's homestead,
the present and future. Behind the wolves are the mountains and the
past. The dream wolves attempt to return to the past, and their aura —
their authenticity, their wolfness— exists only in Billy's memory and
psyche once he awakens.

   In *The Crossing,* the absence of the wolf from the southwestern
United States, with emphasis on southern New Mexico and northern
Mexico, signals the presence of man, not just any man, but European
man; history shows that European man has a cultural bias against the
wolf, and when this bias is conjoined with New World capitalism, he
views the eradication of the wolf as apt and fit. More specifically, the
absence of the wolf indicates the presence of the cattle ranching man,
for in both the United States and in Mexico, the existence of the wolf is
contrary to successful cattle production. Wolves do not know borders

or boundaries and so cross both whenever survival dictates, but the wolf is doomed in either country, on either side of the border. And McCarthy shows that both the Americans and the Mexicans seek the demise of the wolf, specifically here the she-wolf Billy traps and captures. Clearly, man and the wolf cannot coexist, so one species is eradicated while the other species propagates and thrives. Man's intolerance for the wolf leaves little room for man's honor, and both man and the wolves suffer because of the dishonor involved in the eradication efforts; man suffers because man is dishonorable, and the wolf suffers because she is annihilated. McCarthy uses a lone wolf, the pregnant she-wolf, to present his argument that man kills that which he cannot control. The wolf cannot be controlled; therefore, the wolf is eradicated. Again, man succeeds in his brutal control of the natural world. In *The Crossing,* the controlled animal may be different from the animals of other McCarthy texts, but the controller is always the same.

In the final text of the Border Trilogy, *Cities of the Plain,* McCarthy offers two very different hunting passages. Each passage contains a different bounty, theme and result, but paradoxically the very different passages argue the same thesis—the ballet of the hunt. For, in McCarthy's literature, other than the horse, the only animal that coexists honorably with man is the domesticated, trained hunting hound. Domestic dogs exist within their own hierarchy, but hunting hounds exist isolated from the pueblo curs and beasts of *Blood Meridian, All the Pretty Horses* and *The Crossing.* From McCarthy's earliest texts forward, the author argues that hunting wild and feral animals with trained hounds is a ballet between hound and man; the hound is immediately labeled an animal of honor, one that coexists in harmony with man. McCarthy furthers this thesis through all of his works up to the penultimate and ultimate hunting scenes in his eighth novel. As the hunt is man's organized attempt at control of the natural world, in conjunction with trained hounds, which of course are specifically bred by man to hunt, the hunt evolves into a ballet between trained domestic animal and man. Again, man is seeking to control the natural world through killing, and as such, man is a creature easily captured in McCarthy's texts; man seeks control, and in *Cities of the Plain,* man appears to achieve control.

9

The Hunt as Ballet in
Cities of the Plain

In *Cities of the Plain*, McCarthy's eighth novel and the final text of
the Border Trilogy, the author offers two very different hunting scenes,
the first pits coonhound against mountain lion, and the second pits
coonhounds against a pack of feral dogs. The first hunt in the text is one
where the hounds are set loose to hunt in the Franklin Mountains of
New Mexico, relying only on the pack and the cumulative results of
man's domestication and training. This hunt resembles the hunts from
the Southern texts, where the hounds are set loose to hunt raccoons.
Man releases the hounds to tree the prey animal, and through their bays
and howls, the hounds notify man of the status of the hunt. In contrast
to the hunts of the Southern texts, the hunt here is one where the prey
animal is a wild feline, a mountain lion. Of course the term, mountain
lion, is a provincial label, synonymous with the term, panther; the former is regional to the Border Southwest, and the latter is regional to the
southeastern United States. McCarthy uses the dominant wild feline in
the feline hierarchy to oppose the hunting hound; in doing so, McCarthy
elevates the trained hound, while he transforms the master feline predator into a prey animal. Thus, man, through the hound, attempts to
control the natural world. The theme of the first hunt in *Cities of the
Plain* is one of bounty. While the bounty-value of the mountain lion is
not specifically alluded to in the scene, an interpolated tale of a jaguar
hunt seems to bear out the assumption that bounty is the basis for the
mountain lion hunt. As well, the passage is one in which the nobility of

the hunting hound is repeatedly articulated by the characters present in the scene. And as noble warriors, the hounds in the first hunt, hunt and battle and are wounded in honor, even though their prey eludes them.

In the second hunting scene of the text, the hounds are set loose after a pack of calf-killing, feral dogs. This hunt is quite different from the first in that this hunt incorporates man and horse into the fray. As in McCarthy's previous novels of the Border Southwest, the horse is a warrior animal, but in *Cities of the Plain,* the equine is conjoined with man and hound. In this scene of the hunt, the hounds are set free, while the men on horses trail the hounds and kill the feral dogs in a number of brutal ways. The feral canines are killing calves, and man cannot tolerate intrusion into man's commercial world, so the feral dogs must die. The theme of this hunt is one of the kill, and the men in the scene actively compete to catch and kill the feral canines. The primary result of this bloody ballet is the eradication of the adult feral dogs; McCarthy leaves no doubt that all of the adult feral dogs are slaughtered; for the good of man, there can be no other way. In both of the hunting scenes in *Cities of the Plain,* man —for different reasons— seeks to control the natural world through killing. The goal of the hunt is to kill the hunted, and in this text, two hunts produce two results, but the ballet of the hunt is extant in both scenes.

Each passage contains a separate bounty, theme and result, but paradoxically, the very different passages argue the same thesis— the ballet of the hunt. For, in McCarthy's literature, other than the horse, the only animal that can coexist honorably with man is the domesticated, trained hunting hound. And while domestic canines exist in their own hierarchy, hunting hounds— Walker hounds, Blueticks, Redbone hounds, and Greyhounds— exist independent from the pueblo curs and beasts of *Blood Meridian, All the Pretty Horses* and *The Crossing.* Consequently, in McCarthy's body of work, hunting hounds and town curs rarely meet. This textual fracture isolates the hunting hounds from the town and city canines, while the treatment of the hounds by man elevates the hunting hound over the abject cur. As such, McCarthy, as is his habit, romanticizes the rural over the urban. From McCarthy's earliest texts forward, the author argues that hunting wild and feral animals with trained hounds is a ballet between hound and man; the hound is immediately labeled an animal of honor, one that coexists in harmony with man and disharmony with the natural world. McCarthy posits this argument through the novels of the South and the novels of the Border Southwest, up to the penultimate and ultimate hunting scenes in *Cities of the Plain*, rarely presenting hunting hounds in a negative light. The hunt is an action, as the hunt is man's organized attempt at controlling the natural world, in conjunction with trained hounds, which of course are specifically bred by man to hunt. Over eons, the hunt evolves into a ballet between trained domestic animal and man. The hounds are equalizers, with which man quells the savage. With the domestication of the horse, the hunt further evolves into a tripartite ballet.

The domestication of hounds for the specific purpose of hunting is an action practiced by man for more than five thousand years, and the Greyhound is the oldest known purebred hunting hound (Greyhounds 0:00–00:30), with a documented history to the third millennium b.c. in Egypt, where tomb hieroglyphs contain passages of Greyhounds (Greyhound). As well, in pre–Christian times, Greyhounds were favored by both theocrats and dictators, and were to be found in the courts and palaces of Egypt, Greece and Rome. By the ninth century, Greyhounds were to be found throughout Western Europe and England. As a hunter, the Greyhound hunts by sight, and historically, its prey consists of goat, fox, deer, and hare. While Greyhounds are not often present in McCarthy's texts, the hounds do play an important role in *All the Pretty Horses* (see below).

More broadly, the term hound is the name of one of the two classes of dog used for hunting purposes; one class includes pointers, retrievers and spaniels, and the other class includes hounds, most of which hunt through their olfactory sense (Hound). Commonly, the term, coonhound, refers to members of a number of hound breeds that "instinctively hunt raccoons squirrels, and opossums, and other tree-climbing animals by scent" (Hound). The coonhound "traps the animal by cornering it in a tree. Remaining at the base of the tree, the dog barks until the hunter locates the prey and makes the kill. The coonhound's hunting instinct is so strong that often the dogs must be trained not to hunt rabbits, foxes, and other kinds of game that are not tree climbers" (Coonhound). McCarthy refers often to three specific types of coonhound, the Bluetick, the Redbone and the Walker. The Bluetick has a white coat, mottled with blue-black, and resembles a Bloodhound; the Redbone is red in color, and the Walker has a white coat with black and tan markings (Coonhound). Redbones and Walkers fall under the category of Black and Tan Coonhounds. Typically, coonhounds have short, dense coats, hanging ears, are deep chested, and weigh between seventy to eighty-five pounds (Black and Tan Coonhound). Behaviorally, coon-hounds are loud, bold, intelligent and instinctual, courageous, loyal, and ferocious at times. McCarthy's coonhounds display all of these honorable traits, as the author sees fit to glorify the canines though the characters' voices and actions and the narrator's omniscient textual commentary. Of course, McCarthy is not the first author to glorify the hunting hound. The late, cultured man of letters, Siegfried Sassoon, for instance, identifies himself in his memoirs as a man enamored with the ballet of the hunt.

In his fictionalized autobiography, *Memoirs of a Fox-Hunting Man*, the British war-hero and poet Siegfried Sassoon fondly reminisces upon the joys of the fox-hunt. In doing so in print, Sassoon sets precedent for the theme of the ballet of the hunt, while he also lovingly describes the action and atmosphere and the rituals of the hunt: "Ringwell cubbing days are among my happiest memories. Those mornings now reappear in my mind, lively and freshly painted by the sunshine of an autumn which made amends for the rainy weeks which had washed away the summer. Four days a week we were up before daylight" (202). Here, the hunt is a ritual action undertaken by the men on a scheduled basis, and as such, the hunt is an action incorporated into the men's lives. Sassoon continues, out of doors:

> In the kennels the two packs were baying at one another from their separate yards, and as soon as Denis had got his horse from the gruff white-coated head-groom, a gate released the hounds—twenty-five or thirty couple of them, and all very much on their toes. Out they streamed like a flood of water, throwing their tongues and spreading away in all directions with waving sterns, as though they had never been out in the world before.... Then, without any apparent lull or interruption, the whirlpool became a well-regulated torrent flowing through the gateway into the road, along which the sound of hoofs receded with a purposeful clip-clopping [203].

This scene is both similar and dissimilar to McCarthy's scenes of the hunt. What is similar is the behavior of the hounds. In both the Sassoon and in McCarthy's texts, the hounds are salivating and screaming, literally, for the action of the hunt. In this scene, through the behavior of the dogs themselves, Sassoon shows the hounds' willingness and desire to hunt. The hounds bay until released, and in their escape from the confines of the cages, the hounds flow from their kennels like rushing water. These hounds are eager to hunt; Sassoon makes their love of the hunt evident. As it will be argued below, in both the novels of the South and the novels of the Border Southwest, McCarthy's hounds also love the hunt and also are eager hunters. What is more, Sassoon's hunting scene also includes ridered horses, not unlike a number of McCarthy hunting scenes. The use of the horse — a warrior animal — as a tool with which man can control the natural world, is a literary device often used by McCarthy, most often in the Border texts. Obviously, though, authors who pre-date McCarthy, such as Sassoon, set the precedent for this type of man, horse, hound hunt. Dissimilar from McCarthy's hunters is Sassoon's narrator's point of reference, for Sassoon's narrator is gentried and is using the hunt neither for sustenance nor for commercial bounty. However, what unifies the Sassoon ballet of the hunt and the McCarthy ballet of the hunt is the "Naturalistic Attitude" (Kellert 6) exhibited by the characters in each author's texts.

According to Professor Stephen R. Kellert, author of "Perceptions of Animals in America," "the creation of a discrete set of categories that permit both the description and measurement of fundamental human attitudes towards animals" (5) is needed in order to identify how human beings perceive and interact with animals. Kellert breaks down "Attitude Categories" (6) into ten distinct groups, of which the Naturalistic Attitude warrants attention, because many of McCarthy's characters who hunt exhibit this sort of attitude towards the natural world. In *Cities of the Plain*, this attitude is explicitly expressed in both extended hunting scenes. Kellert defines the Naturalistic Attitude:

> The primary characteristic of this attitude is a strong interest in and affection for the outdoors and wildlife. Active contact with natural settings is especially valued; thus the naturalistic attitude is closely related to both wilderness and the outdoor recreational benefits of wildlife. A sense of permanence, simplicity, and pleasure derived from unspoiled natural beauty is typically associated with this perspective. Most of all, observation and personal involvement with wildlife are key to the naturalistic interest in the outdoors, with animals providing the context and meaning for active participation in natural settings. Thus wildlife offers the intellectual content and challenge for seeking the outdoors and wilderness experience [6].

This Naturalistic Attitude is not literary naturalism, but is a method of defining man's relationship with the natural world. And clearly, many of McCarthy's primary characters, from Ather Ownby, Marion Sylder and John Wesley Rattner to John Grady Cole and Billy Parham, possess an extremely powerful affection for the natural world, and subsequently, spend much of their professional and personal lives in the natural, not manmade, world. As a result, these characters value their proximity to the wilderness. However, in contrast to Kellert's emphasis on the recreational benefits of the wilderness, McCarthy's characters are quite often fixated on the commercial or use-value of the animals in the wilderness. As such, McCarthy's characters hunt for bounty or food, rather than sport. Yet the characters do, in all of the texts, enjoy a sense of permanence, simplicity and pleasure, which is gleaned from the natural world. Next, McCarthy's characters, with emphasis on those who hunt, are deeply and personally involved with the wildlife with which the characters share the wilderness; one need look no further than *The Orchard Keeper* and Ather Ownby's conscious and unconscious fear of natural and legendary wild cats to realize the depth with which McCarthy's characters are socially and psychologically contextualized with the wildlife of the natural world. Thus, is can be ascertained that, while flora is omnipresent in the texts, fauna is that which is symbiotic to the lives and existences of the characters in the texts. As such, Kellert's Naturalistic Attitude of man towards nature predominates in the important characters in McCarthy's texts, and in addition to Kellert's defining characteristics of man's Naturalistic Attitude toward wildlife, McCarthy adds the use of the hunting hound to allow man to better hunt the wild or feral animal.

In McCarthy's first book length work of fiction, *The Orchard Keeper*, hunting hounds play an important role in the lives of the rural characters, especially Ather Ownby, for Ownby personifies the naturalistic attitude towards wildlife, and his hunting hounds, Scout and Buster are companion animals and tools for the hunt, with which Ownby controls the natural world via killing for sustenance and use-value:

> Night. The coombs of the mountain fluted with hound voices, a threnody on the cooling air. Flying squirrels looped in feathery silence from tree to tree above the old man sitting on a punk log, his feet restless trampling down the poison ivy, listening to Scout and Buster flowing through the dark of the flats below him, a swift slap slap of water where they ghosted through the creek, pop of twig or leaf-scuttle brought to his ear arcanely — they were a quarter mile down — and the long bag-throated trail-call again.
> ... Abruptly the yap of hounds treeing [44, 45].

This brief passage illustrates the relationship between hound and nature, man and nature, and man and hound. The coonhounds run the hunt at night, baying as they seek their prey. McCarthy's choice of language indicates the melodiousness of the hounds' calls, which do not crash through the mountain air, but flute through the mountain air. This harmony with the natural world, however, is illusory, for a threnody is a song of lamentation for the dead. And of course, in this scene, the coonhounds' lamentation is directly conjoined to the coon the hounds are pursuing. For when the coonhounds tree their prey, their bays become frantic. So while the coonhounds' bays flute musically through the mountain air, their call is actually a funerary elegy. This beautification of the hunt is extraordinary because of the subtleness of the language, for both fluted and threnody are onomatopoeic and suggest beauty, not the brutality of the hunt. As such, McCarthy posits the hounds within nature, but against nature. For the hounds are man's tool to control the natural world through killing. Thus, the scene is situated at Ather Ownby's locus, not the hounds' locus. But notice that the subject of the sentence that incorporates Ownby into the scene is, flying squirrels, not Ownby. As well, McCarthy places the squirrels above Ownby, literally, for the squirrels loop through the air above the man. The squirrels are above Ownby in the sentence and in the action of the scene. But Ownby and the squirrels co-exist at peace with one another. As with the hounds and nature, man and nature seem to be symbiotic, but are not, for McCarthy has Ownby trampling the poison ivy on the forest floor. Again, as with the hound and nature above, the author is arguing that man, the hunter, is in a symbiotic relationship with nature, yet the relationship between man and nature is also a brutal blood-battle. As such, squirrels "loop in feathery silence" as man battles and crushes poison ivy.

Next, notice that the coonhounds are named. In McCarthy's fiction, but for a small number of horses in the texts of the Border Trilogy, animals go nameless. For animals are merely animals, but hounds and horses are unique because the animals are both companions and tools; as well, both coonhounds and horses are warrior animals, animals that fight and die beside man. In this text, but for Warn Pulliam and John Wesley Rattner, Scout and Buster are Ownby's only companions, and the old man is closer to the hounds than he is to the two boys. Here, he listens arcanely to the pair run the raccoon through woods and water; that is, Ownby listens as one who possesses a secret knowledge, the knowledge of the hunt and that language of the hunting hound. With this secret knowledge, the hounds and Ownby communicate, even though he is not with the animals during the chase. Ownby and the hounds are a symbiotic man and animal pair, for when the hounds tree the raccoon, Ownby will shoot the critter. As well, the hounds will receive care and respect from the old man; this care and respect from man to animal is rare in McCarthy's texts, and in the Southern fiction, is only shown between man and hunting hound. As the final cited sentence indicates, the hounds have treed the raccoon, and this example of the ballet of the hunt climaxes and concludes. This precedent creating passage, culled from the opening of McCarthy's earliest text, is one that identifies the complex — symbiotic yet oppositional — relationships between hound and nature, and man and nature. Also identified here is the symbiotic relationship between man and hound. Finally, this passage clearly creates the theme of the ballet of the hunt, a ballet that utilizes both man and hunting hound, and a theme that becomes an *oeuvre*-wide theme for McCarthy.

Coonhounds and scenes of the hunt are to be found in *Outer Dark* and *Child of God*, but the primary characters of the texts are not symbiotically and oppositionally conjoined to the natural world, as is Ather Ownby. In the bleak *Outer Dark*, hounds haunt the text peripherally, another evil presence in a very evil world: "Two hounds watched him [Culla Holme] with bleeding eyes, muzzles flat to the scoured and grassless soil in the yard" (117). As Holme enters the yard, the hounds rise "surly and mistrustful" (117). Here, McCarthy demonizes the animals with bleeding eyes, while he also labels the pair as surly. In doing so, the author posits the hounds in the bleak text-scape that is *Outer Dark*. However, later in the scene, the author returns to the symbiotic relationship between man and hunting hound. Culla asks if the old man lives alone, and the man replies, "Not exactly. I got two hounds and a ten-gauge double-barrel that keeps me company" (119). The elderly gentleman clearly identifies the roles the hounds play in his life. The hounds, like the shotgun, serve to protect the old man. As well, the hounds provide needed companionship to the old man, for as the old man states, "... I reckon it's all right to talk to a dog..." (119). And of course, the hounds are coonhounds, so there can be no question that the hounds hunt with the man. Ironically, the hounds provide little protection as the old man is slaughtered by The Three (129).

In *Child of God*, Lester Ballard, lonely, alone and mean, is isolated by McCarthy as a failure, in contrast to men with dogs, who practice the ballet of the hunt: "He stood in the crossroads listening to other men's hounds on the mountain. A figure of wretched arrogance in the lights of the few cars passing ... the men tightly shouldered in the high old sedans with guns and jars of whiskey among them and lean tree-dogs curled in the turtleback" (41). Here, the companioned relationship between the men and their hounds is evident through the contrast with Ballard. Ballard is bitter, angry and alone. Conversely, the hunters have autos, booze and coonhounds. Lester is surrounded by the social actions and sounds of the hunt, yet he is utterly alone. Later in the text, Ballard watches the ballet of the hunt from above the fray:

> The hounds crossed the snow on the slope of the ridge in a thin dark line. Far below them the boar they trailed was tilting along with his curious stifflegged lope, highbacked and very black against the winter's landscape. The hounds' voices in that vast and pale blue void echoed like the cries of demon yodelers.
>
> The boar did not want to cross the river. When he did so it was too late. He came all sleek and steaming out of the willows on the near side and started across the plain. Behind him the dogs were falling down the mountainside hysterically, the snow exploding about them. When they struck the water they smoked like hot stones and when they came out of the brush and onto the plain they came in clouds of pale vapor.
>
> The boar did not turn until the first hound reached him. He spun and cut at the dog and went on. The dogs swarmed over his hindquarters and he turned and hooked with his razorous tushes and reared back on his haunches but there was nothing for shelter. He kept turning, enmeshed in a wheel of snarling hounds until he caught one and drove upon it and pinned and disemboweled it. When he went to turn again to save his flanks he could not.
>
> Ballard watched this ballet tilt and swirl and churn mud up through the snow and watched the lovely blood welter there in its holograph of battle, spray burst from a ruptured lung, the dark heart's blood, pinwheel and pirouette, until shots rang and all was done. A young hound worried the boar's ears and one lay dead with its bright ropy innards folded upon the snow and another whined and dragged himself about. Ballard took his hands from his pockets and took up the rifle from where he had leaned it against a tree. Two small armed and upright figures were moving down along the river, hurrying against the fading light [68–9].

This exquisite scene, cited in its entirety, displays the frenzied passion of the hounds during the act of the hunt. These hounds are bloodthirsty, and the hysterical hounds chase the boar to its inevitable brutal death. Moreover, the hounds show themselves to be warrior animals through the courage they exhibit at the tusks of the boar. McCarthy's hounds will battle, even after being wounded, and even after their allies are mortally wounded. Further, the hunting brutality present in this scene is unmatched in the literature, but for the second hunt in *Cities of the Plain*, a hunt analyzed below. In regard to the first three novels of the Border Southwest, hunting hounds of all sorts exist in the texts.

In McCarthy's first three novels of the Border Southwest, hunting hounds are peripherally present in the text, but do not dominate the canine presence. In *Blood Meridian*, city curs, doomed puppies, wretched Chihuahuas, Glanton's large and vicious canine, and Dr. Lincoln's half-mastiff dominate the canine presence, while hunting hounds, coon-hounds, are nonexistent. However, it must be noted that coonhounds, by that title, have only been recognized in the United States since the early twentieth century (Black and Tan Coonhound). Logically, in *Blood Meridian*, the author chooses not to name most of the canines by breed title.

In *All the Pretty Horses*, coonhounds are rarely if ever cited in the text, but Greyhounds are present in a number of scenes in and around Don Héctor Rocha y Villareal's La Purísima ranch. As John Grady Cole and Lacey Rawlins ride into the estate, the pair is "attended by a pack of greyhound dogs and the dogs were lean and silver in color and they flowed among the legs of the horses silent and fluid as running mercury ..." (97–8). The hunting hounds flow like liquid, language McCarthy uses to describe the coonhounds during the boar hunt cited above. McCarthy allows that the physical ability of these hounds to hunt is not in question, for in a later scene, the dogs come upon a campsite inhab-ited by Cole, Rawlins and the vaquero, Luis: "Suddenly three greyhounds trotted into the light one behind the other and circled the fire, pale and skeletal shapes with the hide stretched taut over their ribs and their eyes red in the firelight" (148–9). Unknown to the reader, and to the charac-ters in the scene, these three hunting hounds are on the hunt for John Grady Cole. Cole has been intimate with Don Héctor's daughter, and Don Héctor seeks blood vengeance. As such, McCarthy describes the trio as death-like and emaciated, with blooded eyes— not horsemen but hounds of the apocalypse. McCarthy continues, "The dogs vanished as suddenly as they had come" (149); this ability to disappear lends the hunting hounds a mystical, powerful aura, and in no way can the reader not associate the hunting hounds in the scene with death. These Grey-hounds are not coonhounds, but nonetheless, these hounds are intimate with the ballet of the hunt.

In *The Crossing*, Bluetick coonhounds are mentioned early in the text, but fighting breeds and town curs dominate the canine presence in the text. In the brief passage that includes a reference to coonhounds, Billy Parham rides traps, looking for the she-wolf, when an old man in a Model A pickup appears and stops for a brief chat; the old man states, "My nephew's got some dogs. Got some blueticks out of the Lee Brothers' line. Pretty good dogs. He don't want em walkin in no steel traps though" (38). The point to Billy is obvious; traps ruin expensive coonhounds. The point to the reader is subtle. First, the scene introduces the Lee Brothers' line of coonhounds, hunting hounds par excellence. In a scene analyzed below, the Lee Brothers' line will be positively alluded to in *Cities of the Plain*. Additionally, the coonhounds are labeled good dogs by the old man, a gentleman who, one can easily assume, possesses and offers rare and faint praise. The result of the obvious and the subtle is a renaissance of the coonhound, reborn in the novel of the Border Southwest. The coonhound has been displaced from the southeastern United States and laterally relocated to the Border Southwest. However, what remains constant is the value — in Tennessee or in New Mexico— of the coonhound; the coonhound is an expensive tool and a good dog and companion. The old man knows so, as does the reader. In McCarthy's forth novel of the Border Southwest, the coonhound is again elevated above the animal fray, and the author sees fit to present the animal's use-value in characters' words, but sees fit to present the hunting hound via its ultimate exercise, the ballet of the hunt.

In *Cities of the Plain*, the ballet of the hunt is epitomized in two extended scenes of the hunt, both of which utilize coonhounds. Writing in regard of coonhounds and the hunt, and the relationship between the hounds and McCarthy's characters, Vereen M. Bell notes that in the text, coonhounds and human characters share "a special affinity that is significant in itself, since coonhounds are independent and solitary hunters as well as game dogs and the coon hunt therefore a ritualized contest between trained predator and prey, an ancient bridge between the human and the feral one" (17). Coonhounds can hunt without man, but coonhounds can also hunt with man. As such, the coonhounds are both instinctual and trained hunters. The hunting instinct may have been bred into the coonhound, but regardless, man behaviorally trains the coonhound after the canine is born. The result is the human and the "not-human are ... commingled" (17). Further, the human and the coonhound are bridged, commingled, balanced against nature in a brutal and bloody ballet, a ballet practiced since ancient times.

McCarthy opens the first hunting scene (87–92) with an allusion to the ancient past: "They sat against a rock bluff high in the Franklins with a fire before them that heeled in the wind and their figures cast up upon the rocks behind them enshadowed the pretroglyphs carved there by other hunters a thousand years before. They could hear the dogs running far below them" (87). Here, conjoined to the hunters of the ancient past and identified as such, the twentieth century human hunters sit around the fire — a totem of man's power over the natural world — while the hounds run and bay in the valley below. The hunt is on, and both the men and the hounds are the predators. What is more, the hunt is for specific prey, a mountain lion that the hunters have hunted before:

> Archer had stood and turned toward the running dogs the better to listen and after a while he squatted again and spat into the fire.
> She aint goin to tree, he said.
> I don't believe she will either, said Travis.
> How do you know it's the same lion? Said JC.
> Travis had taken his tobacco from his pocket and he smoothed and cupped a paper with his fingers. She's done us thisaway before, he said. She'll run plumb out of the country.
> They sat listening. The cries grew faint and after a while there were no more [87–8].

Archer and Travis, two likable characters who own the dogs, are able to testify to what the dogs and the prey are doing during the hunt, regardless of the fact that the hunt occurs off-scene. The hounds and the men are still in communication, even though the hounds and the men are out of sight, so the ballet of the hunt is not sight dependent, but is sound dependent:

> I hear em, Travis said.
> I do too.
> She's crossed at the head of that big draw where the road cuts back.
> We wont get that Lucy dog back tonight [88].

Here, she refers to the prey, the mountain lion, and the hunters can detail her movement through the direction from which come the bays of the coonhounds, so a ballet of sound, movement and communication is occurring between the hunters and the hounds. Unlike the prey animals in the novels of the South — raccoons, opossums, boars and feral felines, the prey here is one of the predator animals at the apex of the feline hierarchy, a mountain lion/cougar/puma. Additionally, the mountain lion is one that Travis and Archer have previously hunted. Thus, the recursive nature of the ballet of the hunt is emphasized in this passage where both prey and predators return to hunt again. With this thematic recursiveness in mind, the author continues the scene with Travis and Archer telling of legendary hounds and previous hunts:

> We wont get that Lucy dog back tonight.
> What dog is that?
> Bitch out of that Aldridge line. Them dogs was bred by the Lee Brothers. They just forgot to build in the quit.
> Best dog we ever had was her granddaddy, said Archer. You remember that Roscoe dog, Travis?
> Of course I do. People thought he was part bluetick but he was a full leopard cur with a glass eye and he did love to fight. We lost him down in Nyarit. Jaguar caught him and bit him damn near in two.
> You all don't hunt down there no more.
> No.
> We aint been back since before the war ... Lee Brothers had about quit goin. They brought a lot of jaguars out of that country, too [88–9].

The first lines of this passage allude to the heart and never-quit hunting passion of the coonhound, Lucy. The warrior animal will hunt until the hunting is done, regardless of the chase and the distance involved. Also mentioned here is the Lee Brothers line of dogs, and again, as in *The Crossing*, all involved highly praise the Lee Brothers' coonhounds. Unique to this text, though, is the hunt within the hunt, the metafictive tale of the hunt, within McCarthy's tale of the hunt. Archer and Travis lament the hunts of yore, while the pair concurrently elevate the status of the coonhound, for only great hunters from a great line would be able to take so very many jaguars from the jungles of Mexico. Additionally, this scene shows that the ballet of the hunt is not a ballet limited by geographic locale, for the ballet need only include man, coonhounds and prey; as such, the ballet can and does occur in Tennessee and Texas and New Mexico and old Mexico. The coonhounds are trained warriors, as is evidenced by the closing passages of this scene, when the walking wounded return from the hunt.

As the coonhounds return from the hunt, the reader will notice that the prey animal, the mountain lion, has not been treed, and as such, the hunt, within the action of the scene, is a failure, because man and canine have failed to control the natural world through killing. However, paratextually, the scene — if not the hunt — is a great success, because the reader is able to measure and ascertain the importance of the hunting hound in the textual and intertextual existences of McCarthy's characters. As such, the reader can recognize an *oeuvre* honoring and mythol-

ogizing the hunting hound in general, and the coonhound in particular. As the scene continues, the hounds return from the hunt: "Two of
the dogs came in out of the night and passed behind the hunters. Their
shadows trotted across the stone bluff and they crossed to a place in the
dry dust under the rocks where they curled up and were soon asleep"
(90). The weary hunting hounds begin to trickle in, and the weary
hunters are immediately asleep. As well, notice that McCarthy labels the
men around the campfire hunters. In doing so, the author is allowing
the fact that the men and the coonhounds are a team, and that without
the other, the ballet of the hunt would cease to exist. As the scene progresses, more exhausted coonhounds enter the campsite: "Three more
dogs passed the fire and sought out beds under the bluff" (91). Again
the hunting hounds enter the scene and immediately go to sleep. Then,
a wounded warrior returns to the campsite: "... and after a while another
dog came in. He was favoring a forefoot and Archer got up and walked
up under the bluff to see about him. They heard the dog whine and when
he came back he said they'd been in a fight" (91). Interesting here is
McCarthy's use of vague pronouns. Archer could tell the men that the
dogs has been in a fight, but, actually, the dog tells the men that there
has been a fight, because the dog is quite obviously wounded, so it is
the dog that tells them that he had been in a fight; a wounded warrior's
wounds tell tales of the battle, of course. So the he in this scene can refer
to the hound or to Archer. As time passes, more hounds enter the site:
"Two more dogs came in and then all were in save one" (91). Of course,
the missing hound is the coonhound named Lucy, a true and resilient
hunter:

> The dog they were waiting for came in limping badly and circled the
> fire.... There were four bloody furrows along her flank. There was a flap of
> skin ripped loose at her shoulder exposing the muscle underneath and
> blood was dripping slowly from one ripped ear onto the sandy dirt where
> she stood.
> ... She carried the only news they would have of the hunt, bearing wit-
> ness to things they could only imagine or suppose out there in the night.
> She winced when Archer touched her ear and when he let go of her she
> stepped back and stood with her forefeet braced and shook her head.
> Blood sprayed the hunters and hissed in the fire. They rose to go [91].

Lucy enters the scene the last and the ultimate hunter coonhound,
and she too, carries the wounds of the hunt. Appropriately, as the ultimate coonhound in this caste of hounds, Lucy is named and is, as well,
the coonhound with the severest wounds. Lucy has been lacerated mul-

tiple times, but yet, she has survived to return for medical care, and as such, Lucy will live to see another hunt. Lucy is also witness to the hunt. By identifying the coonhound as witness, McCarthy is elevating the animal, because, while the theme of the witness is a prominent one in the fiction, rarely is an animal acknowledged by the narrator as a witness. Lucy is witness and participant to the hunt, and in a symbolically inclusive act, she splashes the human hunters with her blood, thus including the men in the ballet of the hunt. As the scene closes, Archer and Travis are chaining the hounds, while the bloodied Lucy rests her head on Cole's lap. The penultimate hunting scene is over, and the ballet has yielded only wounded dogs, but the ultimate hunting scene — in the text and in the *oeuvre*— is yet to come, and in this ultimate hunting scene (158–69), as the ballet of the hunt continues, much canine blood will be spilled, and many canines will die.

Writing in regard to the second hunt in *Cities of the Plain*— a hunt for a pack of cattle-killing feral canines— Edwin T. Arnold addresses the motive of the human hunters:

> The hunt itself stands as the central and highly problematic action in the novel.... Although it is a great action episode, described and paced with all of McCarthy's controlled artistry, the almost unconscious brutality of the characters makes us confront their motive to violence as effectively as anything in *Blood Meridian* [226].

The motive of the human hunters is clear and simple: control over the natural world through killing. This motive of man attempting to dominate the natural world appears in the McCarthy *oeuvre* repeatedly. And in *Cities of the Plain*, when the feral dogs begin to kill calves, the feral canines must be controlled, that is, killed. McCarthy's ultimate ballet occurs as Part III of the text opens. In a scene reminiscent of the opening of *The Crossing*, Cole rides upon "the flyblown carcass of a new calf" (153), but the predator(s) in the latter text is not a lone she-wolf, but is a pack of feral dogs. Billy Parham, late of *The Crossing*, diagnoses the predators that are to become prey immediately. Cole asks, "You think it's been a lion?" (154), and Billy replies, "No" (154). McCarthy's narrator informs the reader, "The calf had been cut out and run down and killed in open country" (154). Cole continues, "You don't think it's just been coyotes?" (154), and Billy again replies in the negative, "I don't think so" (154). The dialogue continues:

> What do you think it's been?
> I know what it's been.

What?
Dogs.
Dogs?
Yep.
I aint never seen no dogs out here.
I aint either. But they're here [154–5].

In a passage comic and brilliant in understatement, tone and diction, the cowboy detective Billy deduces the identity of the predators through the crime scene, and the narrator includes the reader in the gathering of evidence. The narrator continues, "In the days that followed they found two more dead calves.... They found tracks of the dogs but they did not see them. Before the week was out they'd found another freshkilled calf not dead a day" (155). The feral dogs are clearly a commercial bane, and as such, the feral dogs must be eliminated from the natural world and the man-made world. And in another scene reminiscent of *The Crossing*, Billy cleans, waxes and lays traps, but the prey is too wiley for traps, and the traps do no good. Subsequently, Cole asks Billy, "You think Travis's dogs would run em?" (155), and the hunt is on in an ultimate action of the feral and natural versus the domesticated and man-dominated.

The stakes are simple in this scene of the ballet of the hunt. For the coonhounds and the men and the horses, victory is counted in feral dogs dead, and for the feral dogs—as with the elusive and savage mountain lion from the first hunt—survival is victory. At pre-dawn on a Tuesday, the men and the dogs and the horses enter the valley of the feral dogs. The coonhounds sense the hunt is about:

> The dogs backed and danced and whined and some raised their mouths and howled and the howls echoed off the rimrock and back again and Travis halfhitched the first cast of dogs to the front bumper of the truck where their collective breath clouded whitely in the headlamps and the horses standing along the edge of the dark stamped and snorted and leaned to test the yellow lightbeams with their noses [158].

The coonhounds are frenzied with the pre-hunt because the hounds are acutely aware of the ritual. Concurrently, the horses seem to be quite edgy and alert, and not fearful of the frenzied hounds. As Billy and Cole show Travis and Archer the placement of the dead calf, "they came down the wash with the big bluetick and treeing walker hounds lunging at their leads and slobbering and sucking at the air with their noses" (159). Here, McCarthy names the breeds so that there may be no error; what is more, after releasing the hounds, Travis tells Billy, "If Smoke wont run

em they aint goin to be run" (159). For the third time in the text, a coonhound has been named. Again, it bears mention that McCarthy commonly names horses and coonhounds, but rarely, if ever, names other
canines or domestic animals. What is interesting though about the coonhound named Smoke is what Travis tells Billy, "But he's the dog for the
job.... Cause he's run dogs before" (159). Coonhounds are like men in
that they hunt and kill their own, and givin the opportunity, repeat the
acts of killing. Before the men and the horses enter the canyon, Archer
states calmly, "There's goin to be one godawful dogfight up in them
rocks" (160), and he is correct of course, and as the seven men — Cole,
Billy, Archer, Travis, Joaquín, JC, Troy — ride into the canyon on their
horses, they hear the feral dogs barking in answer to the coonhounds'
bays, "I guess they want to be in on the race, Archer said. Dumb sum-
bucks don't know they are the race" (160).

At this point in the hunt, McCarthy limits the dialogue, while the
narrator describes most of the brutal action: "By the time they reached the
foot of the stone palisades the hounds had already driven the dogs out of
the rocks and they could hear them in a running fight and then a long
howling chase up through the broken scree and boulders" (160). As in the
first scene of the hunt, the human hunters follow the course of the chase
via the bays and howls of the coonhounds. The communication here is
aided by the men's use of the horses to follow the hounds, for as the scene
plays out, it is the men on horses who kill the feral dogs, not the Blueticks
and Walkers. Also important in this passage is the fact that the coonhounds
have immediately driven the feral dogs from the safety of their rock lairs.
As well, the coonhounds are chasing the feral dogs, and as the coonhounds
chase the feral dogs into the open area below the rocks, the men on horses
await, prepared to lasso and throttle the feral, problematic canines. Cole
readies his horse for battle: "Three yellowlooking dogs were loping ahead
in tandem before him up a long gravel wash. He leaned and spoke again
to the horse but the horse had already seen them" (161). In a mannerism
reminiscent of the warrior bounty hunter, Captain John Joel Glanton, Cole
prepares his warrior horse for battle by speaking to the animal. But the warrior horse is prepared and is willing for battle, and as Cole attempts to lasso
the cur, the horse is aware of the action: "When the horse saw the rope loft
past its left ear it laidback its ears and came hauling down upon the running cur with its mouth open like some terrible vengeance" (161–2). The
horse, a willing warrior, is bloodthirsty, and as such, the warrior horse runs
down the cur. Cole loops the cur, and the horse aids in the killing of the

dog: "The dun horse tossed up its head and set its forefeet in the gravel and squatted and John Grady dallied the home end of the rope about the polished leather of the pommel and the rope popped taut and the dog snapped into the air mutely" (162). In this example of the ballet of the hunt, the coonhounds ran the feral dog from the rocks, and then Cole, aided by the bloodthirsty horse and its seemingly consciously malicious actions, loops and throttles the cur. The three predators in this action co-hunt in a balance of timing and movement, and as the hunt progresses, "the outlaw dogs" (162) are systematically hunted down by the men on horses.

After Billy kills a feral dog and Cole kills a second, a second cast of hounds is also at work: "The second cast of hounds were now tracking the dogs along the lower end of the floodplain, running them down among the boulders and scree and fighting and going on again" (163). McCarthy reminds the reader that the coonhounds are part of the ballet of the hunt, and that the coonhounds are crucial to this hunt, for as previously noted, neither Cole nor Billy had ever seen the feral dogs, but the coonhounds needed only scent to locate and run the curs. So, without the coonhounds, the hunt would fail, but with the coonhounds, the hunt is an overwhelming success, and the feral dogs are killed. As well, notice that McCarthy takes care to label the coonhounds, hounds, and the feral canines, dogs. There is a particular distinction between the warrior hounds and the feral curs, and McCarthy posits one animal close to man and one animal beneath man. The hounds are indicative of man's ability to control the natural world, and the feral dogs are symbolic of man's failure to control the natural world, for man must kill that which man cannot control. And for man, control through killing is perfectly acceptable, especially at times when commercial property — cattle — is at stake. And in this scene of the hunt, man, hound and horse cooperate in a balance that is gruesomely effective.

Later in a scene that takes place upon the mesa above the valley, near the end of the hunt, McCarthy includes another episode that incorporates hound, man and horse:

> The spotted dog seemed to see no way down from the tableland and it looked to be tiring as it loped along the rim. When it heard the hounds it turned upcountry again and crossed behind Joaquín and Joaquín brought his horse around and in a flat race overtook it and roped it in less than a mile of ground....
> They came riding back across the mesa with the hounds at the horses' heels. Joaquín trailed the dead dog through the grass at the end of his rope [168].

Again, the hounds run the dog, and the man and horse catch and kill the feral cur. Teamwork, a balance between man and beasts, this is how the work of killing gets done in the McCarthy fiction, and the ballet of the hunt is a ballet where man and domesticated animals kill the animals of the natural world. After much blood and brutality, the scene closes on a light note. It seems that after the hunt has finished, a coonhound is missing: "Joaquín leaned and spat and turned his horse. Let's go, he said. He [the missing coonhound] could be anywhere. There's always one that don't want to go home" (169). And on that thought, the ultimate hunt comes to a close, as does the scene. Of course, the comment by Joaquín is an intratextual allusion, as the same thought is narrated during the first hunt, when Lucy does not return from the Mountain Lion hunt (91). As well, the comment maintains the coonhounds' status as a willing, ready and able hunter. For these hounds will hunt.

In McCarthy's eighth novel, *Cities of the Plain*, the author uses two very different hunting scenes to argue the same thesis—the hunt as ballet between man and hunting hound. In the former hunting scene, the author offers a nighttime hunt in which the coonhounds—Walkers, Blueticks and Redbones—are set loose in the Franklin Mountains to run and possibly tree a mountain lion. In the hunt, the hounds communicate with their keepers through their bays and howls. As such, the keepers can track the progress of the hunt, regardless of the hounds' locale and proximity. In this hunt, two of the hounds are wounded, and the prey animal eludes the prey. Nonetheless, the men in the scene articulate the status of the coonhound in the lives of the characters. Coonhounds are honored co-hunters with the men, and the men respect and care for the hounds. This respect and admiration for the hounds does not diminish, regardless of the fruitless hunt. In the second scene of the hunt, the coonhounds are after feral dogs in a dawn hunt. In this hunt, the men actively participate with the coonhounds, aided by their warrior horses, of course. Here, the men and hounds and horses make short work of the feral dogs, as the coonhounds run the curs, and the man and horse teams catch, lasso and throttle the feral dogs. This hunt, like the former hunt, balances the men and the hounds as co-hunters, while the latter hunt also assimilates the warrior horse into the ballet of the hunt. The hunt is man's organized attempt at control of the natural world, in conjunction with trained hounds, which of course are specifically bred by man to hunt; the hounds are equalizers, with which man quells the savage, in a savage ballet.

Chapter 10 will discuss animal precedent in *No Country for Old Men*.

10

Following Animal Precedent in
No Country for Old Men

An initial reading of Cormac McCarthy's ninth novel, *No Country for Old Men*, leaves the reader wondering about the lack of animal presence in the text. McCarthy's previous eight novels are rife with animal presence and imagery, and it seems that the author deviates from literary precedent with this latest text. However, a closer examination of *No Country for Old Men* reveals in fact that McCarthy is closely following precedent, although he is doing so without the animal omnipresence of the previous novels. As with the previous novels, animals and death are conjoined. More specifically, animals and death are proximal to the hand of man. Man kills animals—domestic, feral, wild, and stock, and this dyad of man and animal death is found often in *No Country for Old Men*. So in this way, McCarthy is indeed following precedent. And he does so in other ways. Previous study of both *The Stonemason* and *The Gardener's Son* reveals that not all of McCarthy's works contain animal omnipresence, but all of the works contain the theme of animals and death. In the drama and the teleplay, animals play important roles linked to death, but do so less explicitly than in the novels. In *No Country for Old Men*, living animals are less prevalent, but animal imagery is not. Thus, McCarthy negates the animal, while he keeps the animal imagery. This negation of the living, breathing, dying animal in favor of the image of the animal—in boot skin (often an endangered animal) or vehicle name (Barracuda or Bronco or Ram) or character thought or narration—is significant because it is McCarthy's argument that man has killed off the fauna, especially the predatory fauna, of the Border Southwest. By 1980, the year of the action, there are no bears, no cougars, no jaguars, no wolves left in the Border Southwest. And the few animals present in the text are dying rapidly at the hand of man. In the first eight novels, McCarthy uses the theme of omnipresent animals and death, but he often qualifies this use of animals and death with animal death specifically, which occurs directly at the hand of man. The motif that man kills animals—wild, feral, domestic, and stock—is recurrent within each novel and is genre-wide. In McCarthy's fiction, it is clearly dangerous to be an animal around man. Over the course of the first eight novels, McCarthy repeatedly shows how proximity to man is life threatening to an animal; accidentally or on purpose, man kills animals. As well, as the chronology goes from the middle nineteenth century to the late twentieth century, wild animals cease to be omnipresent in the text, because they cease to be omnipresent in the wild. In *No Country for Old Men*, set in 1980, McCarthy continues the theme of animal death at the hand of man, but he does so without animal omnipresence.

Very early in the text, Llewelyn Moss is introduced while stalking a herd of antelope. Moss's tools are cataloged: "a pair of twelve power german binoculars ... a harnessleather sling ... a heavybarreled .270 on a '98 Mauser action with a laminated stock of maple and walnut ... a Unertl telescopic sight ... a Canjar trigger set to nine ounces ... 150 grain bullet[s]" (8, 9, 10). McCarthy introduces Moss as a hunter, not some lazy slob in a blind. The reader later learns that Moss was a sniper in Vietnam, and in this scene, Moss carries a sniper's nomenclature and behavior. But Moss is a flawed sniper: "He ... lowered the forearm of the rifle down into the leather and pushed off the safety with his thumb and sighted the scope. They stood with their heads up, all of them, looking at him. Damn..." (9). Rather than be patient, Moss nearly immediately takes the shot and misses his target. But through ricochet, he wounds a random antelope: "One of the animals had dropped back and was packing one leg.... He leaned and spat. Damn ..." (10). As a conscientious—but flawed—hunter, Moss is obligated to track down the wounded animal to finish the job. And Moss tries—but fails—to do so, because, "the animals had vanished" (10). Notice McCarthy's language here; the antelope do not bound or gallop away; they vanish, never to re-appear. Seeing no blood trail, Moss looks to the direction the herd has fled, but he sees no antelope, wounded or otherwise. This calls into question two things: First, did Moss actually wound the animal? If so, where is the blood trail? Second, if the animal is wounded, what is to become of it? Quite likely, it will die secondary to a wound infection, a lá Sproule in *Blood Meridian*. And what of this animal's death? Well, Moss misses his shot, but in a typical McCarthian way, an antelope dies nonetheless, but not because of man's skill. What is also of note in this scene is that Moss has no rangefinder, a rather inexpensive piece of equipment. So Moss the hunter is flawed in a number of ways, yet he kills the antelope by accident.

The antelope scene gives way to a scene in which McCarthy introduces two dogs into the action. As is common in the *oeuvre*, the dogs do not fare so well. Moss looks over the terrain for the antelope: "Crossing that ground was a large tailless dog, black in color. He watched it. It had a huge head and cropped ears and it was limping badly. It paused and stood. It looked behind it. Then it went on" (11). At this point, this dog seems to be the luckier of the two canines, because this dog is still alive. McCarthy describes the beast vaguely, as to let the reader's imagination take hold. The animal is large, black, and tailless, with a huge head and cropped ears. From this vague description, one can reasonably surmise that the dog is bred for violence. Large is a subjective term, and each reader has his or her immediate image of a large dog. Black is denotative, plus the pejorative meaning of black as evil or scary resonates. The three remaining descriptors identify the animal as a fighting animal. The dog is tailless, and its ears are cropped. Dogs bred for battlesport are often de-tailed and de-eared so that the opposing animal does not rip off the first animal's ears or tail. The dog is huge headed. In other words, the animal's huge head is disproportionate to its large body. A fighting dog needs a huge head with massive jaws, with which the beast can chomp its foes, be those foes canine or human. McCarthy further de-domesticates the animal by using the vague third person pronoun, it, seven times in five sentences to refer to the beast. In all, McCarthy creates the image of a predatory animal. However, the dog is wounded and is scared, as is evidenced by the animal's look back for pursuers, human pursuers. The frightened, wounded dog keeps moving, even without pursuit, most likely to meet the same fate as the wounded antelope. As Moss notices and approaches the scene of the shootout, he encounters another dog, this one past being wounded: "There was a large dead dog there of the kind he'd seen crossing the floodplain. The dog was gutshot" (12). In addition to being bred to be a better, more efficient weapon, in addition to being butchered and maimed as a puppy, and in addition to being forced to participate in gun-battles in the name of narco-economics, this dog is gutshot. And as any fan of Cowboy 101 well knows, "bein' gutshot is the worst wound there is." As a consequence, this animal suffers before death, as will the wounded antelope and the wounded dog.

As one warrior dog dies and one takes flight in a probably futile attempt to elude death, so do two predatory birds in two contrasting scenes. In the first scene, Sheriff Ed Tom Bell comes across a hawk dead in the highway:

> He saw the feathers move in the wind. He pulled over ... and looked at it. He raised one wing and let it fall again.... . It was a big redtail. He picked it up by one wingtip and carried it to the bar ditch and laid it in the grass. They would hunt the blacktop, sitting on the high powerpoles and watching the highway in both directions for miles. Any small thing that might venture to cross. Closing on their prey against the sun. Shadowless. Lost in the concentration of the hunter. He wouldn't have the trucks running over it [44–5].

Again, an animal dies accidentally, proximal to man. It is a rare act for a McCarthy character to show compassion towards an animal, living or dead. And McCarthy refers to the dead bird as an "it" until Bell removes the animal from the road. The animal is de-animated, without the Latin *anima*, life force. But, when McCarthy interpolates a micro-scene of the species' hunting process and prowess, the master predators become "they" and "their," animated, identifiable, and plural in number. But, even with the master predator's eyes, killing ability and shadowless flight, a red tail is no match for a speed limit-busting tractor and trailer. Random death waits. And man killing birds in the McCarthy is not uncommon, as Judge Holden shoots birds to dress and to catalog and Billy Parham arrows a hawk, in another random, but much more malicious act. Here, though, the mismatch between bird and semi is quite outrageous, and the randomness of the hawk's death is tragic and well noted by the reader. Another master predator fades from the landscape, secondary to man's presence. It is as if McCarthy is arguing that man's very existence dooms many species. And so it does, if this red tail hawk is metonymic, and it is.

In the next bird-hunting scene, Anton Chigurh, killer magnificent, takes aim at a nocturnal avian:

> The headlights picked up some kind of large bird sitting on the aluminum bridgerail up ahead.... . He took the pistol from beside the box and cocked and leveled it out the window, resting the barrel on the rearview

mirror.... . He fired just as the bird crouched and spread its wings. It flared
wildly in the lights, very white, turning and lifting away into the darkness.
The shot hit the rail and caromed off into the night.... . Chigurh laid the
pistol in the seat and put the window back up again [98–9].

Shooting out of spite or boredom, rather than his business model, Chigurh misses his shot. And it is a rare miss indeed, for his human targets are
never so lucky. As with the wounded dog, McCarthy uses vague language
to describe the bird. It is large and very white, and as this scene occurs at
night, most likely an owl of some sort. The size befits a predator bird that
has survived into maturity, and the color implies purity and innocence.
Again, the animal is referred to as an "it." The bird is resting on a bridgerail,
a man-made instrument, on the side of the highway. This perch is a mistake by the bird, for any reliance by a wild animal upon man, in any way,
is life threatening. As well, we know how vehicles and birds match up. The
bird is alertly moving to fly away from the oncoming vehicle, but the shot
is unexpected, as the bird flares wildly at the muzzle-flash, concussion, and
ricochet of the gunfire before moving up and into the night. Silencers do
not suppress all concussion or muzzle-flash. This bird, aware of the danger of man's vehicles, has lived to learn a new lesson, that of the gun. The
randomness of the killing act against the animal is a very human behavior, for most animals do not murder for pleasure. But humans do.

The final animal death scene, or near death scene, to examine is
one where Sheriff Bell and Deputy Torbert discuss the method with
which Bill Wyrick is killed. After reading the coroner's report from
Austin, Sheriff Bell and Torbert have this brief discussion:

> I know what's happened here, he [Bell] said.
> All right.
> Have you ever been to a slaughterhouse? Yessir. I believe so.
> You'd know it if you had.
> I think I went once when I was a kid.
> Funny place to take a kid.
> I think I went my own self. Snuck in.... . They had a knocker straddled
> the chute and they'd let the beeves through one at a time and he'd knock
> em in the head with a maul. He done that all day.
> That sounds about right. They don't do it thataway no more. They use a
> airpowered gun that shoots a steel bolt out of it. Just shoots it out about
> so far. They put that thing between the beef's eyes and pull the trigger and
> down she goes. It's that quick ... [105–6].

The report does not state that a cattlegun killed Wyrick. It most likely
states that he was killed by a metal projectile which pierced his skull and

brain tissue by a distance of "about so far." Remember, Deputy Haskins told Bell of Chigurh's cattlegun (5). So from the opening of the text, the leitmotif of the cattlegun is the image of death, human death and animal death. For in a great case of situational irony, the assassin Chigurh uses a device designed to execute cattle by the thousands each week, to execute humans. As eras evolve from the modern to the postmodern, so evolve man's methods of killing animals for mass human consumption. Imagine this, the assassin Chigurh carrying around a cattle maul to whack his victims. The element of surprise might be gone. The cattlegun leitmotif is a great example of animal negation. The tool as it is designed, negates cattle from life. As well, the repetitive naming of the tool through the text continually calls forth the image of the bovine, sans the bovine. As such, the image of the animal is present in the text, but the living, or dying, beef is not.

So, paradoxically, in *No Country for Old Men*, Cormac McCarthy minimalizes animal presence, but he does so while following his ongoing themes of animals and death, and animal death at the hand of man. The result is a text that seems devoid of animal imagery, yet is not.

Chapter 11 will be a conclusion to chapters 1 through 10.

11

Conclusion

In the fiction of Cormac McCarthy, clearly the author's dominant literary theme is death. For as McCarthy states, literature that does not "deal with life and death ... to me, that's not literature" (Woodward 31). Consequently, very rarely do McCarthy's human characters die of old age. However, human characters do die in a wide variety of ways. Animals in the text live only to die as well, and as such, McCarthy's theme of omnipresent death and dying is appropriately applied to the animals that inhabit the texts. Specifically, as has been previously argued, McCarthy uses four modes by which he presents animals and animal death in the fiction. The first mode with which he presents animal death is a biologically deterministic manner. McCarthy uses feline hierarchies, canine hierarchies and horses as warriors to argue and present biological determinism. Often, as well, McCarthy posits the animals in the hierarchies through the animals' proximity to man. As such, the closer an animal is to man, the lower that animal is on the animal hierarchy. Next, McCarthy uses animals to preface human death, and the animals become harbingers for human deaths in the text. A particular animal will appear in the text, and a human being will soon die. In this study, McCarthy's use of swine and mules as harbingers of human death has been the focus, although, other animals in the texts can preface human death. Additionally, through the presentation of man's capture and killing of many animals of the natural world, McCarthy emphasizes man's ceaseless desire to control the natural world. Man wants to control the natural world, and will capture, domesticate, attempt to kill, or kill those animals which he cannot control, such as birds, bats, wolves,

174

and, humorously, certain bovines. Finally, McCarthy uniquely uses coonhounds to control the natural world through the ballet of the hunt, the balance between human hunter and trained coonhound in the pursuit of wild prey. These four manners of textual animal presentation meet at the nexus of death, McCarthy's dominant textual theme, and all of the major and minor texts contain death-centric animal presentation.

Animal presentation based upon biological determinism — events causally determined by natural laws, which are themselves determined by a combination of environment and genetics—can be found in *The Orchard Keeper, Blood Meridian, All the Pretty Horses,* and *The Stonemason.* In *The Orchard Keeper,* McCarthy uses a feline hierarchy composed of domestic, feral and wild felines to argue that proximity to man and dependence upon man can be bad for a feline's existence. As such, domestic kittens, absolutely dependent upon man, are presented as doomed and diseased, and not long for this earth. A feral feline, free from man's control, yet nonetheless dependent upon man for survival, is next on the feline hierarchy. And even though the feral cat has, at the least, survived to adulthood, the feral cat is used as prey by a great hunting owl. Small wild felines, the lynx and the bobcat, make up the lower order of the wild felines on the hierarchy. Neither bobcat, nor lynx appear in the text, although Warn Pulliam and John Wesley Rattner refer to both types of wild feline. Higher yet on the hierarchy are the legendary wampus cat and the real-life panther. Characters in *The Orchard Keeper* fear the legendary wampus cat, though none really knows if the wild cat exists. Regardless, the animal, in legend and lore, does exist to strike fear into the folks of McCarthy's Appalachia. Utmost on McCarthy's feline hierarchy are the wild panthers that roam rural Tennessee. These felines do exist in reality and in the text, and the predatory prowess of one she-panther in particular serves to enhance the symbiotic dyad of the theme of death and McCarthy's presentation of the feline hierarchy. This she-panther hunts without sound and kills without being seen. McCarthy's feline hierarchy in *The Orchard Keeper* is similar to his canine hierarchy in *Blood Meridian.*

In *Blood Meridian,* the author again uses an animal hierarchy to present death, biological determinism and animal proximity to man, but in this text, the author conjoins domestic canines to each canine's master. As such, socially and behaviorally, and deterministically, the canine is conjoined to its master. Lowest on the canine hierarchy are the domestic curs found in the border towns and pueblos of northern Mexico. These abject curs, here in puppy form, are conjoined in the text to the little child urchins that the judge kills. The children in the text are doomed, as are the puppies nearly drowned by the judge, then shot by Bathcat. Neither town cur puppy nor town urchin is very deterministic. Next on the canine hierarchical scale is a pair of circus dogs that travel with a company of *bufones*. Captain John Joel Glanton is unimpressed with both the human and the canine performers, yet he sees fit not to kill the entire lot, perhaps because the canines and their human handlers are sans dignity. Higher on the canine hierarchy is the river ferry-master Lincoln's half-mastiff. This canine is owned by a man of social and economic power, and as such, is provided some honor and dignity, that is, until both are massacred by the Yuma Indians at the Colorado River crossing. Highest on the *Blood Meridian* canine hierarchy is Glanton's unnamed, breedless warrior canine. Glanton's dog is one who fights and kills as the gang of scalphunters fights and kills. Aptly, the warrior canine dies with the warrior Glanton, who also is killed by the Yumas. As well, *All the Pretty Horses* has warrior animals in the text, but unlike *Blood Meridian*, the warrior animals in *All the Pretty Horses* are horses not canines.

In *All the Pretty Horses*, the horse as warrior animal is a dominant theme of the text, and McCarthy uses Indian, Mexican and Anglo riders to articulate this argument. From the onset of the text, the horse is promoted as a warrior, and McCarthy uses an extended paragraph on the People — the Comanche — to present the horse in a manner in which the animal is an integral part of a warrior society, for in Comanche society, horses, men, women, children, all participate in war or in the communal promotion and propagation of war. Additionally, McCarthy uses Luís, a Mexican cowboy and war veteran, to further promote the animal as warrior, for this veteran, a veteran of the Mexican Revolution and numerous other cavalry battles, promotes the horse as an animal that is a warrior by birth and by communal soul; all horses are warriors. Finally, McCarthy uses his young Anglo characters, John Grady Cole, Lacey Rawlins and Jimmy Blevins, to show that the horse is a warrior animal in a violently deterministic world. For in a number of scenes the boys, alone or together, must fight on horseback, and in each instance, the warrior horses perform honorably and exceptionally under fire. In *All the Pretty Horses*, McCarthy uses a trio of cultural viewpoints to argue, articulate, and finally, to prove the horse a warrior animal. In McCarthy's drama, *The Stonemason*, there are no warrior animals and there are very few wars, but there is the end stage of biological determinism, death by old age of a family dog.

The Stonemason is a drama that revolves around and is built upon the theme of death. A number of people and things die in the drama, and animals are not excluded from the theme of death. In the drama, the art and practice of stonemasonry dies, a large number of the Telfair family dies, dead ancestors are continually alluded to and referred to by the living, the large tree in the front yard dies, and finally, the family dog dies as well. The death-centric drama is inclusive of the dog's death, in that the drama is of the death of the Telfair family. As such, when the dog dies, McCarthy is calling attention to the fact that the dog was a loved and valued member of the family. And as biological determinism is based upon survival in a brutally violent world, the fact that the dog dies of old age is important because death by old age is the ultimate act of determinism, for one must survive to old age to die of old age. In addition to presenting animal death and survival in a deterministic world, in a number of texts, McCarthy uses animals to preface human death.

In *Outer Dark* and in the teleplay *The Gardener's Son*, McCarthy uses specific types of animals as harbingers of human death. In the former text, McCarthy uses swine to preface the deaths of a number of human characters. For example, early in the text, a screaming sow announces the imminent death of the squire. McCarthy later rewrites the scene, again with the swine's scream, followed by the squire's death. Later in the text, a tusked boar chases Culla Holme, but it is not he who dies, but a pair of wandering millhands. Still later, McCarthy posits Rinthy Holme in a scene with a hog that has drowned her hoggets; the implication is clear, the hog has killed her offspring, and Rinthy is guilty of killing her infant son (who dies later in the text). Finally, McCarthy has a great herd of pigs enter the textual action and then sees fit to have the pig-drover Vernon stampeded off of a cliff by the very pigs that he has tended. In each instance in *Outer Dark*, the appearance of a swine — or swine — in the text is a harbinger of human death. In *The Gardener's Son*, McCarthy uses the mule as a signifier or harbinger of human death.

In the teleplay, McCarthy frames the opening and closing scenes of the text proper with passages in which mule teams are prominently displayed and play the role of harbinger to human death. Thus McCarthy continues his presentation of animals and death, while he also continues his motif of particular types of stock animals as harbingers of human death. Here, the focus of the action revolves around the murder of wealthy James Gregg by poverty-struck Robert McEvoy, and McEvoy's subsequent execution by hanging. Prior to each man's death, mule teams are situated in either the text or the stage direction, signifying the death(s) to come. In Gregg's case, the opening direction posits a photograph of a mule-drawn wagon with a coffin being loaded upon the wagon, with the entrance of Gregg into the action of the drama. Gregg is fated to die before the text is to close. In McEvoy's case, the mule as harbinger of human death motif is used more than once. While in jail, a coffin is brought by a team; of course the coffin is McEvoy's. Later, McEvoy's corpse is carried off in a mule-drawn wagon. Finally, at the close of the drama, a team of mules deconstructs the Gregg family monument. In all of the cases above, the mule, death, and more specifically, human death are interwoven; the mule first appears in the text as a harbinger of human death and is inter-associated with human death until the very close of the text. In *Outer Dark* and *The Gardener's Son*, animals, so to speak, control the deaths of human characters, but a more dominant McCarthy model is man controlling the fauna of the natural world through capture and killing.

In *Child of God, Suttree, The Crossing,* and the early short story "Bounty," McCarthy presents animals and the theme of death, here animal death, through man's ceaseless attempts to control—for various reasons—the natural world. Man constantly seeks to control animal behavior and action, to the point where man kills in his attempt to control. In *Child of God,* the author comedically includes three scenes in which human characters attempt to control bovines. In the first scene, Lester Ballard is going to shoot some fresh-water fish in a clear creek; however, his plan is thwarted by a number of cattle who muddy up the creek as Lester gathers his rifle. Lester, in an act of animal control, attempts to move the cattle by shooting one. The cattle move, and one dies. Later in the text, Lester attempts to move a cow by attaching a rope to the animal's neck, and by pulling the rope taught with a tractor. The result is another controlled, but dead, bovine. Finally, in an interpolated first-person tale, a boy attempts to move a team of oxen by lighting a fire under the pair. While working the fire, the oxen team runs over the not too bright boy. In each of these three scenes of bovine levity, man attempts to control an animal through violence or force. Success at control is subjective. In *Suttree,* though, flying animals are quite successfully controlled through intended death.

In *Suttree*, the character of Gene Harrogate controls birds and bats through various means of killing; as flying is the ultimate act of natural freedom, and as killing is man's ultimate act of control, McCarthy has Harrogate control pigeons and bats, and thus control their flight (an insult to man) via the killing of the flying animals. In the case of birds, pigeons specifically, McCarthy has Harrogate kill two ways. First, Harrogate kills the pigeons with grain as bait and rat traps as the killing devices; subsequently, Harrogate's belly is filled with dead, ultimately controlled, pigeons. Harrogate's second method to kill the birds is one which utilizes electricity — an aspect of the natural world which man controls — to electrocute the birds as they land on electrical wires. The method works, and the flying animals are rendered permanently flightless. In regard to Harrogate's control of bats, he also devises a number of schemes, the most effective involving strychnine laden globs of pig's liver, which he shoots into the air with a slingshot; the dying bats fall from the sky. Harrogate controls the pigeons and the bats through the act of killing the animals; this extreme method of control is not a unique one for man or for McCarthy.

However, in the titled short story "Bounty," McCarthy has a character control an animal through capture, not killing. In the text, a young boy finds a wounded sparrowhawk, and he controls the animal through capturing it and then placing it in a box — a cell. Not surprisingly, the confined bird shortly dies. So even when man attempts to do something that is perhaps honorable, nursing a wild bird back to health, man's attempts go awry. For a wild animal, with emphasis here on a creature that flies, is not meant to be imprisoned in a box. Such an animal is better dead than captured, for most wild animals cannot be controlled through capture. In *The Crossing*, man's control through the killing of the untamable wolf has left the southwestern United States devoid of the wild predators.

In *The Crossing*, a lone she-wolf is metonymous for all of the Mexican Grey wolves eradicated by nineteenth and twentieth century Euro-American man. Man, through the federal government sanction bounty system, sought to eradicate the wolf from the southwestern United States and man succeeded. The wolf was the bane to sustenance and commercial livestock, and as such, impeded the westerly progress and destiny of man. In *The Crossing*, the she-wolf is fated from the moment she enters the text, and from the moment she enters southern New Mexico. In the text, the wolf is also a metaphor for man's unquenchable appetite and need to control the natural world. Consequently, the absence of the wolf from southern New Mexico signals the presence of man, European man; history shows that European man has long feared the wolf, and thus, has attempted to control the feared animal through slaughter. Finally, the wolf is a wild animal that cannot be controlled or domesticated; man — because he is man — must kill the uncontrollable animal. So, McCarthy presents a number of reasons why the wolf must be controlled through killing. And as man will allow, that which must be killed, eradicated, and thus controlled, will be killed, eradicated and controlled. Man, as he is man, evolves to the point where he uses living tools to aid in the killing of wild or feral animals, and this balance between man and trained animal, to kill the wild animal — the ballet of the hunt — is a major theme in *Cities of the Plain* and "The Dark Waters."

In the novel *Cities of the Plain* and in the short story "The Dark Waters," man uses the domesticated dog, specifically the trained coonhound, to assist with the control of wild and feral animals. As the texts are McCarthy's, the attempts at control involve killing the animals being controlled. In *Cities of the Plain*, McCarthy uses coonhounds to first hunt a mountain lion and then to hunt a pack of feral dogs. The former scene shows the coonhounds as deterministic, as the beasts fight to the death when called upon as warrior animals should, while the scene also shows the animals in the ballet of the hunt, working with man to control the natural world. For the ballet of the hunt is one in which man does not necessarily hunt within sight of the dogs, but hunts within earshot of the dogs. This is evidenced by the characters' descriptions of the ongoing hunt, descriptions made while sitting around the campfire. The trained dogs hunt, as they are trained to do, and the men are to follow when the coonhounds tree the prey animal. In this scene, the prey eludes the hunters. In the second scene of the ballet of the hunt in *Cities of the Plain*, John Grady Cole and his band of hunters hunt a pack of feral dogs — dogs that are killing stock and therefore must be killed. In this scene of the ballet, the coonhounds run the feral dogs into sight of the human hunters, and the hunters kill the feral beasts. What is similar in both scenes of the ballet of the hunt is that the coonhounds seek and locate the prey, and the man or men kill the prey. This balance of hunting duties is evident as well in "The Dark Waters."

In the short story, a man takes a teenage boy on his first raccoon hunt, a ritual rite of passage. As the hunters listen to the chase, the man ascertains that a coonhound is in trouble, and one is, for the raccoon attempts to drown a coonhound in icy water. The boy, risking his life, rescues the coonhound from the depths. What is important here is that the human listens to the chase and realizes the danger to the dog. The ballet of the hunt here is auditory at first. The boy rescues the coonhound because the coonhounds and the men work in tandem, and one does not willingly let one's teammate perish. So here, the man does not kill the treed prey, but rescues the felled hunting partner. Either way, though, the ballet of the hunt has been effective as a balance between man and hunting hound.

McCarthy's latest work, *No Country for Old Men,* continues the theme of animal death at the hand of man but does so without the animal omnipresence of the previous works. As with the previous works, animals and death are conjoined. Specifically, animals die at the hand of man. Man kills animals, and this dyad of man and animal death is found throughout *No Country for Old Men.* From the first scene with Llewelyn Moss, where he is stalking antelope and later comes upon the wounded dog and the dead dog, to the scene where Sheriff Bell removes the dead hawk form the highway, to the scene where Anton Chigurh shoots at the wild bird, to the scene where Bell and Deputy Torbert discuss slaughterhouse killing methods, the text is lined with animal death at the hand of man. In the work, McCarthy minimalizes animal presence, while he continues his ongoing themes of animals and death, and animal death at the hand of man. The result is a novel that follows thematic precedent, but does so in a world where man has killed off great populations of animals, hence, the lack of animal omnipresence.

Death is McCarthy's central literary theme, and the motif of animal presence and death is a major motif in the author's work. All of McCarthy's texts contain this motif of animal presence and death. McCarthy adroitly utilizes biological determinism, animals as harbingers of human death, man's control of the fauna of the natural world through killing, and the hunt as ballet between man and trained coonhound, to emphasize the presence of animals in a human dominated world. Human beings may dominate McCarthy's literary universe, but animals, via their presence in the texts in conjunction with death, are thematically, symbolically and literally as important to the outcome of the stories as are many of the human characters in the text.

Bibliography

Aristotle. *The History of Animals.* Trans. D'Arcy Wentworth Thompson. Book 6, Part 2. http://classics.mit.edu/Aristotle/history_anim.6.vi.html 10 October 2004.

Arnold, Edwin T. "The Last of the Trilogy: First Thoughts on *Cities of the Plain.*" *Perspectives on Cormac McCarthy.* Eds. Edwin T. Arnold, and Dianne C. Luce. Revised Edition. Jackson: University Press of Mississippi, 1999. 221–47.

Associated Press. "Endangered Mexican Gray Wolves Step Away from Release into Wilds." *Lubbock Avalanche-Journal* 6 April 2002: B15.

Audubon, John Woodhouse. *Audubon's Western Journal, 1849–1850: Being the MS. Record of a Trip from New York to Texas, and an Overland Journey through Mexico and Arizona to the Gold-fields of California.* 1906. Tucson: The University of Arizona Press, 1984.

Bell, James Luther. *Cormac McCarthy's West: The Border Trilogy Annotations.* El Paso: Texas Western Press, 2002.

Bell, Vereen M. *The Achievement of Cormac McCarthy.* Baton Rouge: Louisiana State University Press, 1988.

Berger, Joel. "The Horse: Noble Steed or Wild Menace?" *Perceptions of Animals in American Culture.* Ed. R. J. Hoage. Washington, D.C.: Smithsonian Institution Press, 1989. 101–12.

Bierce, Ambrose. "The Eyes of the Panther." *The Complete Short Stories of Ambrose Bierce.* 1970. Ed. Ernest Jerome Hopkins. Lincoln: Universitry of Nebraska Press, 1984. 38–46.

"Black and Tan Coonhound." *Microsoft Encarta Encyclopedia.* 2000.

Campbell, Neil. "Liberty beyond its Proper Bounds: Cormac McCarthy's History of the West in *Blood Meridian.*" *Myth, Legend, Dust: Critical Responses to Cormac McCarthy.* Ed. Rick Wallach. New York: Manchester University Press, 2000. 217–26.

"Cat Family." *Microsoft Encarta Encyclopedia.* 2000.

Chamberlain, Samuel E. *My Confession: Recollections of a Rogue.* 1956. Ed. William H. Goetzmann. Unexpurgated and Annotated Edition. Austin: Texas State Historical Association, 1996.

Ciuba, Gary M. "McCarthy's Enfant Terrible: Mimetic Desire and Sacred Violence from *Child of God.*" *Sacred Violence: A Reader's Companion to Cormac McCarthy.* Eds. Wade Hall, and Rick Wallach. El Paso: Texas Western Press, 1995. 77–85.

"Coonhound." *Microsoft Encarta Encyclopedia.* 2000, p. 244.

Darwin, Charles. *The Voyage of the Beagle.* 1909. Intro. H. James Birx. New York: Prometheus Books, 2000.
"Greyhound." *Microsoft Encarta Encyclopedia.* 2000.
"Greyhounds." *Breed All about It. Animal Planet Television.* 29 July 2002.
Hardy, Thomas. *Tess of the d'Urbervilles.* 1891. New York: Norton, 1991.
"Hound." *Microsoft Encarta Encyclopedia.* 2000.
Howey, M. Oldfield. *The Horse in Magic and Myth.* New York: Castle, 1958.
Isaacs, Ronald H. *Animals in Jewish Thought and Tradition.* Northvale: Aronson, 2000.
Jarrett, Robert L. *Cormac McCarthy.* New York: Twayne, 1997.
Kellert, Stephen R. "Perceptions of Animals in America." *Perceptions of Animals in American Culture.* Ed. R. J. Hoage. Washington, D.C.: Smithsonian Institution Press, 1989. 5–24.
Kirves, Kyle. "Index of Character Names in the Novels." *Myth, Legend, Dust: Critical Responses to Cormac McCarthy.* Ed. Rick Wallach. New York: Manchester University Press, 2000. 303–85.
Klinghammer, Erich. "The Wolf: Fact and Fiction." *Perceptions of Animals in American Culture.* Ed. R. J. Hoage. Washington, D. C.: Smithsonian Institution Press, 1989. 77–91.
Lang, John. "Lester Ballard: McCarthy's Challenge to the Reader's Compassion." *Sacred Violence: A Reader's Companion to Cormac McCarthy.* Eds. Wade Hall, and Rick Wallach. El Paso: Texas Western Press, 1995. 87–94.
"The Legend of the Wampus Cat." http://ksks.essortment.com/wampuscat_rvmr.htm 14 May 2002.
Lopez, Barry Holstun. *Of Wolves and Men.* New York: Scribner's Sons, 1978.
Luce, Dianne C. "The Vanishing World of Cormac McCarthy's Border Trilogy." *The Southern Quarterly* 38.3 (2000): 121–46.
Maxwell, Gavin. *Ring of Bright Water.* London: Reprint Society Ltd., 1961.
McCarthy, Cormac. *All the Pretty Horses.* 1992. New York: Vintage, 1993.
_____. *Blood Meridian or The Evening Redness in the West.* 1985. New York: Vintage, 1992.
_____. "Bounty." *The Yale Review* 54.3 (1965): 368–74.
_____. *Child of God.* 1973. New York: Vintage, 1993.
_____. *Cities of the Plain.* New York: Knopf, 1998.
_____. *The Crossing.* 1994. New York: Vintage, 1995.
_____. "The Dark Waters." *The Sewanee Review* 73.2 (1965): 210–16.
_____. *The Gardener's Son: A Screenplay.* Hopewell, NJ: Ecco, 1996.
_____. *No Country for Old Men.* New York: Knopf, 2005.
_____. *The Orchard Keeper.* 1965. New York: Vintage, 1993.
_____. *Outer Dark.* 1968. New York: Vintage, 1993.
_____. *The Stonemason: A Play in Five Acts.* Hopewell, NJ: Ecco, 1994.
_____. *Suttree.* 1979. New York: Vintage, 1992.
Montaigne, Michel de. *Apology for Raymond Sebond.* Trans. Roger Ariew and Marjorie Grene. Indianapolis: Hackett, 2003.
Owens, Barcley. *Cormac McCarthy's Western Novels.* Tucson: University of Arizona Press, 2000.
"Pliny the Elder." *Biographies.* http://library.thinkquest.org/11402/bio_pliny_old.html 17 July 2002.
Pliny the Elder. *Natural History.* Eds. And Trans. John Bostock and H. T. Riley. Book VIII, Ch. 71. http://perseus.tufts.edu/cgi-bin/ptext?doc=Perseus%3Atext%3a 1999.02.0137&query=head%3D%23404 11 October 2004.

Potter, Beatrix. *The Tale of Samuel Whiskers or, The Roly-Poly Pudding.* 1908. London: Penguin, 1991.

Raverat, Gwen. *Period Piece.* New York: Norton, 1953.

Robisch, S. K. "The Trapper Mystic: Werewolves in *The Crossing.*" *Myth, Legend, Dust: Critical Responses to Cormac McCarthy.* Ed. Rick Wallach. New York: Manchester University Press, 2000. 288–92.

Ruxton, George Frederick. *Adventures in Mexico and the Rocky Mountains.* New York: Harper & Bros., 1855.

Sassoon, Siegfried. *Memoirs of a Fox-Hunting Man.* London: The Folio Society, 1971.

Sepich, John E. *Notes on Blood Meridian.* Louisville: Bellarmine College Press, 1993.

Sewell, Anna. *Black Beauty.* New York: Dodd, Mead and Co., 1941.

Shakespeare, William. *The Two Gentlemen of Verona. The Complete Works of William Shakespeare.* Ed. William Aldis Wright. New York: Doubleday, 1936. 247–76.

Trimmer, Sarah. *Fabulous Histories.* 1786. New York: Garland, 1977.

Tripp, Edward. *The Meridian Handbook of Classical Mythology.* New York: Meridian, 1974.

Voltaire. "Bêtes: Animals." *Philosophical Dictionary.* 1972. Ed. and Trans. Theodore Besterman. New York: Penguin, 2004.

Warner, Sylvia Townsend. "Letter to Joy Chute. 21 October 1976." *Letters.* Ed. William Maxwell. New York: Viking, 1983. 291.

Waterton, Charles. *Wanderings in South America.* 1852. London: Oxford University Press, 1973.

Wood, J. G. *Bible Animals: Being a Description of Every Living Creature Mentioned in the Scriptures from the Ape to the Coral.* New York: Scribner, 1870.

Woodward, Richard B. "'You Know about Mojave Rattlesnakes?'": Cormac McCarthy's Venomous Fiction." *The New York Times Magazine* 19 April 1992: 28–31.

Young, Thomas D., Jr. "The Imprisonment of Sensibility." *Perspectives on Cormac McCarthy.* Rev. ed. Eds. Edwin T. Arnold and Dianne C. Luce. Jackson: University Press of Mississippi, 1999. 97–122.

Index